Religious Freedom
after the Sexual Revolution

A CATHOLIC GUIDE

RELIGIOUS FREEDOM AFTER THE SEXUAL REVOLUTION

HELEN M. ALVARÉ

Catholic University of America Press
Washington, D.C.

Nihil Obstat:
Rev. Christopher Begg, S.T.D., Ph.D.
Censor Deputatus

Imprimatur:
Very Reverend Daniel B. Carson
Vicar General and Moderator of the Curia

The Roman Catholic Archdiocese of Washington

March 30, 2022

The *nihil obstat* and *imprimatur* are official declarations that a book or
pamphlet is free of doctrinal or moral error. There is no implication that
those who have granted the nihil obstat and the imprimatur agree with the
content, opinions or statements expressed therein.

Cataloging-in-Publication Data available at the Library of Congress

ISBN 978-0-8132-3497-7 | eISBN 978-0-8132-3498-4

Book design by Burt&Burt
Interior set in Meta Serif Pro and Good Pro

TO MY LATE FATHER,
LOUIS J. ALVARÉ,
WHOSE LOVE FOR
HIS FAMILY,
FOR GOD,
AND FOR THE CHURCH
IS WITH ME EVERY DAY

INTRODUCTION

NOT SO VERY LONG AGO IN THE UNITED STATES there was a broad consensus about sexual responsibility. Catholic proposals were unremarkable. Even after contraception entered the mainstream of law and culture, and the US Supreme Court located a right to abortion in the Constitution, non-Catholics generally associated Catholic sexual norms with virtue and with positive outcomes for children and adults.

Today, however, governments and other powerful institutions increasingly insist that human freedom, dignity, equality, and health depend crucially upon individuals' realizing their subjective sexual interests, desires, and beliefs, often without reference to the well-being of others. They are attacking long-standing laws and customs fostering links between sex, marriage, and parenting. They are supporting unlimited abortion as well as the notion that one's sex is subjectively determined.

The Catholic Church, however, has thus far refused to be carried along with the tide. Onlookers seem perpetually shocked by this. In 2021, when the Holy See's Congregation for the Doctrine of the Faith issued a statement reaffirming that the Church could not bless same-sex unions,[1] the statement was front-page "news" worldwide. Statements by Pope Francis affirming the Church's teachings on abortion, gender ideology, and contraception have received similar treatment.

---

1 Holy See Press Office, Summary of Bulletin, "Responsum of the Congregation for the Doctrine of the Faith to a Dubium Regarding the Blessings of the Unions of Persons of the Same Sex," February 22, 2021. This document, as well as many other documents produced by persons or entities associated with the Catholic Church that are cited herein, may be found at www.vatican.va.

Today it is no longer acceptable in the US to disagree with the "powers that be"—the state, the media, the academy, and many corporations—on matters touching on sex, sexual identity, marriage, parenting, or abortion. (For brevity I will call these "sexual expression" matters throughout.) Instead, the powers that be continually target individuals and institutions who refuse to heel with both legal and reputational penalties. In this environment, the Catholic Church has become a preferred target, even as her institutions continue to provide nearly universally acclaimed services for tens of millions of Americans annually, and even as her pope is an internationally acclaimed voice for peace and human rights. The Church is targeted even though there has never existed as much empirical evidence as we have right now that the Church's prescriptions regarding sexual responsibility foster freedom, dignity, equality, and health and provide relief and comfort, especially to children and to vulnerable adults.

Thus has it come to pass in the US that the most frequent and visible challenges to Catholic institutions' religious freedom take the form of laws or regulations related to sex, sexual identity, marriage, parenting, or abortion. Weekly, the federal government or a state or local government somewhere, is demanding that one or another Catholic institution cooperate with the state's new sexual orthodoxy. In response, institutional leaders have to articulate both for courts of law and courts of public opinion—which often include their own Catholic members—the reasons that they cannot obey the state.

But in far too many cases, leaders' responses are insufficient and onlookers' respect for religious freedom and for Catholic sexual responsibility norms are diminished. Consequently—and even though the Church has never asked to speak day and night about sex, marriage, and parenting—she must do better than she is doing presently.

This is not to say that Catholic institutions caught in the maelstrom always lose in courts of law. Sometimes they win, and rightly so. The attorneys involved in these winning cases are satisfying judges' need to know what Catholic "rule" a particular law burdens or transgresses. In the end, however, both in courts of law and public opinion, Catholic institutions are winning individual challenges while simultaneously losing observers' sympathy for and understanding of the larger causes of religious freedom and human flourishing in the arena of sexual expression.

How is this happening? Too often, Catholic institutions respond to demands to cooperate with problematic sexual expression with a brief recitation of the relevant Catholic "rule" or "ban"—for example, the Catholic "rules" against contraception, abortion, same-sex marriage, cohabitation, or transgender surgery. Onlookers regularly believe that these rules are negative, sex-obsessed, unloving, unrelated to the core religious mission of the Church, irrational, retrograde, and targeted to hurt the already vulnerable. They judge them highly unattractive by comparison with the laws they challenge. These include laws banning discrimination in employment, housing, and public accommodations and laws mandating institutions to provide and/or provide insurance for contraception or abortion or transgender surgery—all promoted as advancing equality, dignity, freedom, and health for historically vulnerable groups. Onlookers also wonder why institutions they understand as just-another-service-provider—schools, hospitals, social services—are concerning themselves at all with issues seemingly unrelated to delivering quality services.

To better meet these stiff challenges, Catholic institutions sorely need to change the way they speak about their refusals to cooperate with sexual expression laws. They should speak differently not only in their formal legal pleadings, but also in their statements to members, employees, clients, patients, students, and the public. Their responses should go way beyond a mere recitation of the religious teaching at issue. Instead, they need first to distinguish themselves from other service providers and describe what they *are*: communities responding in unity to the call of Christ; communities called to make the living Christ present in the world today; and communities whose practices manifest the inbreaking of the reign of God; that is, the person of Jesus and His Kingdom. Catholic institutions are all of these things even as they also dedicate themselves to a particular human service in response to Jesus's call to love God and neighbor.

In addition, Catholic institutions need to articulate briefly and clearly—which is very hard to do—how their observance of Catholic sexual responsibility norms is an *integral* part of their mission to love God and neighbor, part of the very same mission that inspires them to provide high-quality health care, social services, and education to the community, especially to the neediest. When Jesus is asked in the Gospel of Matthew which is the greatest commandment, He articulates two interrelated commands: "You shall love the Lord, your God, with all your heart, with all your soul, and with all your mind. This is the greatest and the first commandment. The second is like it: You shall love your neighbor as yourself. The whole law and the prophets depend on these two commandments" (Mt 22:37–40).[2] Catholic institutions have to credibly explain how these commandments require us to love both our families and our nonfamily neighbors with the same radical love that Jesus demonstrated.

With these two moves, Catholic institutions should be able to turn current charges against them on their head. They should be able to explain clearly, positively, and with enthusiasm and emotional intelligence how the Catholic approach fosters authentic love, freedom, happiness, dignity, health, and equality—the very values lionized today in the US. This is the way to increase respect and affection not only for the religious freedom of Catholic institutions, but also for their teachings on sexual responsibility.

If Catholic institutions can thus show that they cannot "be what they are" by cooperating with sexual expression laws hostile to their beliefs, they have an excellent set of religious freedom arguments available to them. But again, they have first to articulate what a Catholic community really *is*, in addition to being a service provider, and to further articulate how Catholic sex, marriage, and parenting norms help shape that communal life and identity. Recent Supreme Court decisions protect religious institutions' "church autonomy" over their own internal operations, personnel, faith, and doctrine.[3] Without a doubt, the Church has the necessary scriptural and theological resources, and a sufficiently developed social teaching, to frame a winning church autonomy argument cognizable to a court. These resources also showcase the many ways in which Catholic beliefs promote equality, dignity, health, and freedom, particularly with respect to the vulnerable who suffer the most under the new sexual orthodoxy. At the same time, the Church can draw significant support and explanatory power from human experience and from

---

2 All scripture quotations in this book are drawn from the New American Bible as available online from the U.S. Conference of Catholic Bishops at https://www.usccb.org/offices/new-american-bible/books-bible.

3 Hosanna-Tabor Evangelical Lutheran Church and Sch. v. EEOC, 565 U.S. 171 (2012); Our Lady of Guadalupe Sch. v. Morrissey-Berru, 140 S. Ct. 2049 (2020).

various empirical sciences to construct arguments displaying an inter-play of faith and reason comprehensible to both legal and popular interlocutors.

But even if these arguments win the day in court some of the time, it is still a challenge for Catholic institutions to speak about religious freedom and sexual expression in a way that inspires affection or respect for their stances on both. This is due in part to a growing conviction in the US that a person's self-constructed "sexual iden-tity" and his or her attainment of sexual desires are central markers of human freedom and ought to lie beyond the influence of the church and the state.[4] Proponents of this novel set of beliefs about human nature—this "anthropology"—regard sexual expression nondiscrimi-nation laws, and mandates commanding institutions to provide abor-tion, contraception, and transgender surgeries, as natural outgrowths of preexisting, inviolable human rights.

Furthermore, many audiences will remain hostile for what may be good reasons. These include at least the Church's ongoing sex abuse crisis and cover-up and its history of denying or slow-walking the possibility that human sexuality might be a good thing, even though God *did* design it.

There is also the matter of disunity within the Church. The Church is a collection of individuals and institutions with widely varying levels of resources and talents, as well as widely varying interests respecting communications in these areas. A not insignificant number of Cath-olic institutions might not want to walk the path I map out in this book. Some of their leadership no longer agree with Catholic thinking about sexual expression, or if they do, they think it's pointless to spit into the tsunami that is our contemporary, highly sexualized culture. Alternatively, a given Catholic institution might believe that teachings in these areas are separable from the central Catholic commitment to love God and neighbor. Or an institution is eager only to demonstrate its expertise in its chosen service to the relevant powers that be: the government, accrediting agencies, professional associations, potential hires, clients, and others. Or the institution disagrees that employees

---

4   See generally, Carl R. Trueman, *The Rise and Triumph of the Modern Self: Cultural Amnesia, Expressive Individualism, and the Road to Sexual Revolution* (Wheaton, Ill.: Crossway, 2020).

or services or operations that contradict Catholic beliefs relating to sexual expression matter to its Catholic witness.

This raises the important matter of conversion. Before Catholic institutional leaders can speak in a more compelling way about their religious freedom to observe Catholic sexual expression norms, they must first believe that these are expressions of love. It is not simply a matter of a better public relations campaign or a willing attorney. Whether due to their absorption in other responsibilities or even a lack of personally appropriated faith, many Catholic leaders have failed to first seek convincing answers to these questions for themselves from within the Catholic intellectual tradition. How many Catholic leaders have examined the close relationship between sexual responsibility and love of neighbor? How many understand how the sufferings of the most vulnerable in our society, especially children, are linked to the new sexual orthodoxy? How many have examined the resources of various empirical sciences in order to construct arguments displaying an interplay of faith and reason comprehensible to their own hearts, and also to legal and popular interlocutors? It is one thing to obediently observe a rule, but it is another to have drunk deeply from the waters of the Catholic tradition, found them life-giving, and responded in kind.

This book is intended to foster such a conversion, as well as to practically assist Catholic institutions and leaders when they take up their responsibilities, despite obstacles. Explaining the place of sexual expression norms in the life of the Church and her institutions is an important part of the contemporary vocation of Catholics. *This is not because sexual expression is the most important facet of the Catholic life, but because the world's need is great.* The need is great for an intelligent, compassionate voice on a subject currently preoccupying culture and law, and wreaking havoc in many lives. But few voices or institutions have sufficient theological and intellectual gifts to understand these problems, or an available network of respected institutions through which to speak. Fewer still have the endurance to withstand the penalties and even abuse that today face those willing to defy current orthodoxy. At its best, however, the Church has all of these resources and qualities.

Demands to conform to the new orthodoxy are not going away anytime soon. Although the sexual revolution has taken hold of major institutions relatively quickly, it has been percolating for hundreds of years, and will persist for a long time to come. As theologian Louis J. Cameli has observed:

> Every epoch in the history of the Church has faced a particular challenge in trying to understand the revelation of God in Jesus Christ and its implications. In the early centuries of the Church, this challenge had to do with coming to terms with an understanding in faith of who God is for us and who is Jesus Christ. For the last five hundred years . . . there has been a double and connected process of doctrinal development. The Church has come to a greater and more explicit self-awareness of who she is as Church. At the same time, the Church has grappled with a faith understanding of the human person, technically identified as theological anthropology. . . .
>
> At this moment, . . . the faith understanding of the human person continues to develop but with a focus on human sexuality. . . .
>
> The central issue has to do with the distinctive meaning that men and women have for each other and how, in the order of sign and symbol, this distinctive meaning assumes sacramental significance in . . . Marriage and Holy Orders. This development is far from complete. . . .
>
> . . .We who are in the Church today find ourselves in an uncomfortable position. What makes us uncomfortable is our location in the middle of a process of development . . . This development does not mean the reversal of the Church's faith but rather its unfolding.[5]

Answers to the issues raised by Cameli are important not only for Catholics but for the common good. Yet critics will greet every effort of the Church to grapple with these matters with the charge that she is obsessed with pelvic issues, that she has reduced the words and witness of Jesus Christ to a list of sexual dos and don'ts. This is unreasonable.

It is the powers that be in the US who are harming men, women, and children every day by supporting practices and beliefs concerning

5   Louis J. Cameli, *Catholic Teaching on Homosexuality* (Notre Dame, Ind.: Ave Maria Press, 2012), 141–43.

sex, marriage, and parenting that fly in the face of common sense, personal experience, and empirical findings. They are especially harming the poor, the lonely, the confused, and children. They rightly insist that we show love and practice social justice toward our "neighbors" outside the family, but ignore those nearest neighbors we are certainly going to deeply impact for their whole lives—parents, children, spouses, and romantic partners who may become family.

It would be irresponsible for the Church—with all her resources and talents—to fail to take up these challenges at this time in history. She must respond to them both with great compassion and great sophistication. She must defend religious freedom so that Catholic communities can continue to exhibit to onlookers new ways of living interpersonal relations that manifest the love of Christ.

Perhaps the Church can take consolation and strength from the fact that early Christians shouldered a similar burden. According to leading historical accounts,[6] early Christians too faced disbelief and hostility when they sought to live out sex, marriage, and parenting norms quite foreign to those prevalent in the Greco-Roman world. In his marvelous *The Rise and Triumph of the Modern Self: Cultural Amnesia, Expressive Individualism, and the Road to Sexual Revolution*, theologian and historian Carl Trueman writes that Christians today are living in a moment reminiscent of the second century:

> A pluralist society has slowly but surely adopted beliefs, particularly beliefs about sexuality and identity, that render Christianity immoral and inimical to the civic stability of society as now understood. The second-century world is, in a sense, our world, where Christianity is a choice—and a choice likely at some point to run afoul of the authorities.

Trueman encouragingly reminds us, though, that "it was that second-century world . . . that laid down the foundations for the later successes of the third and fourth centuries" and those beyond.[7]

---

6 Rodney Stark, *The Rise of Christianity: A Sociologist Reconsiders History* (Princeton: Princeton University Press, 1996); Kyle Harper, *From Shame to Sin: The Christian Transformation of Sexual Morality in Late Antiquity* (Cambridge, Mass.: Harvard University Press, 2013).

7 Trueman, *The Rise and Triumph of the Modern Self*, 407.

This book is intended to assist leaders at Catholic institutions (and their lawyers too) to better understand and articulate their objections to facilitating the new orthodoxy of sexual expression, so that they might shore up respect and affection for religious freedom and for Catholic teachings on sexual expression. It takes strength and examples from both early and more contemporary Christian communities. It is also intended as a service to all those individuals and families struggling personally as a result of the new orthodoxy. Capacious institutional religious freedom would increase the likelihood that they might hear the good news about sex, marriage, and parenting from Catholic institutions, and even see Catholic communities living out this good news in ways that might provoke curiosity, reflection, and even admiration.

This book tries to explain Catholic teachings about neuralgic sexual topics in helpful and not overly complicated ways. I am not a credentialed theologian, but only a lawyer—albeit one with extensive experience communicating "Catholic things" to lawmakers, judges, and the public. I have labored to avoid platitudes and obscure theological terms whenever possible. Instead, leaning on a wide array of marvelous theologians, popes, historians, sociologists, economists, and others, I try to speak in positive terms about how Catholic institutions share in the Church's mission to witness Christ to one another and to the world and how our sexual expression norms are part of this mission, while also better satisfying the goals that current laws claim they are pursuing—freedom, happiness, dignity, health, and equality in particular.

I do not and cannot offer advice about counseling persons, couples, or families who do not accept Catholic teachings on sexual expression. I do not have the talent or training of a counselor or pastor. At the same time, it is possible that the facts and reasoning I offer about Catholic institutions and Catholic sexual expression norms will prove helpful to those undertaking the delicate and crucial work of speaking directly with persons in need of loving and informed advice.

And again, allow me to emphasize that I am *not* writing this book to argue that matters of sexual expression are the heart and soul of the Catholic faith. They are not. But they are too often understood as a set of rules separate from the great commandments to love God and one another, when in fact they are an inseparable part of these.

Of course, many human actions demonstrate devotion to God and neighbor. Catholic social teaching and the wide variety of Catholic ministries, institutions, and other charitable efforts testify to this. At the same time, however, and realistically speaking, very few actions that most of us undertake in our daily lives, year in and year out, are as likely to affect other human beings in indelible ways, at profound levels, and over the course of their entire lives, as are decisions in the realm of sexual expression. These include, among other things, decisions regarding whether to be or not to be committed to a person we have sex with; to conceive or not to conceive a child; to give birth to a child in or outside of a marriage; to abort or to give birth to a child; to raise a child or to place him or her for adoption; to be or not to be faithful to a spouse; to remain married or to divorce; and to accept or reject the sex that God fashioned us. All of these behaviors and decisions profoundly impact our own and others' happiness, freedom, health, and sense of personal dignity and worthiness over the course of entire lives. All resound decades and even generations later in the lives and families and even communities that they profoundly shape. All concern justice to our nearest neighbors—probably the largest group of "neighbors" most of us will actually impact over the course of our entire lives.

But even as Catholic teachings on sexual expression are important, they cannot be promoted without a proper context. Pope Francis spoke wisely when he cautioned Catholics against a "disjointed"[8] expression of Catholic moral teachings. This would not only be untrue to Catholic theology—in which morality emerges from a community's *prior* conversion to Christ and the neighbor[9]—but would fall prey to the common complaint that our sexual expression teachings are "mean" and "unloving." Instead, it is especially necessary today to say that we are unwilling to cooperate with the new sexual orthodoxy *because* the commandment to love God and neighbor instructs us otherwise. Catholics further believe that our marital and parent-child

---

8   Laurie Goodstein, "Pope Says Church is 'Obsessed' with Gays, Abortion and Birth Control," *New York Times*, September 19, 2013, https://www.nytimes.com/2013/09/20/world/europe/pope-bluntly-faults-churchs-focus-on-gays-and-abortion.html.

9   Luigi Giussani, *Morality: Memory and Desire*, trans. K.D. Whitehead (San Francisco: Ignatius Press, 1986), 87–98, 163–74.

relationships are privileged sources of understanding how God loves us and wants us to love Him.

In order, therefore, to assist Catholic institutions confidently and succinctly to do what is required to better secure religious freedom in the context of challenges related to sexual expression, and to advocate for the wisdom of Catholic teachings on sexual responsibility, the itinerary of this book is as follows.

Chapter 1 will set forth the legal and cultural situations in the US that are generating so many battles between religious freedom and sexual expression. It will also summarize the variety of sexual expression laws affecting religious institutions, as well as the current state of religious freedom law at both the federal and the state levels. In particular, it will describe the "church autonomy" doctrine, which provides significant protection for Catholic institutions' decision-making respecting services, operations, and personnel, within due limits.

Chapter 2 will describe specific conflicts between Catholic educational, health care, and social service institutions and the demands of various sexual expression laws. It will illustrate the typical and insufficient religious freedom defenses these institutions offer and characterize the types of backlash and misunderstandings these generate.

Chapter 3 offers three ways of portraying the religious nature of Catholic institutional communities, in order to help courts and the public distinguish them from secular service providers. Unless observers apprehend these institutions' religious foundations and missions, they will be at a complete loss to grasp why they cannot cooperate with behaviors seemingly bearing little relation to their ability to deliver quality services. I will describe these three models in simple terms derived from leading Church documents and theologians. These characterize Catholic institutions as communities who are united in response to Christ's call, seek to manifest His living presence in the world today, and live at the intersection of divine and human relations in a way that reveals the inbreaking of the Kingdom of God.

Chapter 4 lays out the empirical evidence that further supports a religious institution's assertion that it must retain final authority specifically over personnel decisions in order to maintain its religious character. This evidence consists of research from the "social influence" and "psychology of religion" literature that shows the crucial importance of personnel to an institution's efforts to realize its mission. This chapter is sui generis in the book, as it is the only one comprised almost completely of empirical material. But it is important for religious institutions to claim the benefit of the studies it describes given the government's frankly ridiculous and frequent claims that governmental control of an institution's employees will not interfere with or impair the institution's religious mission.

Chapter 5 shows how Catholic educational, health care, and charitable institutions in the US share in the Church's ecclesiological self-understandings while also being dedicated to the *particular* demands of Christ: to heal the sick, care for the poor, and spread the Gospel. Painting with a broad brush because there is a great deal of history and theology involved, this chapter will show how both ancient Catholic institutions and those operating today in the US manifest the traits of Catholic communities.

Chapter 6 performs the difficult work of explaining how Catholic sexual expression teachings are an intrinsic element of Catholic communal life because of their essential role in demonstrating the love of God and neighbor. It will attempt to answer the objection that these norms are simply extrinsic "rules" unrelated to the great commandments. This chapter relies on three of the leading metaphors scripture uses to help Christians grasp how to love God and/or other human beings: as the bride and bridegroom love one another, as parents and children love one another, and as the Good Samaritan loves the neighbor strewn upon his path. It also demonstrates how early Christians understood the norms of sex, marriage, and parenting that they observed—and that we still observe today—as *responses* to scripture and to other lessons from the life and words of Jesus Christ. This ancient material is quite inspiring and relevant to the Church's current situation. Both then and today, Christians have found themselves in the midst of a highly sexualized, exploitative, and misogynistic environment, as well as an environment in which the stronger easily overpower the weaker. Both then and today, Christian sexual responsibility practices at their best offer dignity, freedom, and equality between the sexes, as well as among diverse socioeconomic groups. Chapter 6 is intended to help solve a problem that has troubled Catholic life and communications a great deal during the late twentieth and early twenty-first centuries: the artificial division between Catholic sexual expression norms and Catholic social teaching to "love thy neighbor." It is a big and enduring problem, and I can only throw my ideas into the ring, along with years of experience with public communications about Catholic matters. Obviously, I cannot provide the final word. But I can help advance a conversation I hope others will join, especially if they care strongly about the future of Catholic institutions, and about the well-being of people suffering under the pressure of the new sexual orthodoxy.

Chapter 7 offers concrete suggestions about how Catholic institutions can speak about the sexual expression challenges that are *most frequently* posed today—cohabitation/premarital sex, contraception, abortion, same-sex relations, and transgender identity—in ways that might better respond to the current backlash against the Church. Here I should remind readers that this is neither a textbook of moral theology nor of pastoral theology; it does not fully explore the theological disputes relating to each of these contested issues, nor does it provide advice for counseling individuals acting against Catholic beliefs. Instead, it summarizes the leading complaints about and misunderstandings of the relevant Catholic teachings. It clarifies what the Church is asking for when it launches a religious freedom defense, provides language and evidence to help Catholic institutions demonstrate that their teachings are loving, and argues that Catholic sexual expression norms are more likely to promote the outcomes that lawmakers claim they are seeking to realize via contemporary sexual expression laws: health, happiness, freedom, equality, and human dignity.

Finally, chapter 8 will summarize the most important arguments made throughout the book and describe their application in the course of typical legal contests pitting religious freedom against sexual expression laws. It will also highlight additional opportunities offered by these contests for advancing the appeal of religious freedom and the norms of Catholic sexual expression.

Two final and interrelated thoughts about tone and about the audience for this book. I understand that even some Catholic institutions that support both religious freedom and the Church's sexual expression norms will fear raising their heads above ground. They will be charged with being in the "surveillance" or "witch-hunting" business when it comes to their employees. They will be told that sex is an "obsession" with the Church, or "all we do." They fear being accused of the "disjointed" expression of moralistic rules that Pope Francis rightly laments.

But it is likely that Catholic institutions should not be so pessimistic with respect to how employees or potential employees might regard them. Most still have a positive impression of these institutions' mission and methods. And the Church should never forget that it enjoys the gratitude of innumerable women, men, children, and families for continuing to teach and promote—both within and outside its community—love that is radically faithful, permanent, creative, generous, forgiving, and self-sacrificing. Love that answers consistently expressed human needs. Love of the quality human beings were made to receive. This should not be overlooked. At the same time, vocal segments of the public, especially today's "powers that be," will be just as harsh as Catholic leaders fear. Every religious freedom contest involving sexual expression will feature both realities.

There are, additionally, some Catholic institutions or individuals—including some involved in politics—who *do* want to speak out on these issues, but by their aggression tend only to exacerbate the problem of credibility this book addresses. When St. Paul writes to the Christian Corinthians, "Avoid giving offense, whether to Jews or Greeks or the church of God" (1 Cor 10:32), he does not mean that Christians should abandon their controversial beliefs or practices, but that their default position should not be adversarial. When we must disagree with or resist the claims of law or culture that are contrary to the Gospel, in the course of our seeking to love God and neighbor, we can only witness effectively by following the admonition of Pope Benedict XVI to "give [others] the look of love which they crave,"[10] while leaving judgment to God, demonstrating the mercy of the Gospel and respect for interlocutors and for reason, and seeking the goodwill of others wherever it can be found.

Still, institutions with the will to work on the problems I have identified can succeed. They can fully embrace Pope Francis's admonition to behave like a "field hospital" for sinners, while also promoting joyful, personal witness to the faith, and helping individuals and groups struggling with the consequences of sexual and familial dysfunction. These are the institutions, I am convinced, that will

---

10 Benedict XVI, Encyclical Letter *Deus Caritas Est* (December 25, 2005), 18.

lay the foundation for future centuries of Catholic community and service to society. Sincere conversion to the radical implications of the Christ event is indispensable to this task, as is the patience and skill to craft truthful and explanatory communications. I hope this book provides inspiration and help for both. For better inspiration than I can offer, however, allow me to close with the words of Saint John Henry Newman speaking to the Catholics of his day about their pressing challenges. They are as applicable to clergy, religious, and laity today as to the laity he was addressing then:

> As troubles and trials circle round you, He will give you what you want at present—"a mouth, and wisdom, which all your adversaries shall not be able to resist and gainsay." "There is a time for silence, and a time to speak;" the time for speaking is come. What I desiderate in Catholics is the gift of bringing out what their religion is; it is one of those "better gifts," of which the Apostle bids you be "zealous." You must not hide your talent in a napkin, or your light under a bushel. I want a laity, not arrogant, not rash in speech, not disputatious, but men who know their religion, who enter into it, who know just where they stand, who know what they hold, and what they do not, who know their creed so well, that they can give an account of it, who know so much of history that they can defend it. I want an intelligent, well-instructed laity; I am not denying you are such already: but I mean to be severe, and, as some would say, exorbitant in my demands, I wish you to enlarge your knowledge, to cultivate your reason, to get an insight into the relation of truth to truth, to learn to view things as they are, to understand how faith and reason stand to each other, what are the bases and principles of Catholicism and where lie the main inconsistencies and absurdities of [the opposing view], . . . I have no apprehension you will be the worse Catholics for familiarity with these subjects, provided you cherish a vivid sense of God above, and keep in mind that you have souls to be judged and to be saved.[11]

---

11 John Henry Newman, "Lecture 9: Duties of Catholics Towards the Protestant View," in *Lectures on the Present Position of Catholics in England* (London: Burns & Lambert, 1851), 362.

-1-

THE LEGAL
AND CULTURAL
CONTEXT

A MIX OF LEGAL AND CULTURAL FACTORS is giving rise to a large number of contests pitting Catholic institutional religious freedom against claimed sexual expression rights. Each of the cultural factors at play both merits and has received book-length treatment. The legal side is a complicated and dynamic phenomenon involving every branch of the government at both the state and federal levels. For reasons of length, therefore, this chapter provides only enough information to understand the ways in which law and culture are currently interacting to confront religious institutions with demands to affirm, facilitate, or cooperate with the new sexual expression regime sweeping the US. Those interested in reading more deeply about any legal or cultural point raised below can "enjoy" reading the books and articles cited in the footnotes. I have endeavored throughout to be complete and to avoid legal jargon. But make no mistake, the legal material is not simple and will require some concentration.

Numerous cultural factors have also helped to shape our current fixation on sexual expression. They influence the law and are influenced by it. They come from the fields of psychology, anthropology, philosophy, sociology, history, and economics, among others. Together, they have upended deeply rooted moral and legal norms shared by believers and nonbelievers alike. They exert powerful influence even though they regularly contradict both common sense and empirical data. As a result of their influence, religious institutions today maintaining norms admired until recently are often deemed socially pernicious. I will begin with a discussion of these and then move to the law.

Readers will likely be familiar with most, but not all, of the factors described below. They are not arranged in any particular order, but together constitute the most influential ones.[1] The list is neither "conservative" nor "liberal." It is rather soberly realistic and supported by sound empirical data, as well as by the research and reflections of many eminent thinkers. [2]

Cultural Factors

INDIVIDUALISM

Individualism, the turn toward the self, bears important responsibility for the rise of our national preoccupation with sexual expression. Individualism holds that individual success and happiness is the measure of all things. Persons are not primarily to be understood as oriented to relationship with others, including God. "Progress" is not about good relationships or virtue (in relation to a transcendent God) or the common good. It is self-focused: "finding" and becoming oneself is the real source of progress.[3] Individualism also tends toward subjectivism: taking one's subjective opinion as the only important or even the final word on a subject. One might tolerate others' opinions,

---

1   For a more extended discussion of the cultural factors and their interplay with US law's declining concern for children in favor of increasing support for adults' rights in the arenas of sex, marriage, and parenting, see Helen M. Alvaré, *Putting Children's Interests First in U.S. Family Law and Policy: With Power Comes Responsibility* (Cambridge: Cambridge University Press, 2018), 50–57.

2   A book providing an excellent, cohesive treatment of the path that has led to our current situation is Carl Trueman's *The Rise and Triumph of the Modern Self: Cultural Amnesia, Expressive Individualism, and the Road to Sexual Revolution* (Wheaton, Ill.: Crossway, 2020). It contains a masterful history of the West's movement from the individual psychological self to the sexual self, and then to the sexual as political, thereby accounting for the relentlessness and strength of current efforts to undercut both the family and Christian sexual mores in the name of achieving human freedom.

3   Steven Seidman, *Romantic Longings: Love in America, 1830–1980* (New York: Routledge, 1993), 73.

but, in the words of philosopher Charles Taylor, the self is not terribly "porous"; it is instead relatively disengaged from everything but its own mind. The purposes and meanings of things arise *within* the person.[4]

Americans are rather famous for being individualists. One can see it in our thoughts and actions, even respecting family and friends. Today we are more likely to marry later or not at all. We live alone more often. We claim fewer close friends. We highly value individual material and career success and revolve other decisions around this. It is thus not at all surprising that individualism should also affect Americans' approach to human sexuality.

Sometime during the mid- to late twentieth century, some influential Americans concluded that our sexual interests and behaviors are the most significant features of our person. Taking cues from Sigmund Freud, who was inclined to explain all human behavior as a function of sexual matters, some concluded that our authentic selves, our dignity, and our freedom are importantly determined by our ability to stay closely in touch with and even to act out our sexual desires.

Sociologist Pitrim A. Sorokin (the founder of Harvard University's Department of Sociology) argued as early as 1956 that, with respect to sex in particular, the American was coming to "regard[] himself as law giver and judge entitled to juggle all moral and legal standards."[5] Later, Cambridge sociologist Anthony Giddens in the 1990s,[6] and American sociologist Mark Regnerus more recently,[7] wrote extensively about the influence of individualism in contemporary thinking about sex. Giddens introduced the notion of "plastic sex": sex with individual, subjectively moldable meaning, unmoored from its physical structures, which would otherwise link it with the partner and with procreation. Giddens observed that modern contraception and assisted reproductive technologies directly enabled plastic sex. By severing sex from reproduction, these also sever sex from kinship

4 Charles Taylor, *A Secular Age* (Cambridge, Mass.: Belknap Press of Harvard University Press, 2007), 38.

5 Pitrim A. Sorokin, *The American Sex Revolution* (Boston: Porter Sargent, 1956), 6.

6 Anthony Giddens, *The Transformation of Intimacy: Sexuality, Love, and Eroticism in Modern Societies* (Stanford: Stanford University Press, 1993).

7 Mark Regnerus, *Cheap Sex: The Transformation of Men, Marriage, and Monogamy* (Oxford: Oxford University Press, 2017).

and from intergenerational awareness. Sex has no communal implications; its meaning is reduced to pleasure. Sexuality thus becomes "a property of the individual" and "internally referential," which leads to it becoming a tool for forging self-identity.[8]

Regnerus' 2017 book, *Cheap Sex*, updates and further delimits Giddens's observations.

He maps sexual practices and preferences among 25- to 34-year-old Americans and concludes that sexual acts are becoming "cheaper" in the sense of their being more widely accessible at a drastically lower "cost" than ever before in human history, and because they are regularly separated from children and marriage by means of contraception and abortion. Thus, sex less often fosters relationships with spouses or children or extended families. Increasingly, it even takes place without any contact with another human being, via pornography.

Another aspect of American individualism that affects our understanding of sex is the decline in the salience of the transcendent. The person does not understand herself as intrinsically in relationship with the divine. More Americans report that they consider themselves atheists or agnostics or "spiritual but not religious." In 2021 the press breathlessly reported that for the first time ever, less than 50 percent of Americans were affiliated with any particular religion. When one believes that a divine author is responsible for all of creation, including the human body, the body is a "given" to which one looks for norms. But if one rejects or ignores the transcendent, the "givenness" of creation likely also goes away. The body becomes a matter for personal interpretation. It can even become a mere resource or an object of investigation, manipulation, improvement, or even mining. A person might begin to understand herself as largely "self-made." The meanings and purposes of biological realities—such as the functioning of the body, the existence of two sexes, and the link between sex and procreation—point neither to the transcendent nor to behavioral norms. At a certain point, the body can even become an obstacle, a barrier, to self-realization, as reported by individuals suffering gender dysphoria or simply demanding that sexual identification is a wholly subjective conclusion. Likewise, procreative processes and marriage itself, with their usual or expected structures, become a

---

8   Giddens, *The Transformation of Intimacy*, 2, 27, 112, 144, 156, 174, 175, 178–80.

problem because they are handed down and have a typical and natural structure seemingly limiting self-expression.

HAPPINESS

Another important cultural idea in the US is the centrality of "happiness" to human welfare, aligned with the belief that sexual satisfaction is a core element of happiness. The philosopher Charles Taylor writes of the historical importance in the US of the right to happiness generally, pointing to its appearance even in the Declaration of Independence. He opines that while Americans had previously conditioned their enthusiasm for happiness with shared ethics concerning good citizenship, self-rule, and sexual morality, these limits, especially those regarding sexual mores, were set aside after World War I.[9] In Taylor's view, the modern "triumph of the therapeutic"[10] is a closely related phenomenon; people are inclined to subordinate traditional, including religious, ideas about morality with the psychological imperative of personal fulfillment and becoming our "authentic selves."[11]

Although Americans are not actually likely to rate sexual experiences as their chief source of happiness when asked by researchers,[12] they are influenced by important messengers who valorize sexual happiness. Margaret Sanger, for example, the founder of the Planned Parenthood Federation of America, is one of the most well-known exponents of the centrality of sexual freedom to happiness, a point that was made in the context of her arguments promoting birth control. She opined that, through sex separated from the fear of conception by means of contraception, "mankind may attain the great spiritual illumination which will transform the world, which will light up the only path to an earthly paradise." She continued: "We look forward in our vision of the future to children brought into the

---

9 Taylor, *A Secular Age*, 485.
10 Taylor, 618, citing Phillip Rieff, *The Triumph of the Therapeutic: The Uses of Faith After Freud* (New York: Harper and Row, 1966).
11 Taylor, *A Secular Age*, 618–20, 507–8.
12 Patrick Van Kessell and Adam Hughes, "Americans Who Find Meaning in These Four Areas Have Greater Life Satisfaction," Pew Research Center website, November 20, 2018, https://www.pewresearch.org/fact-tank/2018/11/20/americans-who-find-meaning-in-these-four-areas-have-higher-life-satisfaction/.

world because they are desired, called from the unknown by a fearless and conscious passion, because women and men need children to complete the symmetry of their own development, no less than to perpetuate the race. They shall be called into a world enhanced and made beautiful by the spirit of freedom and romance."[13]

Later feminists—Betty Friedan in her *Feminine Mystique* and Simone de Beauvoir in *The Second Sex*—also predicted significant, positive transformations of male/female relations if sex could be separated from children.[14] And of course a right to sexual happiness was vigorously asserted by the man who invented the term "the sexual revolution." In his book *Die Sexuelle Revolution*, Freudian disciple Wilhelm Reich wrote that the "core of life's happiness is sexual happiness."[15]

SEX AS REVOLUTIONARY

The idea that once-taboo sex is itself a tool for progress in overthrowing problematic authority is likely a less familiar aspect of the rise of our national preoccupation with sexual expression. But a surprising number and diversity of thinkers have explored it.

Hebrew University sociologist Eva Illouz, for example, has written that the idea of socially forbidden sexual expression originated with popular stories about taboo or star-crossed love—stories in which love is irruptive and has the potential to undermine authority and cross social lines.[16] Think Romeo and Juliet.

Early twentieth-century journalist and social critic Walter Lippman wrote about the tendency in the 1920s to associate overthrowing traditional sexual mores with women's empowerment.[17] And philosopher Charles Taylor describes the growth of the belief that persons formerly

---

13 Margaret Sanger, *The Pivot of Civilization* (1922; repr., Oxford: Pergamon, 1969), 271, 274.

14 Betty Friedan, *The Feminine Mystique* (New York: W.W. Norton, 1963), 86; Simone de Beauvoir, *The Second Sex,* trans. and ed. Howard M. Parshley (1949; repr., New York: Vintage Books, 1989), 724–31.

15 Wilhelm Reich, *The Sexual Revolution: Toward a Self-Regulating Character Structure,* trans. Therese Pol (New York: Farrar, Straus, and Giroux, 1945), 88.

16 Eva Illouz, *Consuming the Romantic Utopia: Love and the Cultural Contradictions of Capitalism* (Berkeley: University of California Press, 1997), 8.

17 Walter Lippmann, *A Preface to Morals* (New York: Macmillan Company, 1929), 290–307.

cast out of polite society on the grounds of their sexual conduct—or anyone repressed by bourgeois conventions—could be liberated by transgressive sex.[18] It was a reaction against old taboos and the double standard.

American literature professor Robert Oscar Lopez highlights several landmarks of American culture that communicate the belief that transgressive sex is revolutionary. He dwells particularly upon the huge popularity of pornography, the constant use of women's bodies in advertising, and classics of American literature such as *The Crucible*, which "reinforced the association in Americans' minds between sexually judgmental Puritans and their penchant for political persecution."[19]

Contemporary treatments of sexual practices and identities formerly hidden regularly communicate the conviction that smashing old sexual taboos equals progress per se. Disclosures about gay or bisexual or transgender preferences are regularly labeled as "brave," or as "coming out of the closet." They are hailed as decisions to "become one's true self" and equated with freedom and progress.

A REDUCED VALUATION OF CHILDREN

Americans' declining interest in bearing children has likely helped to valorize sex unrelated to children. The early twentieth century witnessed a spike in the public's acceptance of eugenics in order to produce only "fit" children. In the 1960s, several authors stoked fears of a "population bomb." Increasing numbers of feminists depicted children as first and foremost hindrances to women's growing opportunities in education and employment. By this time too, due to the decline of the family farm and child labor, children rarely contributed to a household's income. They became consumers, not producers. Not surprisingly, as sex became decreasingly associated with children, it was increasingly associated with attaining personal satisfaction.

---

18 Taylor, *A Secular Age*, 502–3.
19 Robert Oscar Lopez, "Civil Rights and the Sexual Revolution Need a Divorce," *The Federalist*, April 19, 2016, http://thefederalist.com/2016/04/19/civil-rights-and-the-sexual-revolution-need-a-divorce/.

TECHNOLOGY

Americans regularly accept that what is characterized as "science" is objectively true and necessary to achieve progress. Consider the zero-sum fights over "what the science shows" during the nation's recent experience with COVID-19. This is sometimes referred to as the "technological imperative." Therefore, when technology makes possible outcomes like sex without children and transgender surgeries, these are readily associated with "progress." To oppose these is to be retrograde.

MATERIALISM

Several scholars have explored a twentieth-century predilection to conceive of sex and its positive effects as a consumer item. In a capitalist society like the US, capitalist materialism—including the notion that consuming is pleasure and self-expression and self-fulfillment—easily invades the sexual arena. To have sex is to consume. Sex is used to sell consumer items, and consuming certain things is claimed to make a person sexy.[20]

All of the cultural factors reviewed above have played a role in the growing conviction in the US that sexual freedom is extraordinarily important for individuals' overall happiness, freedom, and progress. In such a milieu, those who oppose or even doubt the wisdom of any consensual sex or any choice of sexual identity become enemies of freedom and happiness and progress.

Yet culture did not do all the work to establish the context in which religious freedom contests unfold today. The law was also important. It both reacted to and provoked various cultural moves. In what follows, I will briefly describe the series of cases, laws, and regulations (i.e. rules issued by state and federal agencies) issued between the 1960s and today that have interacted with the above-described cultural phenomena.

The Law as a Powerful Force Promoting Sexual Expression Unlinked to Marriage or Children

The legal part of the story about how our nation became so preoccupied with sexual expression rights runs from about 1965 to the present. During these years, lawmakers incrementally but ultimately concluded that the state has no interest in preserving any links between sex, marriage, and children, that fulfilling one's sexual desires is nearly a human right, and that an individual's sexual identity is self-created. For brevity's sake, I call this set of ideas "sexual expressionism."

US SUPREME COURT DECISIONS

The legal story of sexual expressionism begins with the 1965 *Griswold v. Connecticut* decision in which seven members of the Supreme Court held that married couples have a constitutional right to buy and to use birth control.[21] While the Court acknowledged that the text of the Constitution does not speak about birth control, it reasoned that there were "penumbras and emanations" emitted from several other explicit guarantees in the Bill of Rights, which, together, pointed to married couples' possessing a right of "privacy" extending to their relationship and their bedroom and expansive enough to include the right to use birth control.

Griswold is easily characterized as the case kicking off the Supreme Court's high level of interest in sexual freedom as individual liberty. There the Court proved willing to create a constitutional right without explicitly supporting constitutional text. This exercise is not only fraught with uncertainty, but easily invites judges to substitute their personal predilections for the actual meaning of the Constitution and at the same time to trespass into the rightful sphere of legislatures. Note that the US Constitution is *supreme*: no federal or state law or state constitution may contradict what the Supreme Court holds the US Constitution to require. No law may provide *fewer* rights than the

---

21 Griswold v. Connecticut, 381 U.S. 479 (1965).

US Constitution commands. Thus, *Griswold*'s conclusions affected Americans and American law from coast to coast. At the same time, relative to the Supreme Court's later pronouncements, *Griswold* is a modest holding: the Court confined the right to use contraception to *married* couples and spoke of the sacred quality of *marital* relationships and bedrooms.

The Supreme Court's decision in *Eisenstadt v. Baird* exhibited no such modesty.[22] In *Eisenstadt*, the Court held that single persons have a constitutional privacy right to use contraception. In the course of its holding, for the first time, the Court separated sex from both marriage and childbearing. It stated that

> the marital couple is not an independent entity with a mind and heart of its own, but an association of two individuals each with a separate intellectual and emotional makeup. If the right of privacy means anything, it is the right of the individual, married or single, to be free from unwarranted governmental intrusion into matters so fundamentally affecting a person as the decision whether to bear or beget a child.[23]

Eisenstadt also dramatically altered the "right of privacy" so as to locate it not in a marital relationship or bedroom, but in the mind of the individual. In its holding that single persons had a "liberty" right to use contraception under the Fourteenth Amendment to the Constitution, it stated that this liberty included the right to make "decisions about matters so fundamentally affecting a person" in her "intellectual and emotional makeup."

For purposes of clarity, I should pause a moment to explain how the Court interprets the Fourteenth Amendment to provide for substantive rights not appearing in the text of the Constitution. One provision of the Fourteenth Amendment guarantees that "nor shall any State deprive any person of life, liberty, or property, without due process of law." It was originally understood to guarantee fair *procedural* process; for example, the right to know the charges brought against you and to be heard in a court of law. Over time, however, the Supreme Court held that the due process guarantee also promises

---

22 Eisenstadt v. Baird, 405 U.S. 438 (1972).
23 *Eisenstadt*, 453.

certain *substantive* rights implied by America's long-standing history and tradition. These are announced by a vote of a majority of the justices on the Court. The additional cases below will show that the Court has often altered its articulation of this test and that what is now called "substantive due process" has become the leading vehicle for the Supreme Court's inventing new "rights" regarding sex, marriage, and parenting that do not only appear nowhere in the text of the Constitution, but that also contradict America's history and tradition, rather than respect them.

Returning to the subject of *Eisenstadt*, its hallmark is individual choice regarding sexual matters. The Court's decision separated sex from marriage and from children, and moved the constitutional right of privacy out of the relationship between the marital couple and out of the marital bedroom, and into the mind of the individual, married or single.

Following *Eisenstadt*, the Court used Fourteenth Amendment substantive due process reasoning to declare the existence of a federal constitutional right to abortion in 1973's decision in *Roe v. Wade*. It held that even in the last trimester, a woman has a right to an abortion necessary for her "health," which the Court defined in *Roe*'s companion case, *Doe v. Bolton*, to include "all factors—physical, emotional, psychological, familial, and the woman's age—relevant to the well-being of the patient."[24] In short, *Roe* and *Doe* granted constitutional protection to all abortions for any and all reasons throughout pregnancy. The Court's "rationale" consisted largely of a litany of the physical, psychological, social, and emotional miseries it linked with unwanted pregnancy and parenting.

Legal abortion further assures that sex stands alone—without links to children or marriage. Contraception fails more often than people imagine, either because of the method or the user. But abortion ensures that a particular child is not born. While "shotgun marriage" formerly and regularly linked unexpected procreation with a subsequent marriage, abortion rendered even this practice irrelevant. Fathers instead often anticipate that their pregnant girlfriends can and should obtain an abortion.

---

24 Doe v. Bolton, 410 U.S. 179, 192 (1973).

The next abortion decision, *Planned Parenthood v. Casey*,[25] went further than *Roe* in the direction of elevating the importance of sexual expression, identifying sexual intercourse unlinked to children with freedom, dignity, and even identity formation. The Court wrote that women have "organized" their lives assuming the freedom to have an abortion if their contraception fails. It also linked women's ability to avoid childbearing by means of abortion with their social and economic progress and standing. In its most famous (and most frequently mocked) passage, it reaffirmed abortion as a Fourteenth Amendment "liberty" interest linked to identity formation and universe shaping. Justices O'Connor, Kennedy, and Souter wrote: "At the heart of liberty is the right to define one's own concept of existence, of meaning, of the universe, and of the mystery of human life."[26]

The *Casey* court gave voice to every one of the above-described cultural factors promoting sexual expressionism. It was individualistic in the extreme, suggesting that persons shape not only their own identities, but even their own "universe[s]." It linked women's happiness and social and material success with sex, free of children. It celebrated the links between women's progress and their contemporary, transgressive sexual and procreative rights. And it took into account the role of technology—contraception and abortion—in women's progress as it measured such progress.

While *Casey* merely suggested that nonprocreative sex was a constitutional right (requiring abortion to guarantee it), the next major Supreme Court sexual expression case explicitly announced it. In 2003, the Court's *Lawrence v. Texas* opinion overturned a Texas law banning homosexual sodomy.[27] The Court once again used a substantive due process rationale to discover a nontextual right in the US Constitution—in this case the right of two persons of the same sex to have consensual sex. Neither procreation nor marriage were in the picture.

While *Lawrence* directly constitutionalized a right of homosexual sex, the opinion is also regularly relied upon to affirm a right to consensual sex between *any* adults. This is because the Court

25 505 U.S. 833 (1992).
26 *Casey*, 851.
27 Lawrence v. Texas, 539 U.S. 558 (2003).

explicitly relied upon *Casey*'s "mystery of life passage" to conclude that consensual sex forms a person's identity and that the state has no business interfering in such a fundamental act.

Lawrence, like *Casey*, exhibits hyperindividualism respecting sex in its claim that individuals form their identity and even their universes by means of sex. Also, as in *Casey*, children are nowhere on the scene. Sex is important for an individual's happiness and sense of self, not because it has any connection with making the human race or enhancing a marital bond. Finally, *Lawrence* is filled with language affirming that being one's sexual self and breaking old taboos is the stuff of human progress.

The most recent case of importance to the shaping of contemporary sexual expressionism is the same-sex marriage opinion, *Obergefell v. Hodges*.[28] The *Obergefell* court declared the existence of a federal constitutional right to marriage, not based upon the text of the Constitution, but rather upon a 5–4 majority opinion about what the Fourteenth Amendment's due process clause requires. The Court specifically eschewed consulting history and tradition in favor of a new method of finding constitutional rights *not* articulated in the text of the Constitution. The new method simply consults the beliefs of the current majority of the justices on the Court. Opined the *Obergefell* majority: "The generations that wrote and ratified the Bill of Rights and the 14th Amendment . . . entrusted to future generations a charter protecting the right of all persons to enjoy liberty as we learn its meaning."[29]

Despite being an opinion about *marriage*, *Obergefell* indicated that it recognized same-sex marriage as a constitutional right because doing so ratified *individuals'* subjective sense of dignity and equality. In order for the state to affirm this dignity, the Court redefined marriage as sexual intimacy plus commitment, without any necessary or usual link to procreation. *Obergefell* thus represents the definitive separation of sex from children from marriage: the couple involved is biologically incapable of sexually producing children; every recognized marriage of this type will be free of children born of the marriage; if children are brought into the couple's household,

---

28 576 U.S. 644 (2015).
29 *Obergefell*, 664.

they will be separated from their natural mother or father or both in every single case. And no state is any longer permitted to declare that procreation or natural parent-child bonds have special value.

Obergefell—like the contraception, abortion, and sexual intercourse cases described above—reflected nearly all of the cultural influences leading to our current fixation upon sexual expression. The Court repeatedly stressed the importance of the individual's desire for sexual and relational happiness. It held that public licensing of same-sex unions is a necessary vindication of homosexual persons' individual rights. And it portrayed legal protections for homosexual sex and marriage as signs of human progress.

LAWS AND REGULATIONS

As already noted above, the Supreme Court's constitutional decisions about sex, marriage, and parenting provide the baseline for all other similar laws in the US, whether state or federal, legislative or regulatory. No lawmaker at any level can provide lesser rights than those guaranteed by the US Constitution. Frequently, however, supporters of the new sexual expression norms want more than the right to do this or that act. They want to project these new norms into more areas of law and society by means of statutes and regulations. They want to require others to facilitate their protected behavior. They are especially keen to bring these norms to bear upon laws affecting employment, services, and operations at every kind of social institution, including the kinds of institutions that Catholics frequently sponsor: health care, education, and social services. These types of services and institutions—whether religious or secular—are subject to state licensing and accreditation requirements. They employ many people and serve many others. They regularly provide health insurance for their employees. Higher-educational institutions regularly provide housing for students. And many institutions seek federal grants or contracts to provide services of interest both to the government and to the religious institution, including, among other things, refugee resettlement, halfway houses for ex-prisoners, care for single pregnant women and their children, food programs, antipoverty programs, and many others.

In recent decades, more governmental bodies have given interest groups promoting sexual expression more of what they demand. Laws are moving beyond recognizing particular citizens' "rights" to consensual sex, contraception, abortion, same-sex marriage and—today—transgender recognition and surgeries. Now they are requiring institutions, including religious institutions, to cooperate with or facilitate or provide the means for others to exercise their "rights." Thus, for example, laws will make birth control, sterilization, abortion, and/or transgender surgery the standard of care expected of all health insurance, health care facilities, or physician training programs aspiring to professional accreditation or licensing. Employment nondiscrimination laws will require employers to hire or retain same-sex married persons and to give identical benefits to same- and opposite-sex spouses of employees. Schools and sports programs might be required to treat males who identify as females equally to females. Marriage counseling or adoption services might be required to be made available to same-sex couples. Landlords might have to provide bedrooms for unmarried, cohabiting couples. And social services for youth might have to provide contraception and abortion services or referrals. If a Catholic entity seeks a federal grant or contract to provide services of interest both to the government and the religious institution, the grant or contract might come packaged with its own set of nondiscrimination or service requirements. This is not an exhaustive list.

In what follows, I offer a general summary of these myriad laws and regulations, highlighting the most common types that Catholic institutions face. But first, a brief preamble is in order for the many nonlawyer readers who might benefit from a review of the distinction between federal and state laws and of the body of law known as "nondiscrimination law." Both of these matters figure importantly in any understanding of why Catholic institutions are facing so many sexual expression-related lawsuits, and how they might respond with religious freedom claims.

Looking first at federal versus state lawmaking authority, Article I of the Constitution sets forth the limited subjects upon which Congress can legislate. For our purposes, the most relevant areas include Congress's power to legislate concerning interstate commerce (under the "Commerce Clause"), and its power to spend, which is accompanied by its power to place conditions on the receipt of federal money.

Simplifying matters greatly, it is fair to say that Congress exercises broad powers under the Commerce Clause upon a showing that a subject matter affects interstate commerce. Congress can, for example, regulate parts of the health care industry on the basis of its interstate effects. A federal nondiscrimination law passed by Congress can affect an employer in a particular state.

Congress also exercises a great deal of power over local matters by way of its spending power. The government can place numerous conditions upon its grants and contracts with private institutions, including religious institutions. Today, federal money flows to a vast number of educational institutions, hospitals, and state social service organizations, including Catholic ones. Increasingly, the government is deciding that it will only award grants or contracts to organizations willing to cooperate with the provision of abortion or contraception or even transgender surgeries.

Federal agencies—usually part of the executive branch—are responsible for rulemaking and other activities that implement laws passed by Congress. For example, a federal agency—the Department of Health and Human Services—was charged with interpreting the "preventive services mandate" of the 2009 health care reform law.[30] This agency decided that the mandate should be interpreted to require a large body of employers—including many religious ones—to provide contraception, sterilization, and some early abortifacients for free to female employees and the daughters of employees. This is the famous "contraception mandate," which has taken the Little Sisters of the Poor to the Supreme Court more than once.[31]

Turning now to state law, state legislative powers are broader than federal powers, and include the ability to make laws regarding any matter affecting "health, safety, and welfare." This is called a state's "police power" and every state has it.

The police power is an exceedingly broad authority, covering everything from motorcycle helmet requirements to day care licensing to shopping-bag bans, and much more. While the US Constitution,

---

30 The Patient Protection and Affordable Care Act, Pub. L. No. 111–148, 124 Stat. 119 (2010).
31 42 U.S.C. § 300gg–13(a)(4).

Article VI, paragraph 2 (the "Supremacy Clause"), gives the US Constitution, and federal law generally, precedence over state law in matters assigned to federal jurisdiction, there is a great deal of lawmaking left to the states because of their broad police powers. For example, even before federal health care regulations introduced the above-described contraception mandate, many states had already issued such mandates in the name of women's "health" and "welfare."

As the examples immediately above show, federal and state laws and regulations might easily make problematic sexual expression demands upon citizens, including Catholic institutions. One very common type of law provoking religious freedom demands on the part of such institutions is nondiscrimination law. Today, many of these laws require a wide array of individuals and institutions to cooperate with conduct that is contrary to Catholic beliefs, most often in the arena of sexual expression. A brief introduction to this area of law follows.

At law, "discrimination" has both innocent and guilty connotations. Of course, human beings "discriminate" all the time regarding myriad choices—for example, which school, career or food to choose. The law generally leaves people alone to make these decisions on the basis of their tastes and interests.

But there are certain grounds upon which people may not legally discriminate in certain arenas. To wit, in the arenas of employment, public accommodations, health care, housing, and education, both federal and state law provide that Americans may not discriminate on the basis of race, color, sex, pregnancy, religion, national origin, age, disability, or family status. And following the Supreme Court's recent decision in *Bostock v. Clayton County*,[32] "sex" discrimination also includes discrimination based upon a person's sexual orientation or gender identity (a person's subjective determination, unrelated to his or her biology, concerning whether they feel male or female or neither or both). *Bostock* was an employment discrimination case, and it is not yet settled whether its holding applies to other arenas (e.g., public accommodations, education), but it seems likely that it will.

Some state laws ban discrimination on additional grounds; for example, on the grounds of marital status (i.e., being single, married, widowed, divorced or, in some states, choosing to cohabit while unmarried). Citizens, including religious individuals and groups, must comply with both federal and state nondiscrimination laws, and many of the state laws have either narrow or no religious exemptions. Further adding to the religious liberty challenges of both state and federal nondiscrimination laws is that some states had added sexual orientation or gender identity categories, or both, to their nondiscrimination codes even before *Bostock*; some judges, too, decided to interpret the word "sex" to include sexual orientation and gender identity before *Bostock*. And some federal and state courts decided that even if a religious organization bases a decision—for example, to fire someone for entering a same-sex marriage—on that person's *conduct* and *not* their *status* as homosexual, the organization will wrongly be found liable of "sexual orientation *status* discrimination"; that is, firing someone for *being* gay.

Additionally, some laws, regulations, and executive orders forbid discrimination on certain grounds in connection with federal or state workforces, contractors, or grantees. Many religious groups are federal or state contractors or grantees—supplying, for example, expertise and services in the areas of immigration, education, scientific research, or social services. Sometimes these rules mandate some form of cooperation with contraception or abortion or views that are contrary to Catholic teaching on sexual orientation or gender identity. For example, President Obama issued an executive order prohibiting certain federal contractors and subcontractors from discriminating in employment on the basis of sexual orientation or gender identity.[33]

Having surveyed the myriad ways in which federal or state laws or regulations, and especially nondiscrimination law, might bring sexual expression rights to bear upon religious institutions, we now turn to the question of whether religious institutions can refuse to go along with these laws or regulations on the grounds of religious freedom. The general answer under federal and state constitutional and statutory law is sometimes yes, sometimes no, and sometimes maybe. In order to understand this, we will need to take a brief tour through religious freedom law at the federal and state level. Ordinarily, an

---

33 President Barack Obama, order amending section 202 of Executive Order 11246 of September 24, 1965 (April 8, 2014).

entire semester course at a law school is required to grasp this framework, but the following summary will be sufficient for our purposes. It will describe federal and state laws providing specific religious exemptions; the US Constitution's religion clauses (i.e., the free exercise and nonestablishment provisions); federal legislation called the Religious Freedom Restoration Act;[34] and state-level constitutional religion clauses and religious freedom legislation.

Religious Freedom as a Matter of State and Federal Legislative Exemptions and in the Federal Constitution, Together with Some Caveats

LEGISLATION

Sometimes when federal and state legislators pass laws with an obvious potential to infringe upon religious freedom, they incorporate therein specific protection for religious actors. When the Trump administration decided to keep the contraception mandate regulation written by the Obama administration's health agency, for example, it provided explicit protection for both moral and religious conscientious objectors.[35] When Congress passed the civil rights law protecting Americans against employment discrimination on the grounds of religion, it exempted religious employers, who are sometimes permitted to prefer members of their own religion.

This latter exemption,[36] however, is not as straightforward as it seems. On the one hand, it is not limited to hiring that is related strictly to the religious activities of the organization. (For example, a Mormon organization *can* require its janitors to possesses a "temple recommend."[37]) It is believed that Congress designed this exemption as it did in order to prevent courts from exploring the forbidden question

---

34 Pub. L. No. 103–141, 107 Stat. 1488 (1993).
35 See 82 Fed. Reg. 47813–47814; 83 Fed. Reg. 8487; 85 Fed. Reg. 722–723 (2020).
36 42 U.S.C. §2000e–1.
37 Corp. of the Presiding Bishop of the Church of Jesus Christ of Latter-Day Saints v. Amos, 483 U.S. 327 (1987).

of what constitutes a religious activity at a religious institution and what does not. At the same time, however, the exemption does *not* permit religious organizations to discriminate against personnel on the basis of race, color, national origin, sex, age, or disability. Thus, the freedom of religious institutions may be curtailed unexpectedly. For example, post-*Bostock*, if a religious organization asserts that it cannot hire a same-sex married person because this conflicts with its clear religious teachings, the organization might be liable for discrimination on the basis of *sex*, despite the *religious* basis of its objection to the person's *conduct.*

Title VII of the Civil Rights Act of 1964 also contains an exemption permitting religious discrimination in hiring when religion is a "bona fide occupational qualification" pertaining to a particular job.[38] This exemption has not been interpreted by courts to offer broad religious freedom protection; the institution must establish a close nexus between the precise position at issue and the central mission of the organization.

Title VII provides schools a special exemption allowing them to "hire and employ employees of a particular religion."[39] But this is limited by the requirement that the school show that it is "owned, supported, controlled, or managed," "in whole or in substantial part," "by a particular religion or by a particular religious corporation, association, or society," and that it offers a curriculum "directed toward the propagation of a particular religion."

Title IX of the same civil rights law also provides some protection to religious schools respecting their right to teach students in accordance with their religious teachings and moral expectations.[40] But the school must demonstrate that it is controlled by a religious organization and explain how certain Title IX requirements conflict with a specific tenet or tenets of the religious organization.

The federal constitutional guarantee of "church autonomy," as articulated by the Supreme Court in a case involving Our Lady of Guadalupe Catholic School in California, potentially offers the broadest protection for institutions' right to determine "matters of

---

38 42 U.S.C. §2000e–2(e)(1).
39 42 U.S.C. §2000e–2(e)(2).
40 20 U.S.C. §1681(a)(3).

faith and doctrine," "church government," and "internal management decisions . . . essential to the . . . central mission" of religious institutions, free of state intrusion. This doctrine includes, but is not limited to, a "ministerial exception" banning governmental intrusion into the "selection of the individuals who play certain key roles."[41] I will discuss this doctrine in more detail below under federal constitutional religious freedom guarantees. But it should be highlighted here too, because even if Title VII does not sufficiently protect a religious institution's freedom respecting employment, the church autonomy doctrine might.

It should be noted here, however, that some state nondiscrimination laws provide less protection for religious freedom than do federal laws. Some state laws, for example, have narrow definitions of who qualifies as a "religious employer" so that even quintessentially religious institutions are not considered religious. They may exclude organizations like Catholic schools or social services if they employ or serve too many non-Catholics or don't engage in prayer or worship. State laws might protect only those institutions operated solely for the purpose of propagating a religion. Some of these laws may not survive federal constitutional religious freedom scrutiny, but their existence is an invitation to create a religious freedom controversy nonetheless.

Protection for religious institutions against discrimination charges might also be undercut by courts that conflate, for example, a prospective employee's *conduct* with his or her *status*. I mentioned this above but will explain further here. For example, if an institution claims that it is making an employment decision on the basis of an employee's problematic *conduct* (e.g., entering into a same-sex marriage or cohabiting with a romantic partner to whom the employee is not married), a court might conclude instead that the institution is really discriminating on the basis of the employee's "*status*." It might rule that "being" homosexual is indistinguishable from entering into a same-sex marriage, or that because the institution wouldn't fire a married woman living with a man but did fire a single woman doing the same thing, it is guilty of "marital status" discrimination.[42]

41 Our Lady of Guadalupe Sch. v. Morrissey-Berru, 140 S. Ct. 2049, 2060 (2020).
42 Richardson v. NW Christian University, 242 F. Supp. 3d 1132 (D. Or. 2017).

FEDERAL CONSTITUTIONAL LAW AND
THE RELIGIOUS FREEDOM RESTORATION ACT

Now let us consider the scope of religious freedom protection available to religious institutions under the US Constitution. The Free Exercise Clause of the First Amendment in the Bill of Rights provides: "Congress shall make no law respecting an establishment of religion, or prohibiting the free exercise thereof." Pre-1990, the Supreme Court understood this clause to provide strong protection against laws that burdened the free exercise of religion. If the law's application in fact burdened religion, the state had to demonstrate that the law furthered a "compelling state interest" realized by means that were "least restrictive" of religious freedom. This was true even if the law did not target religion on its face.

For example, a law compelling school attendance through senior year of high school—neutral on its face—could not be enforced against the Amish because the state did not have a compelling interest in forcing students who lead successful but separate lives in a long-standing religious community to complete two additional years of school.[43] Likewise, the state could not deny unemployment benefits to a religious believer who refused employment requiring her to work on her Sabbath while benefits went to others who for secular reasons (e.g., job offers inappropriate to their skills) refused employment offers.[44]

This changed in 1990, when it became much harder for a religious individual or group to win a free exercise suit. The Supreme Court held in *Employment Division v. Smith* that if a law is neutral toward religion on its face and generally applicable,[45] then even if it burdens religion *in fact*, the law can stand unless it is not a "rational" means of pursuing a legitimate state interest. This is a very easy burden for governments to meet. Most laws constitute a rational means of pursuing a state interest (e.g., the health, safety, or welfare of citizens). Only if a law targets religion, or allows exceptions to others but *not* to religious actors, must the state meet the previous, more demanding test for burdening religion: the compelling state interest test. As a Supreme Court interpretation of the First Amendment that controls both federal

---

43 Wisconsin v. Yoder, 406 U.S. 205 (1972).
44 Sherbert v. Verner, 374 U.S. 398 (1963).
45 Employment Div. v. Smith, 494 U.S. 872 (1990).

and state laws, *Smith* stated the new constitutional standard that both federal and state laws had to meet. Because religions would have a harder time winning exemptions after the decision, the *Smith* court advised them to try to secure their religious freedom exemptions in the text of laws passed by legislatures, and not to wait to bring religious freedom lawsuits before the judiciary. During the period from 1990 until today, however, it has become harder for religions to convince legislatures to grant them exemptions. This is especially true with respect to sexual expression laws, as opinions and the political environment favoring sexual expression and disfavoring religious objectors have hardened.

Smith was an earthquake. Everyone from the United States Conference of Catholic Bishops to the American Civil Liberties Union joined forces with a nearly unanimous Congress and President Bill Clinton to pass the Religious Freedom Restoration Act (RFRA) in 1993. RFRA prohibits the "government [from] substantially burden[ing] a person's exercise of religion *even if the burden results from a rule of general applicability*" unless the government "demonstrates that application of the burden to the person—(1) is in furtherance of a compelling governmental interest; and (2) is the least restrictive means of furthering that compelling governmental interest."[46]

In a nutshell, this federal law restored the pre-*Smith*, religion-protective test. Even if a law that burdens religion is neutral and generally applicable on its face, religious entities must receive an exemption unless the state can demonstrate a "compelling state interest" realized by means that are least restrictive of religious freedom.

But there are important limits to RFRA's reach. In a later case—for complicated reasons pertaining to the scope of federal legislative power under the Fourteenth Amendment—the Supreme Court held that RFRA is applicable *only* to federal laws and *not* to state laws.[47] And later attempts to pass a federal law that could ban state burdens on religious freedom were stopped largely by interest groups unwilling to countenance religious actors' denial of housing or other services to cohabiting and same-sex couples.

---

46   42 U.S.C. § 2000bb–1(a)-(b) (emphasis added).
47   City of Boerne v. Flores, 521 U.S. 507 (1997).

Another potential limit to RFRA is pending federal legislation called the "Equality Act,"[48] which explicitly bars RFRA's application to lawsuits under the federal Civil Rights Act, including those claiming discrimination on the basis of sexual orientation or gender identity. The Equality Act is pending in Congress as I write this book, but has not yet passed.

There have also been efforts in recent times to eradicate RFRA from federal law or to interpret it so as to weaken its protective effects. For example, many sexual expression interest groups are now claiming that religious individuals and institutions should no longer be permitted to decide if a law "substantially burdens" their religious freedom; rather, judges would make the theological decision about what constitutes an interference with a religious duty or belief. These same interest groups are further arguing that "nondiscrimination" is always a "compelling state interest" sufficient to allow the state to trump any burden a law imposes on religious freedom. And finally, they are arguing that every time the state recognizes a new right or benefit (e.g., free contraception or transgender surgery), a religious institution's refusal to provide it is a sufficient "harm to third parties" to foreclose a religious exemption.

In sum, RFRA is usually useful for protecting religious freedom in the face of problematic *federal* laws or regulations—at least at this moment in time—but not in the face of state laws or regulations. The federal contraception mandate litigation proceeded under RFRA.[49] But states regularly burden religion with laws that appear neutral on their face. After *Smith* and because of RFRA's limited application to federal laws, how do religious actors gain protection for their free exercise rights as against state or local laws?

Religions seeking protection against problematic state and local laws have to hope that their state has either a state-level RFRA statute or a state constitutional provision promising strong religious freedom protection. About fourteen state constitutions are fairly religion-protective, and over twenty states have passed their own RFRAs. These laws were once rather uncontroversial, but the coalition of left and right that fueled their past success has broken down. For example, in

---

48 H.R. 5, 117th Congress (2020).
49 See Zubik v. Burwell, 136 S. Ct. 1557 (2016).

2017, a minor political earthquake erupted when Arkansas and Indiana tried to pass their own RFRAs. LGBTQ interest groups claimed that RFRAs are hate laws and constitute a license to refuse to hire or serve LGBTQ individuals. The governors of both states bowed to protestors who, among other things, threatened to bomb a pizzeria that had answered in the negative a reporter's theoretical question about catering a same-sex wedding.[50] Today, gay and transgender rights activists remain the most visible opponents of religious freedom bills in every state in which they are proposed.

There is one other avenue for religious liberty claims to protect religious institutions from the intrusive effects of both state and federal laws. It is known as the "church autonomy" doctrine, described above, and most recently robustly affirmed by the US Supreme Court's *Our Lady of Guadalupe* decision. As described above, the *Guadalupe* Court affirmed that the religion clauses of the First Amendment preserve a broad right of church autonomy to determine "matters of faith and doctrine," "church government," and "internal management decisions . . . essential to the . . . central mission" of religious institutions, free of state intrusion. It held that this doctrine includes, but is not limited to, a "ministerial exception" banning governmental intrusion into the "selection of the individuals who play certain key roles."[51] In a prior case, *Hosanna-Tabor Evangelical Church and School v. EEOC*,[52] the Supreme Court held that while there is "no rigid formula" for identifying ministers, generally they are those employees who "will personify [the church's] beliefs" and "convey[] the church's message and carry[] out its mission."[53] The *Guadalupe* court concluded that two schoolteachers—Agnes Morrissey-Berru and Kristen Biel—who taught religion and other subjects at two Catholic elementary schools were "ministers" who could not, therefore, pursue age and disability discrimination claims against their employers.[54]

50 See Shekhar Bhatia, "'If A Child of Mine Was Gay, I Would Love Them, But I Still Wouldn't Go to the Wedding': Defiant Indiana Pizza Parlor Owners Who Won't Cater for Gay Receptions REOPEN Store Tomorrow Buoyed by Donations of $842,000," *The Daily Mail* (UK), April 7, 2015, https://www.dailymail.co.uk/news/article-3028925/ If-child-gay-love-wouldn-t-wedding-Defiant-Indiana-pizza-parlor-owners-won-t-cater-gay-reception-REOPEN-store-today-buoyed-donations-842-000.html.

51 *Our Lady of Guadalupe*, 2060.

52 565 U.S. 171 (2012).

53 *Hosanna-Tabor*, 188, 190.

54 *Our Lady of Guadalupe*, 2066.

The scope of the church autonomy doctrine will no doubt remain contested for years to come. Some will try to confine its application to religion teachers or perhaps teachers generally. Some religious institutions will argue that it covers nearly all personnel appointments, as well as a wide array of decisions about services and operations. Given what I write later beginning with chapter 3, I think religious institutions have a strong argument that many or even most of their services, operations, and personnel decisions are protected by this doctrine. All of these components of an institution contribute in a significant way to the organization's ability to preserve and transmit its faith and doctrine.

Conclusion

Together, the legal and cultural developments of the last several decades have valorized and strengthened the influence of new sexual expression norms unlinking sex, marriage, and parenting. Given the sheer number of laws and regulations that affect myriad aspects of religious institutions—health care, employment, insurance, housing, services, operations, and others—these legal and cultural dynamics are pressuring one of the last pockets of resistance to the new norms: the Catholic Church.

Sometimes state or federal statutory or constitutional protection is available. But as the above sketch of religious freedom law suggests, the terrain is tricky. Judges and regulators interpret seemingly clear laws in new ways that are disadvantageous to religious freedom. Local laws may refuse to recognize religious institutions as sufficiently "religious" to enjoy statutory exemptions. Different standards for guarding religious freedom will apply, depending upon whether the law resisted is a state or federal enactment, whether or not a court determines that the enactment is "neutral" on its face respecting religion, and whether a lawsuit is commenced in a state with more or less religion-protective laws.

Furthermore, sexual expression rights are front and center in both law and culture and supported by a wide array of often wealthy, visible, and powerful corporate, media, academic, and political voices.

These voices seem more and more inclined to portray religious freedom as an oppressive opponent of sexual freedom. A statement by Chairman Martin Castro in the last report of the Obama-era Civil Rights Commission sent a chill down the spine of religious liberty advocates. He wrote, "the phrases 'religious liberty' and 'religious freedom' will stand for nothing except hypocrisy so long as they remain code words for discrimination, intolerance, racism, sexism, homophobia, Islamophobia, Christian supremacy or any form of intolerance."[55]

Certainly, state and federal RFRAs are a bright spot, as is the Supreme Court's decision in *Guadalupe* articulating a potentially powerful "church autonomy" doctrine. But sexual expression interest groups are working hard to tarnish the reputation of RFRAs and to ensure that the Supreme Court narrowly interprets the church autonomy doctrine in future cases. The Equality Act looms. In the future, religious organizations may have to demonstrate exceptional integrity and religious character in order to make the case that their faith, doctrine, and mission depend upon their personnel, services, and operations. They will also have to convincingly tie their adherence to the Church's sexual expression teachings to their religious core, and explain how the Church's teachings about sex, marriage, and parenting are not extraneous to the business of being a Catholic institution that exists to witness to Christ while educating, healing, and/or serving the poor.

As already outlined in the Introduction, by these standards, Catholic institutions' current framing of their religious freedom objections to sexual expression laws are insufficient. Not surprisingly, they engender backlash, not only from the public, but also from co-believers employed or served by the religious institution. Chapter 2 will take a closer look at some of the most frequent types of conflicts between Catholic institutions and sexual expression laws in order to illustrate the problems.

---

55 The United States Civil Rights Commission, *Peaceful Coexistence: Reconciling Nondiscrimination Principles with Religious Liberties,* Statement of Chairman Martin Castro (2016), 29, https://www.usccr.gov/pubs/docs/Peaceful-Coexistence-09-07-16.PDF.

- 2 -

BACKLASH

CHAPTER 1 SURVEYED THE WIDE VARIETY OF LAWS and regulations directing religious institutions to bring their employment relationships, operations, and services in line with the new sexual expression norms. It also described the religious freedom defenses available to Catholic institutions confronted with such laws, and the limits to these defenses. This chapter looks at the backlash that has often followed the refusals of Catholic institutions to cooperate with sexual expression laws. It describes and categorizes critics' responses in order to map out a strategy for improving these institutions' future legal and public communications about similar controversies.[1]

The backlash comes from Catholics and non-Catholics alike, and from nonlawyers as well as legal professionals—judges, opposing attorneys, interest groups, and legal academics. It appears to be a function of two misunderstandings: first, about the nature of Catholic institutions, and second, about the substance of Christian love. This chapter will illustrate these misunderstandings as they have unfolded in myriad church/state clashes in recent years, while chapters 3 to 6 will correct them by describing the integrated witness to Christ that animates Catholic communities and the radical and indivisible quality of the love of Christ that Catholics are called to observe.

Catholic institutions unwittingly feed the misunderstandings I outline here. Instead of telling listeners about the religious character of their Catholic communities, they regularly frame their religious

---

1   Some of the material in this chapter was previously discussed in Helen M. Alvaré, "Beyond Moralism: A Critique and a Proposal for Catholic Institutional Religious Freedom," *Connecticut Public Interest Law Journal* 19, no. 1 (2019): 149–98, 156–66. It is used here with the permission of the journal.

freedom defenses in terms of "rules that must not be violated," thin accounts of employees' institutional roles, or the necessity of following the directions of superiors in a hierarchical church. They furthermore shy away from linking Catholic sexual responsibility norms to Jesus's central command to love God and one another and from speaking substantively about Catholic wisdom on this subject. Instead, they often signal ambivalence and/or a shallow grasp of Church teachings, and fail to articulate any link between Christian love of family and/or romantic partners and the love of the many "neighbors" the institution serves.

These responses reduce critics' respect for both religious freedom and the norms of Catholic sexual responsibility. They evidence no pride in these norms, not only as ancient and influential patrimony of the Church, but as empirically and experientially verified paths to greater freedom and love, for Catholics *and* others. They fail to highlight the significant social benefits of allowing religious institutions to maintain their integrity so they can be a light to a world that is suffering from the current sexual orthodoxies. They fail to articulate what Catholic institutions are fully *for*, and how members' witness, and the services and operations of an institution, *together*, are necessary to fulfill the institution's mission.

The amount of backlash is significant and arises even when the institution involved ultimately prevails in a court of law. It is a classic case of "winning the battle but losing the war"—the battle being the immediate lawsuit, but the war being the larger effort to attain respect and affection for both religious freedom and Catholic sexual expression norms. In order to "win the war" in both courts of law and public opinion, it is not only necessary to effectively pursue the religious freedom opportunities described in chapter 1, but also to parse and then respond effectively to the backlash this chapter describes.

This chapter will, first, illustrate the currently problematic ways in which Catholic institutions express their religious freedom defenses. Second, it will classify the backlash coming from legal professionals, Catholics, and the wider public as based upon misunderstandings of the nature of Catholic institutions and/or the nature of Christian love. The second section will be further divided depending upon whether the particular clash between church and state involves the institution's relationship with an *employee* publicly dissenting from Catholic norms or the institution's refusal to cooperate with a legal mandate regarding *services* or *operations*.

The Leading Characteristics of Catholic Institutional Responses

To repeat, Catholic institutional responses to sexual expression challenges at law often display one or more of the following traits: they articulate the "Catholic rule" at issue, describe in technical terms an employee's role in the religious work of the institution, and/or announce a duty to follow hierarchical authority. This is not to say that no US Catholic institution has framed a better or more complete response. It is merely to observe that these tendencies are in fact the usual ones, and that they are insufficient to advance respect for religious freedom and Catholic sexual expression norms.

RULES AND MORE RULES

Catholic institutions' first habit is to articulate a brief, formulaic statement of the Catholic "rule" at issue, followed by a declaration that the government's demand that they violate the rule—or suffer a legal penalty—constitutes a burden on religious freedom. In a case about a Catholic school's refusal to renew the contract of a grade-school teacher who revealed to her employer that she was using in vitro fertilization (IVF),[2] for example, a Catholic school stated that "the Church teaches that in vitro fertilization is gravely immoral, an intrinsic evil which no circumstance can justify."[3] When a church music director in Illinois was fired for entering into a same-sex marriage,[4] the church explained to the former employee that its action was within its rights because "your union is against the teachings of the Catholic Church."[5] A Catholic school in Massachusetts that refused to hire

---

2 Herx v. Diocese of Fort Wayne-South Bend, 48 F. Supp. 3d 1168 (N.D. Ind. 2014).
3 Defendant's Trial Brief, November 24, 2014, Herx v. Diocese of Fort Wayne-South Bend, 2014 WL 7692604, sec. I., Factual Introduction.
4 Demkovich v. St. Andrew the Apostle Par., Memorandum Opinion and Order, 2017 WL 4339817 (N.D. Ill., September 29, 2017).
5 *Demkovich*, citing Complaint, ¶ 25.

a food services director who was in a same-sex marriage called his marriage "incompatible with [the school's] mission and its expectations of its employees."[6] In 2019, when the Archdiocese of Kansas City in Kansas refused to allow a Catholic school to enroll children being reared by a same-sex couple, the archdiocese wrote a press release declaring: "Matrimony is held up by the Catholic Church as a sacrament entered into between a man and a woman," further stating that marriage is "the building block of the family, of society and the heart of the Church," and thus that "same-sex parents cannot model behaviors and attitudes regarding marriage and sexual morality with essential components of the Church's teachings."[7]

The Little Sisters of the Poor framed the burden imposed by the 2012 federal contraception mandate (requiring free contraception as a health benefit or cooperation with federal efforts to send it separately to employees) as "being forced to participate in the provision of health care benefits that conflict with their religious beliefs" or suffer massive fines.[8] They also stated that "in order to stay true to their Catholic faith, they may hire an insurance company only if it will not provide their students and employees with coverage that may destroy human life or artificially prevent its creation."[9]

Finally, a Catholic hospital system claiming a free exercise right to refuse to provide transgender surgeries stated that "as part of its religious practices, Franciscan provides care consistent with its religious beliefs and follows The Ethical and Religious Directives for Catholic Health Care Services, issued by the U.S. Conference of Catholic Bishops."[10] The hospital system also maintained that "to provide or otherwise facilitate these services would also violate our deeply held

---

6 Barrett v. Fontbonne Acad., 33 Mass. L. Rptr. 287 (Mass. Super. Ct., 2015), *7.

7 Archdiocese of Kansas City in KS Media Statement, "Admissions Policies in Catholic Schools in the Archdiocese" (2019), https://www.documentcloud.org/documents/5761141-Archdiocesan-Media-Statement-Regarding-Same-Sex.html.

8 Brief for Petitioners in Zubik v. Burwell, 2016 WL 93988, *29 (US Supreme Court, 2016).

9 Brief for Petitioners, *Zubik,* *36.

10 Plaintiffs' Brief in Support of Their Motion for Partial Summary Judgment or, in the Alternative, Preliminary Injunction, 2016 WL 9049696, sec. F.1, citing Sister Klein Declaration, ¶ 32, in Franciscan Alliance v. Burwell (N.D. Tex., 2016). See also United States Conference of Catholic Bishops, *Ethical and Religious Directives for Catholic Health Care Services,* 6th ed. (Washington, D.C.: USCCB, 2018).

religious beliefs." It would "constitute impermissible material cooperation with evil."[11]

NOTHING BUT MINISTERS AND ROLE-MODELS HERE

The second kind of response, regularly displayed in cases involving an employee, is to articulate a factual link between the employee's work and an obviously *religious* institutional activity, alongside a conclusory statement about it being every employee's duty to serve as a Catholic role model. This is done usually in the hope that such a statement will bring the employee within the scope of the "ministerial exemption" or the "church autonomy doctrine" described in chapter 1.

In a case challenging the Archdiocese of Chicago and a local parish, for example, the Church invoked the ministerial exemption, arguing that it applied to an organist who announced his impending marriage to a man. The Church's reply brief focused on his functions of "convening and leading groups of parishioners to fashion music and liturgy recommendations for the pastor."[12] In another Illinois case involving a same-sex married music director and organist, the parish successfully secured a ministerial exemption after pointing to the relationship between the employee's functions ("selecting, directing and playing the music at Catholic masses") and "convey[ing] the Church's message."[13] In 2020, the Archdiocese of Seattle announced that two teachers at a Catholic high school had "voluntarily resigned" their positions after each became engaged to marry a person of the same sex, maintaining that "those who teach in our schools are required to uphold our teaching in the classroom and to model it in their personal lives."[14] And, as previously noted above, when a Massachusetts Catholic school refused to hire a same-sex married food-services director, the school called his same-sex marriage "incompatible with [the

---

11 Plaintiff's Brief in *Franciscan Alliance*, 2016 WL 9049696, sec. F.1, citing Sister Klein Declaration, ¶ 32.

12 Defendants' Reply in Support of Motion for Summary Judgment as to Ministerial Exception Affirmative Defense, 2016 WL 9445421 (N.D. Ill., Apr. 18, 2017), Argument, sec. A., in Collette v. Holy Family Par. and the Archdiocese of Chicago (N.D. Ill., 2016).

13 *Demkovich*, *3.

14 Juwan J. Holmes, "Catholic School Appears to Force Out Two Gay Teachers Because They're Engaged," *LGBTQNation*, February 17, 2020, https://www.lgbtqnation. com/2020/02/catholic-school-appears-force-two-gay-teachers-theyre-engaged/.

school's] mission and its expectations of its employees."[15] Despite the school's "role-model" argument, the state court refused to apply the ministerial exception on the ground that the functions of a food service employee "do not include formally presenting the gospel values or the ... teachings of the Catholic Church."[16]

JUST FOLLOWING ORDERS

Catholic institutions' third typical response is to point to orders from higher-ups in the Church. For example, with respect to the 2019 Archdiocese of Kansas City's decision not to allow a Catholic school to enroll children from a same-sex household, the pastor's letter noted that other dioceses allow such children into Catholic schools, but stressed that the diocese has final authority in these matters while "individual diocesan schools do not."[17] In a 2019 incident involving an Indiana Catholic school that removed a same-sex married teacher, the school's letter to its community focused substantially on the need to bow to authority:

> It is Archbishop Thompson's responsibility to oversee faith and morals as related to Catholic identity within the Archdiocese of Indianapolis. Archbishop Thompson made it clear that Cathedral's continued employment of a teacher in a public, same-sex marriage would result in our forfeiting our Catholic identity due to our employment of an individual living in contradiction to Catholic teaching on marriage. . . .
>
> Therefore, in order to remain a Catholic Holy Cross School, Cathedral must follow the direct guidance given to us by Archbishop Thompson and separate from the teacher.[18]

15 See *Barrett v. Fontbonne Acad.*, *7.

16 *Barrett*, *8.

17 Rev. Craig J. Maxim (Pastor of St. Ann Parish), Letter to St. Ann School Families, Faculty and Staff, February 27, 2019, https://assets.documentcloud.org/documents/5761765/Letter-from-the-Rev-Craig-J-Maxim-to-St-Ann.pdf.

18 Letter from the Chairman of the Board of Directors and the President of Cathedral High School to Cathedral Family, June 23, 2019, https://www.gocathedral.com/about/news-marketing/school-news/news-post/~board/homepagenews/post/dear-cathedral-family.

WHY ARE THESE RESPONSES INSUFFICIENT?

I am not arguing here that the above statements are always unnecessary—only that they are insufficient and sometimes off-putting. Legally, they are the minimum required to launch a religious freedom claim, in which the religious institution must show that its free exercise is "burdened." This involves showing that the institution will face a legal penalty unless it violates its own religious beliefs, which should be articulated. And in order to make out a ministerial exemption or church autonomy claim in an employment discrimination case, the institution must describe the actual role an employee plays in carrying out the institution's work.

But these statements are not *enough*. Statements about a moral rule that must not be violated fail to explain the wisdom of that rule or how it is loving *in the same way as the institution's services are loving, or in the same way that a nondiscrimination law claims to be loving*. Statements linking an employee's tasks to a narrow religious function of the institution fail to convey the *role of every single member in realizing the institution's religious identity*, particularly their role as a witness to the living Christ and a participant in the interpersonal relations that render the community overall a "new creation," a sign of the reign of Christ. Finally, statements to the effect that "the bishop made me do it" indicate a complete lack of confidence or belief in, or understanding of, Catholic teachings. *They portray the Church as just another bureaucratic service provider.*

It is not necessary to observe that such statements not only fail to elicit respect for religious freedom or Catholic sexual responsibility norms, but often provoke the opposite. Institutional leaders should instead give evidence of their pride in Catholic teachings, not only as ancient and influential patrimony of the Church, but as empirically and experientially verified ways of living in freedom and love. They should emphasize the significant social benefits arising from religious institutions' public witness on these matters in a world where diminishingly few are willing to provide it. And they should describe what a religious institution is—theologically speaking—and why members' witness, and the services and operations of an institution, must work in harmony to fulfill its mission. Instead, they regularly provoke the backlash I describe below.

WHEN CATHOLIC INSTITUTIONS REFUSE MEMBERSHIP IN THE COMMUNITY TO A STUDENT OR EMPLOYEE

Backlash: The Church is Unloving

I will now describe institutional responses according to type of incident and the associated backlash. A first type of incident involves an institution's refusing membership or employment to a particular person on sexual expression grounds.

The most frequently heard complaint about a Catholic institution's decision not to associate with a person—usually an employee but occasionally a student or his or her family—who plans to contradict Catholic teaching in a public manner, is that the Church is being unloving, unmerciful, unkind, and judgmental. It is therefore violating the core Catholic imperative of love.

In early 2020, when the Archdiocese of Seattle announced the departure of two same-sex married teachers from a Catholic high school, the school's letter to its community was exceedingly gentle. But the departures nevertheless led to a massive student walkout and protest featuring the mayor and other local politicians, a well-supported online fundraiser for the teachers, and vocal parent backlash. A banner waved in front of the school summed up the message of the protest: "Who Would Jesus Fire? #LoveisLove."[19]

The 2019 decision of an archdiocese in Kansas not to allow a Catholic school to enroll children being reared by a same-sex couple provoked a letter signed by more than 1,200 people charging that the school was rejecting a Catholic "welcoming culture." Over one-third of the signatories were members of the associated parish or had children enrolled in the school. The pastor's letter characterized the backlash as coming "from a place of love and compassion for the family and the desire for inclusivity within our school and community"[20] without articulating that the school's behavior promoted love of neighbor.

---

19 "Kennedy Catholic High School President Releases Statement about Teacher Resignations," *B-Town Blog*, February 21, 2020, https://b-townblog.com/2020/02/21/kennedy-catholic-high-school-president-releases-statement-about-teacher-resignations/; "Shockwave: How Kennedy Catholic Students Stood Up to Seattle's Archdiocese," June 17, 2020, *Seattle Pride*, https://www.seattlepride.org/news/seattle-pride-magazine-shockwave-how-kennedy-catholic-students-stood-up.

20 Rev. Craig J. Maxim Letter to St. Ann School Families, Faculty and Staff.

A final example of the charge that an institution behaves in an unloving manner by refusing to cooperate with persons publicly contradicting its beliefs, emerges from a Catholic school's decision *to* cooperate. The president emerita of Georgetown Visitation Preparatory School in Washington D.C. (Sr. Mary Berchmans VHM) went so far as to *directly* characterize Church teaching as unloving when she wrote about the school's decision to celebrate graduates' same-sex weddings in its alumnae magazine:

> As I have prayed over this contradiction, I keep returning to this choice: we can focus on Church teaching on gay marriage or we can focus on Church teaching on the Gospel commandment of love. We know from history—including very recent history—that the Church, in its humanity, makes mistakes. Yet, through the grace of God and the power of the Holy Spirit, it learns and grows. And so, we choose the Gospel commandment of love.[21]

Two legal commentators opposed to religious freedom suggest that Sr. Berchmans' arguments provide good grounds for forcing other religious institutions to cooperate with the new sexual orthodoxy in the employment nondiscrimination context. They argue that refusing to maintain a relationship with an employee because of his or her sexual choices is a violation of dignity so great that it qualifies as a "compelling state interest," sufficient to allow the state to trump every religious freedom defense. This argument is summarized in a well-known piece by Yale Law School professors Douglas NeJaime and Reva Siegel:

> Persons of faith are now seeking religious exemptions from laws concerning sex, reproduction, and marriage on the ground that the law makes the objector complicit in the assertedly sinful conduct of others. . . . The distinctive features of complicity-based conscience claims matter, not because they

---

21 Dick Uliano, "Catholic Girls' School in DC Adopts Policy Contrary to Church Teaching," *WTOP News*, May 13, 2019, https://wtop.com/dc/2019/05/catholic-girls-school-in-dc-adopts-policy-contrary-to-church-teaching/; Flo Martinez Addiego et al., "An Open Letter to Georgetown Visitation," *First Things* (May 23, 2019), https://www.firstthings.com/web-exclusives/2019/05/an-open-letter-to-georgetown-visitation.

make the claim for religious exemption any less authentic or sincere, but rather because accommodating claims of this kind has the potential to inflict material and dignitary harms on other citizens.[22]

Backlash: Witch-Hunting Vulnerable Groups

A second, often-heard complaint about Catholic institutions' refusals to accede to violations of Catholic sexual responsibility norms among members of the community is that the Church is witch-hunting for sexual violations, especially among women and LGBTQ persons. In an interview in the widely read *Atlantic Magazine,* a priest familiar with the Indianapolis parish that fired a teacher over her resort to IVF explicitly called the Catholic school's decision a witch-hunt and the policing of private sexual lives.[23] The court deciding the case wrote that because the diocese hadn't terminated any men for participating in infertility treatment, it might have engaged in sex discrimination toward the female plaintiff.[24]

In a case involving a school's separation from a pregnant unmarried teacher, her lawyer told the local newspaper that he "sees the issue as the Scarlet Letter syndrome, that only women can sometimes show signs of premarital sex. 'And for it she is punished, while male employees who engage in it are not—and that is illegal.'"[25]

After the above-mentioned parochial school in Kansas refused to enroll the children of a same-sex couple, the parish Facebook site suggested that LGBTQ persons were being selectively targeted. The pages featured comments like this one: "Wonder how many

---

22 Douglas NeJaime & Reva B. Siegel, "Conscience-Wars: Complicity-Based Conscience Claims in Religion and Politics," *Yale Law Journal* 124, no. 7 (2015): 2516–91, 2516 (Abstract).

23 Jennie Rothenberg Gritz, "Should Catholic Schools be Able to Fire Teachers over Fertility Treatments?" *The Atlantic,* April 27, 2012, https://www.theatlantic.com/national/archive/2012/04/should-catholic-schools-be-able-to-fire-teachers-over-fertility-treatments/256427/.

24 *Herx,* 1178.

25 Kevin Shea, "For Second Time, Court Reinstates Suit by Catholic School Teacher Fired for Being Pregnant," *NJ.com,* November 19, 2020, https://www.nj.com/union/2020/11/for-2nd-time-court-reinstates-suit-by-catholic-school-teacher-fired-for-being-pregnant.html.

parishioners take birth control or eat meat on Fridays? . . . Have any parishioners cheated on spouses? Sooo hypocritical."[26] Some commentators also accuse the Church of being hypocritical and sex-obsessed for failing to draw similar lines respecting employees who disagree with Catholic teachings about immigration or capital punishment. A related criticism asserts the hypocrisy of Catholic institutions' refusals to comply with contemporary sexual expression laws at the same time that horrible clerical sex abuse and cover-ups by Church leaders continue to come to light. There is a great deal of sympathy for this position for obvious and convincing reasons. At the end of an article about a Catholic school teacher asked to leave her position due to her cohabitation and nonmarital pregnancy, for example, a local reporter simply wrote: "[The teacher's] case comes as the Catholic Church faces an onslaught of clergy sex abuse lawsuits that have piled up over the years."[27]

Catholic leaders regularly leave these types of backlash unaddressed. But this only leads to confusion and even animosity among onlookers. Leaders need instead to explain that they only take account of members' *public* behaviors and not their private ones, precisely because they are *not* witch-hunting or surveilling. They also need to clarify that when they assert religious freedom claims in sexual expression controversies, it is because the legal demand *directly* contradicts a clear Catholic commitment—for example, about what marriage is or about nonmarital sex, abortion, or cohabitation. Catholic institutions do not take similar action respecting issues or behaviors admitting of a range of moral solutions. They do not, for example, separate from employees who publicly advocate for less generous immigration policies than the Church endorses, even though, here too, there are lines an employee could not cross, like the use of racist[28] or ethnic slurs.

26 Christine Hauser, "Catholic School in Kansas Facing a Revolt for Rejecting a Same-Sex Couple's Child," *New York Times*, March 8, 2019, https://www.nytimes.com/2019/03/08/us/kansas-catholic-school-same-sex-parents.html.

27 Caleb Parke, "Catholic School Teacher Fired for Unwed Pregnancy Can Sue for Discrimination," *Fox News*, January 29, 2020, https://www.foxnews.com/us/catholic-school-teacher-fired-for-unwed-pregnancy-can-sue-for-discrimination.

28 Edgar Sandoval and Corky Siemaszko, "Ex-Bronx Principal Fired From Pennsylvania Catholic School After Identity Revealed," *New York Daily News*, January 28, 2014, https://www.nydailynews.com/new-york/bronx/racist-ex-bronx-principal-fired-catholic-school-article-1.1594144; Michael Elsen Rooney, "White Headmaster Who Forced

In sum, it is a mistake for institutional leadership to remain silent in the face of backlash that mistakenly conflates public with private behaviors and prudential judgments with clear moral teachings. This aspect of backlash can and should be handled as soon as it arises.

Backlash: Shut Up and Sing

A third, common reaction to institutions' religious freedom claims is to admonish the institution to stop focusing on the lives of its employees or students/clients and get on with its "real" business—its core services of education, health care, or social services. For example, in response to Catholic Relief Services' separating itself from a same-sex married executive, a support group for LGBTQ Catholics opposed to Catholic teaching (New Ways Ministry) urged the "CEO[] and other decision makers to stand by Rick Estridge and other LGBT church workers, whose dedicated service to the Gospel and those in poverty is what matters, not sexual orientation."[29]

A parent at a Miami school that fired a same-sex married teacher likewise reported to the local newspaper: "'We were extremely livid.' . . . [The parent] said that the parents hadn't known [the teacher] was gay, but did not care about her sexual orientation. 'Our only concern was the way she was with our children, the way she taught our children and this woman by far was one of the best teachers out there,' [the parent] said."[30]

A parent at an Indiana Catholic school also stressed the overarching importance of teacher quality in opposing a school's decision to separate from same-sex married teachers: "'The teachers in question are longtime teachers who are highly qualified and highly valued,' said Butch Humbert, who has two children enrolled at Brebeuf."[31]

Black Boy to Kneel in Apology Resigns from L. I. Catholic School," *New York Daily News*, March 24, 2021, https://www.nydailynews.com/new-york/education/ny-long-is-land-headmaster-resignation-20210324-d5gwo5ynbvfs3cbmqxmor7blxy-story.html.

29   Robert Shine, "Tell Catholic Relief Services Not to Discriminate Against Gay Employee," *New Ways Ministry Blog*, May 1, 2015, https://www.newwaysministry.org/2015/05/01/tell-catholic-relief-services-not-to-discriminate-against-gay-employee/.

30   Robert Shine, "Lesbian Teacher Fired by Catholic School Over her Same-Gender Marriage," *New Ways Ministry Blog*, February 13, 2018, https://www.newwaysministry.org/2018/02/13/lesbian-teacher-fired-catholic-school-gender-marriage/.

31   Arika Herron, "Indianapolis Archdiocese Aggressive, But Not Alone, in Firing Gay Teachers, Here's Why," *IndyStar*, July 7, 2019, https://www.indystar.com/story/

Parents and students at Kennedy Catholic High School in Seattle, described above, spoke of the fired teachers in elevated terms, telling the local newspaper and a gay rights journal that the departing homosexual teachers had provided crucial guidance to students.[32] And parents whose children were taught at a Catholic school by a dance coach whose nonmarital cohabitation became public, demanded that the school consider only "the sort of impact teachers have in their schools," and not "who they live with when they're back home."[33] They also accused the school of "selective outrage," asking why they had not fired teachers who had committed "silent" sins.

Backlash: They Can't All Be Ministers?

A fourth common negative reaction to Catholic institutions' religious freedom claims is a disbelief of their broad assertion that all or most employees are "ministers" of an institution's mission and important to the transmission of faith. Critics characterize these claims as opportunistic moves by religious employers seeking only to avoid legal oversight of their unfair treatment of employees.

Many observers noted, for example, that the teacher in the case of *Hosanna-Tabor Evangelical Church and School v. EEOC*[34] was returning from sick leave due to narcolepsy when the church denied her reemployment and then succeeded with its ministerial exemption claim. Similar suspicions were voiced about the teacher in the *Our Lady of Guadalupe School v. Morrissey-Berru* case, who was let go after a cancer diagnosis. In their dissent in that case, Justices Sotomayor and Ginsburg began: "Two employers fired their employees allegedly because one had breast cancer and the other was elderly." They continued, commenting on the majority opinion: "In the Court's view, because the employees taught short religion modules at Catholic elementary schools, they were 'ministers' of the Catholic faith and

---

news/education/2019/07/07/indianapolis-archdiocese-not-first-fire-gay-teachers-but-among-most-active/1555277001/.

32 "Shockwave: How Kennedy Catholic Students Stood Up to Seattle's Archdiocese," *Seattle Pride.*

33 David Gee, "Catholic School Fires Dance Coach for Living with Her Fiancé Before Marriage," *The Friendly Atheist*, June 12, 2018, https://friendlyatheist.patheos.com/2018/06/12/catholic-school-fires-dance-coach-for-living-with-her-fiance-before-marriage.

34 565 U.S. 171 (2012).

thus could be fired for any reason, whether religious or nonreligious, benign or bigoted, without legal recourse."[35]

Backlash: The Teaching is Wrong . . . and Embarrassing

A fifth type of negative reaction to institutional religious freedom claims is simple disagreement with the Catholic teaching involved. A slight variation on this occurs when the institutions involved publicly agree with the teaching, but in a manner that clearly reveals their discomfort.

When a school counselor was fired from a Catholic high school in Indiana, the students "sported rainbow apparel at school and during sporting events. The football team kicked off the season by running onto the field waving a large rainbow flag. A group of students started a nonprofit in [the teacher's] name to advocate for change in the church; they also appeared on Ellen Degeneres' daytime talk show with [the fired teacher]."[36]

When Georgetown Visitation High School decided to celebrate graduates' same-sex unions it wrote, "We know from history—including very recent history—that the Church, in its humanity, makes mistakes. Yet, through the grace of God and the power of the Holy Spirit, it learns and grows."[37]

The pastor at the parish involved in the Kansas City Catholic school decision not to enroll a child reared in a same-sex household wrote a letter to his community suggesting that the Church's teaching in this area is controverted by many of his parishioners and that he himself was "distressed over the division this sensitive and complex issue has caused."[38]

35 Our Lady of Guadalupe Sch. v. Morrissey-Berru, 140 S. Ct. 2046, 2071 (Sotomayor and Ginsburg, JJ., dissenting).

36 Arika Herron, "Roncalli Guidance Counselor, Placed on Leave for Gay Marriage, to Appear on the 'Ellen Show,'" *IndyStar*, September 3, 2018, https://www.indystar.com/story/news/2018/09/03/shelly-fitzgerald-gay-roncalli-counselor-ellen-show-ellen-degeneres-same-sex-marriage/1185038002/.

37 Uliano, "Catholic Girls' School in DC Adopts Policy Contrary to Church Teaching."

38 Rev. Craig Maxim, Letter to St. Ann School Families, Faculty and Staff.

WHEN CATHOLIC INSTITUTIONS REFUSE TO COOPERATE WITH MANDATES TOUCHING ON SERVICES OR OPERATIONS

A second set of negative reactions are provoked by Catholic institutions' refusals to cooperate with legal mandates covering services or operations, such as the 2012 "contraception mandate" under the Affordable Care Act. These reactions largely overlap with the first set, but differ because the former disputes about employment and school admission appear to single out individuals for judgment, while mandates do not directly do so.

Backlash: Even Catholics Don't Believe the Rule

A first common type of backlash charges that the vast majority of Catholics don't even believe in or abide by the Catholic rule at issue in a particular church/state conflict. Both Catholics and non-Catholics have raised this objection. For example, in response to some Catholic institutions' refusals to obey the contraception mandate, an Obama administration official told the press that Catholic women agree more with the administration than with their own institutions, stating her belief that 98 percent of them use birth control.[39]

Backlash: Shut Up and Sing

A second common negative reaction regarding mandates is to claim no connection between the legally mandated services or operations and the religious institution's ability to fulfill its mission. For example, the Obama administration denied that the legal process by which the Little Sisters of the Poor were required to express their objection to the mandate—providing a form to HHS stating their objection, which allowed a third party to give free contraception to their employees—could constitute a "substantial burden" under the Religious Freedom Restoration Act ("RFRA"). A number of lower federal courts agreed with the Obama administration on this point;[40] they could not envision how

39 Becky Bowers, "White House Official Says 98 Percent of Catholic Women Have Used Contraception," Politifact website, February 6, 2012, https://www.politifact.com/factchecks/2012/feb/06/cecilia-munoz/white-house-official-says-98-catholic-women-have-u/.

40 See, e.g., Priests for Life v. U.S. Dep't of Health & Human Servs., 772 F.3d 229, 237, 256 (D.C. Cir. 2014), vacated and remanded *sub nom.* Zubik v. Burwell, 136 S. Ct. 1557 (2016)

the Little Sisters' mission could be impacted or compromised by their facilitating employees' independent decisions to use birth control.

Another aspect of this reaction is the accusation that Catholic institutions resisting a mandate are trying to have their cake and eat it too; to wit, the institutions want both to be part of the professional community—of educational, health care, and social services providers—while refusing to abide by laws and by the minimum standards of professional trade associations. Not surprisingly, the critics usually assume without further discussion that abortion or birth control or transgender surgery is required to meet minimum health care or employment standards.

Conclusion: What More is Needed

As has already been acknowledged above, it is not wrong for Catholic institutions facing sexual expression challenges to describe the Catholic teaching at issue, specify an employee's role in executing the institution's mission, or refer to the authority structure of the Church. These recitations fulfill basic legal and public information requirements for stating a claim of religious freedom.

But it is insufficient and ineffective to stop with these statements. They are not *enough*. Here, one is forcefully reminded of Pope Francis's admonition about the disutility of "disjointed" Catholic moral teachings and how easily they can put observers off the faith.[41] I would add that they can put observers off of religious freedom claims, too.

This is quite evident from the backlash described above, which points to what is missing in current Church communications. I would group all that is missing under two broad headings. First, institutions

---

("We conclude that the challenged regulations do not impose a substantial burden on Plaintiffs' religious exercise under RFRA. All Plaintiffs must do to opt out is express what they believe and seek what they want via a letter or two-page form. . . . The ACA shifts to health insurers and administrators the obligation to pay for and provide contraceptive coverage for insured persons who would otherwise lose it as a result of the religious accommodation." The *Priests for Life* decision also stated that "the regulatory requirement that they use a sheet of paper to signal their wish to opt out is not a burden that any precedent allows us to characterize as substantial.").

41 Laurie Goodstein, "Pope Says Church is 'Obsessed' With Gays, Abortion and Birth Control," *New York Times*, September 20, 2013, https://www.nytimes.com/2013/09/20/world/europe/pope-bluntly-faults-churchs-focus-on-gays-and-abortion.html.

are not broadcasting correct information about or the inspiration around Catholic institutions' essential nature as communities called by Christ to make His person and reign present today. Second, institutions are not providing a more complete and inspiring explanation of the Church's sexual expression teachings, with particular attention to the role they play in demonstrating a robust love of God and neighbor.

Better communication about the first of these issues would help correct the above-described misunderstandings about what the "real mission" of a Catholic institution is and about how its employees are inextricably responsible for the realization of that mission. Better communication about the second issue would speak directly to the accusations that Catholic teachings are unloving, sex-obsessed, and harmful, especially to the dignity and privacy of vulnerable persons. Both would help to contest the claims that Catholic institutions are simply trying to skirt the law.

And the leaders of Catholic institutions should not stop there. They should further and enthusiastically, though not triumphalistically, propose the empirically and experientially verified advantages of Catholic sexual expression teachings for human beings generally and the vulnerable specifically. They should flatly reject the belief that the *new* sexual expression orthodoxy supports health, freedom, happiness, and love. It has been clear for a while to many, many people that the sexual revolution has been a raw deal, especially for women and children, though we increasingly see the harm it has done to men as well. Why not say what more and more people are ready to hear? And support our claims with confidence, with supporting empirical and experiential evidence, and with compassion toward those caught in its web? The next chapters take up the work of crafting these communications.

– 3 –

THE RELIGIOUS NATURE OF CATHOLIC INSTITUTIONS

IN ORDER TO FOSTER GREATER RESPECT FOR THEIR REFUSALS to cooperate with sexual expression laws, Catholic institutions must first explain what they *are* in thicker, religiously determined ways. At the same time, though, their communications to courts of law and public opinion cannot be too theologically detailed and complicated. Courts are not in the business of "doing theology," and neither courts nor the public will be convinced by descriptions lacking language that also engages reason and common sense. This chapter tries to thread this needle by offering three models or theological self-understandings of Catholic institutions that can help them explain to the state and to the public why the state cannot force them to conduct their services, operations, or personnel choices in ways that undercut or eradicate their religious character and mission.

These three models are first, that Catholic institutions are communities of persons gathered in response to God's invitation and a shared conviction that Jesus Christ is Lord and Savior. Second, they are communities in which members understand themselves to be charged to witness by their lives that He is a living presence in the world and not just a beautiful figure in history. And finally, they are communities whose way of living should provide the world a glimpse of the inbreaking of the Kingdom of God among us, that is, Jesus Himself and His reign.[1] By contrast, they are *not*, in the words of Pope Benedict XVI, "just another form of organized social assistance."[2]

Chapter 2 described the common misperception that Catholic institutions are "just another form of organized social assistance," albeit assistance provided "with a heart." This "heart" comes from their being founded and staffed by people who believe that providing humanitarian services is the kind of loving thing that Jesus would do. According to this misperception, these institutions should focus their efforts nearly exclusively upon providing a high quality of services to persons in need in a kind and welcoming manner that looks "loving" to the world's eyes. As such, their cooperation with governmental demands contradicting religious beliefs about sexual expression—whether in their services, operations, or personnel decisions—does not affect their central task of providing quality humanitarian services.

This misperception would fade and perhaps even disappear if confronted by the three models of Catholic institutions described above. With respect to the first model, if such institutions really are composed of persons united in response to a shared conviction that Jesus Christ is Lord and Savior, then they are not merely a collection of individuals who have made an ethical decision to provide human services as a result of human beliefs about what is required to be good. This would be what the Congregation for the Doctrine of the Faith has recently called a new form of "Pelagianism": "In this vision, the figure of Christ appears as a model that inspires generous actions with his words and his gestures," and "the individual, understood to be radically autonomous, presumes to save oneself."[3] Instead, Catholic institutions have emerged and operate as the result of their members' encounter with Jesus Christ, by which they came to see the world with new eyes, and desired to live in a new way according to His words and deeds, and not by their own lights. They are attempting to grasp the obligations of human beings toward their brothers and sisters, especially toward the suffering, in light of Jesus's instructions

---

1   *Catechism of the Catholic Church* (Vatican City: Libreria Editrice Vaticana, 1993), § 763.

2   Benedict XVI, *Motu Proprio: On the Service of Charity*, November 11, 2012, introduction.

3   Congregation for the Doctrine of the Faith, *Letter* Placuit Deo *to the Bishops of the Catholic Church on Certain Aspects of Christian Salvation*, February 22, 2018, 2, 3.

in response to a question from the scribes about what is the first of all the commandments: "The first is this: 'Hear, O Israel: The Lord our God is God alone! You shall love the Lord your God with all your heart, with all your soul, with all your mind, and with all your strength.' The second is this: 'You shall love your neighbor as yourself.' There is no other commandment greater than these" (Mk 12:30–31). An important part of loving God and neighbor concerns the quality of love we share with spouses, children, and romantic partners, in addition to the love shared in the delivery of high-quality health care, education, and social services. Laws and regulations requiring Catholic institutions to facilitate relationships and practices that contradict Christian love therefore attack the very unity of the religious community and its ability to carry out its religious duties.

According to the second model, if Catholic institutions are comprised of persons who understand themselves as charged to be Christ's arms and legs—to witness by their lives that He is a *living* presence in the world—then each person is called to manifest the radical love of Christ to others. This love is no less demanding respecting one's family or romantic partners than it is respecting one's colleagues, students, patients, or clients. Governmental demands to incorporate into the institution persons who openly reject the call to manifest this type of love alter the religious character and operations of the institution.

With respect to the third model, if Catholic institutions are communities whose way of living should provide the world a glimpse of the inbreaking of the Kingdom of God among us—if they each understand themselves as the "bearer of a distinct and peculiar vocation in the world" and as communities "embody[ing] the surprising hope of the new creation"[4]—then the community as a whole must try to transmit this understanding. Its services, operations, and personnel must communicate as much as possible what a society transformed by faith in Jesus Christ might look like. And if (as the song goes) "they will know we are Christians by our love," this has implications for the visible lives and interactions of the institution's personnel, the shape of the health insurance it offers, and all of the services it provides, among

---

4   Richard B. Hays, *The Moral Vision of the New Testament: A Contemporary Introduction to New Testament Ethics* (New York: HarperOne, 1996), 376.

other things. The state's insistence that these elements are unimportant, or can be used to transmit a contradictory message, directly distorts the religious mission and internal affairs of the institution.

I do not claim that these three theological self-understandings exhaust possible Catholic accounts of the identity and purposes of Catholic institutions. For this book's purposes, however—crafting *comprehensible* explanations for courts of law and public opinion about why Catholic institutions cannot cooperate with coercive sexual expression laws—they are very useful. Individually or together, they indicate why these institutions reject the notion that only discrete portions of their personnel or services or operations are the "keepers of the mission." Rather, nearly everything they are and do is part of an attempt to respond to God's saving action in human life, to make the living Christ present in the world today, and to provide onlookers a glimpse of a society comprised of persons living as disciples of Jesus Christ. This is not to say that the state may not impose due limits on the behaviors of any person or group that harms other people.[5] But as chapters 6 and 7 argue, Catholic sexual responsibility norms facilitate love, freedom, dignity, and equality, not harm.

While these overlapping depictions of Catholic community are ordinarily used to describe "churches," they also characterize educational, health care, and social services institutions. Not only do these institutions regularly offer what Catholic parishes offer—the Word of God, evangelization, and often worship—but their services are regularly characterized in documents of the universal Church as a direct sharing in its mission.

For example, a 2012 Motu Proprio (a personal edict of a pope) of Pope Benedict XVI called all Catholic charitable endeavors a "sign of the sharing of all the faithful in the mission of the Church."[6] His encyclical on charity, *Deus Caritas Est* (God is love), referred to charity as an "essential" element of the Church's mission, "as essential to her as the ministry of the sacraments and preaching of the Gospel."[7] Referring to the charitable practices of the first Christian communities, he wrote that

---

5 Vatican Council II, Declaration on Religious Freedom *Dignitatis Humanae* (December 7, 1965), 2.

6 Benedict XVI, *On the Service of Charity*, introduction.

7 Benedict XVI, Encyclical Letter *Deus Caritas Est* (December 25, 2005), 22.

the social service which they were meant to provide was absolutely concrete, yet at the same time it was also a spiritual service; theirs was a truly spiritual office which carried out an essential responsibility of the Church, namely a well-ordered love of neighbour. With the formation of this group of seven, "*diaconia*"—the ministry of charity exercised in a communitarian, orderly way—became part of the fundamental structure of the Church.[8]

More recently, Pope Francis stated in his 2013 encyclical *Evangelii Gaudium* that Catholic social services are "a constituent element of the Church's mission and an indispensable expression of her very being."[9]

Respecting Catholic education, a 1997 document from the Vatican's Congregation for Catholic Education, in a section entitled "The Catholic School at the Heart of the Church," discussed the "ecclesial identity" of Catholic schools, whose mission is evangelization and Christian formation[10] alongside formation in secular disciplines. A later document from Pope Francis's Congregation for Catholic Education stressed Catholic schools' "ecclesial and pastoral mission rooted in a relationship with the Church's pastors."[11]

Likewise, the US Catholic bishops refer to Catholic health care as an "ecclesial mission" of the Church and a "continuation of Christ's mission" that "embod[ies] our Savior's concern for the sick."[12] This is why Catholic health care providers collaborate directly with their local bishops, and why they never attend solely to physical health, but like Jesus, attend also to people's "physical, mental, and spiritual healing" (Jn 6:35, 11:25–27).[13]

---

8 Benedict XVI, 21.

9 Francis, Apostolic Exhortation *Evangelii Gaudium* (November 24, 2013), 179, citing Benedict XVI, *Motu Proprio: Intima Ecclesiae Natura* (November 11, 2012).

10 Congregation for Catholic Education, *The Catholic School on the Threshold of the Third Millennium*, December 28, 1997, 11.

11 Congregation for Catholic Education, *Educating to Intercultural Dialogue in Catholic Schools: Living in Harmony for a Civilization of Love*, October 28, 2013, 85.

12 US Conference of Catholic Bishops, *Ethical and Religious Directives for Catholic Health Care Services*, 6th ed. (Washington, D.C.: USCCB, 2018), Preamble and General Introduction.

13 US Conference of Catholic Bishops, General Introduction.

A 2017 Vatican document about Catholic health care and health care workers described their labors as being "part of the pastoral and evangelizing activity of the Church." It labeled all those working in health care "ministers of life" who "proclaim[]" Christ's redeeming love.[14]

Now of course, the people who make up Catholic institutions are not angels, but rather human beings. They are prey to original sin. They fall down like every human being and need to get up again. Pope Francis's "church as field hospital" image is perfectly apt. But as Francis also notes, these communities are charged with providing the mutual spiritual assistance each member needs to get well again. He wrote that "without detracting from the evangelical ideal," members of the Church must "accompany with mercy and patience the eventual stages of personal growth as these progressively occur."[15] At the same time, he cautions that this "growth" is not to be equated with "therapy": "To accompany them would be counterproductive if it became a sort of therapy supporting their self-absorption and ceased to be a pilgrimage with Christ."[16]

What I have described above as the nature of Catholic institutions, therefore, is what they are called to be, even as they regularly fall short. Of course, some institutions bearing the Catholic label would not describe themselves as I have here, or they would distance themselves from the implications of these descriptions with respect to sexual expression norms. Speaking generally, however, what I have summarized above about the character of Catholic institutions is well-accepted in Catholic theology and social teaching.

Given, then, that Catholic institutions are first and foremost a response to an encounter with Jesus Christ and a community that witnesses to Him individually and together, Catholic schools, health care, and social services should make clear the implications of this when formulating religious freedom claims. They should avoid relying mostly upon brief restatements of a moral rule (e.g., "no contraception here"). And when categorizing an employee as a "minister" they should avoid excessive reliance upon some plausible but thin link between an employee's function and a religious goal of the institution

---

14 Pontifical Council for Pastoral Assistance to Health Care Workers, *New Charter for Health Care Workers* (Philadelphia: The National Catholic Bioethics Center, 2017), 3, 10.

15 Francis, *Evangelii Gaudium*, 44.

16 Francis, 170.

(e.g., "the music teacher picks the songs for the children's Masses"). They should stop implying that "the bishop made me do it." Instead, they should communicate first a thicker and more *integrated* religious description of a Catholic institution as a community "all-in" in service to Christ. This is not only a better explanation of why a Catholic institution cannot deploy its personnel, services, or operations toward ends contradicting the faith, but might also inspire greater respect for religious freedom as a necessary protection for organizations displaying such integrity, which are a light to a world in sore need of it.

In the discussion that follows I provide a far more detailed description of each model of Catholic community introduced above. I draw from scripture, magisterium, and theologians in order to offer descriptions of the Church that I judge most appealing to, useful for, and comprehensible by courts of law and public opinion. In particular, in addition to scripture, I rely on the *Catechism of the Catholic Church*, the *Compendium of the Social Doctrine of the Church*, Vatican II's Constitution on the Church, *Lumen Gentium*, Joseph Cardinal Ratzinger's book, *Called to Communion: Understanding the Church Today*, and Fr. Luigi Giussani's books *Why the Church?* and *Morality: Memory and Desire*,[17] as well as several other sources. Then I propose specific language that institutions can use to explain how their religious self-understandings inform their religious freedom claims.

Three Models of Catholic Community

It is not a simple matter to describe the nature and structure of Catholic institutions briefly. This is not only because I am not a "licensed theologian," as I acknowledged earlier. It is also because it is easy to get lost in a vast body of literature, and not a few metaphors: the People of God, the Body of Christ, the Vine and the Branches, the Sheep and Shepherd, and so forth.

For the limited purposes of this book, however—to explain to courts of law and public opinion why a Catholic institution needs

---

17 Joseph Cardinal Ratzinger, *Called to Communion: Understanding the Church Today*, 3rd ed. (San Francisco: Ignatius Press, 1996); Luigi Giussani, *Why the Church?* (Montreal: McGill-Queens University Press, 2004); Luigi Giussani, *Morality: Memory and Desire*, trans. K.D. Whitehead (San Francisco: Ignatius Press, 1986).

to have authority over its services, operations, and personnel—it is enough to rely upon the three models introduced above.

CALLED TO UNITY BY CHRIST

Since its beginning, the Church has existed as a community united by its members' response to God's call. This is neatly summarized in Vatican II's Dogmatic Constitution on the Church, *Lumen Gentium*, as follows:

> God, however, does not make men holy and save them merely as individuals, without bond or link between one another. Rather has it pleased Him to bring men together as one people, a people which acknowledges Him in truth and serves Him in holiness. He therefore chose the race of Israel as a people unto Himself. With it He set up a covenant . . . . All these things, however, were done by way of preparation and as a figure of that new and perfect covenant, which was to be ratified in Christ, and of that fuller revelation which was to be given through the Word of God Himself made flesh. . . . Christ instituted this new covenant, the new testament, that is to say, in His Blood, calling together a people made up of Jew and gentile, making them one, not according to the flesh but in the Spirit. This was to be the new People of God. For those who believe in Christ, who are reborn not from a perishable but from an imperishable seed through the word of the living God, not from the flesh but from water and the Holy Spirit, are finally established as "a chosen race, a royal priesthood, a holy nation, a purchased people . . . who in times past were not a people, but are now the people of God."[18]

According to the *Catechism of the Catholic Church*, this conception of the Church as a people called by God comprises the core of the Latin word "ecclesia," an "assembly for religious purposes."[19] It is also the essence of one of the earliest popular images of Jesus as the Good Shepherd, and we as His sheep. It is at the heart of Vatican II's

---

18 Vatican Council II, *Lumen Gentium* (November 21, 1964), 9 (citations omitted).
19 *Catechism of the Catholic Church*, § 751.

designation of the Church as the "People of God"; that is, individuals *united* by their being "of God."

During His life on earth, Jesus regularly referred to His followers in communal, familial terms, saying: "For whoever does the will of my heavenly Father is my brother, and sister, and mother" (Mt 12:50). When teaching His followers how to pray, He depicts them as children of one family with one Father: "*Our* Father," "give *us* this day," and so forth.

During and after Jesus's death, resurrection, and ascension, unlike many religious communities in the ancient world, Christians did not understand themselves as having been convened on the basis of race or nation or political party. Theirs was a new unity, an innovation: "There is neither Jew nor Greek, there is neither slave nor free person, there is not male and female, for you are all one *in Christ Jesus*" (Gal 3:28, emphasis added).

St. Paul characterizes this simultaneously horizontal and vertical Christian existence in his famous "body of Christ" passage: "As a body is one though it has many parts, and all the parts of the body, though many, are one body, so also Christ. For in one Spirit we were all baptized into one body, whether Jews or Greeks, slaves or free persons, and we were all given to drink of the one Spirit" (1 Cor 12:12–13).

The behavior of the Apostles and the earliest Christian communities easily suggests their self-understanding as a community continuously called together by Christ.[20] The Apostles replace their lost member, Judas. They meet and pray together despite Jesus's ascension into heaven, believing God to be actually present with them in the person of the Holy Spirit and in the Eucharistic meal. The Acts of the Apostles depicts them as being "of one heart and mind" after the resurrection (Acts 4:32). In the evocative words of Luigi Giussani, a "devout remembrance of an individual would not have been enough to keep that group together under such difficult, hostile circumstances. . . . In the eyes of those men, the only teaching that could not be doubted was the presence of their Master, Jesus alive."[21] He continues: "Here was a group which had never broken up, because the reason for their

---

20 See Giussani, *Why the Church?*, 66–78.
21 Giussani, 67.

union never abandoned them.... He is someone still present and still at work to whom they bear witness."[22]

At Pentecost, the multiple languages spoken manifest the Church's universal call to unite in Christ (Acts 2:4). Peter makes this explicit at Pentecost when he says:

> Therefore let the whole house of Israel know for certain that God has made him both Lord and Messiah, this Jesus whom you crucified. Now when they heard this, they were cut to the heart, and they asked Peter and the other apostles, "What are we to do, my brothers?" Peter [said] to them, "Repent and be baptized, every one of you, in the name of Jesus Christ for the forgiveness of your sins; and you will receive the gift of the Holy Spirit. . . . For the promise is made to you and to your children and to all those far off, whomever the Lord our God will call" (Acts 2:36–39).

These historical beginnings further instruct us that the Church is God's initiative, not ours. It was called into being by someone infinitely higher than ourselves, not by means of our own will and judgment. This points to the primacy of God and God's initiative vis-à-vis any religious community, and to its members' unity "in the name of their acceptance of his Son's coming,"[23] even as He also gives different gifts to members for the good of all. The unity, the community, did not exist prior to the call, as in "we are a group of people of a particular race or nation," *or* "we are a group of people primarily interested in providing health care, and some time after setting up a health care institution, we gave it the name of a holy person we admired."

Catholic unity, in response to the call of the one God, is also distinguished from a religious belief lived as an interior, individual experience, a purely I/Thou interacting directly with God, disconnected from interpersonal relations. Again, Acts 4:32: "The community of believers was of one heart and mind."

Unity of faith also serves the purpose of mutual strengthening. In this way, this first model of the Church overlaps with the third discussed below: a community of mutual witness to Christ. In

22 Giussani, 69.
23 Giussani, 78.

Giussani's formulation, coexistence leads to conviction.[24] He analogizes this dynamic to the mother/child relationship. A child who will not enter a dark room alone will walk into it more easily while holding the hand of his mother: "Only the communital dimension renders the human being sufficiently capable of overcoming the experience of risk."[25] This is no replacement for freedom, personal energy, and decision, but it is the "condition for their affirmation."[26] Here, Giussani recalls the aphorism of G.K. Chesterton: "Two is not twice one: two is two thousand times one."[27]

Today's Catholic communities continue to gather as a response to faith in Christ. Their founders were inspired by His words and deeds to take up a particular ministry of love for the neighbor, whether to heal the sick, lift up the poor, or "make disciples of all nations, baptizing them in the name of the Father, and of the Son, and of the Holy Spirit, teaching them to observe all that I have commanded you" (Mt 28:19–20). To many in the outside world, however, these institutions will resemble secular bureaucracies. But they are not. Obviously, they will have to observe the organizational conventions necessary for the delivery of quality services—in Benedict XVI's words, Catholic charitable services must be "organized" so that they are an "ordered service to the community," and "the Church will constantly have need of human constructions to help her speak and act in the era in which she finds herself."[28] But at the same time, these constructions "risk setting themselves up as the essence of the Church and thus prevent us from seeing through to what is truly essential": "To allow the *nobilis forma*, . . . the living Lord, to appear."[29]

Clearly, an institution operating in service to God and neighbor would betray its essential nature and identity by cooperating with a governmental demand to do or facilitate things that are directly opposed to the unity of its faith. When faced with a demand to do so,

24 Giussani, 80–81.
25 Luigi Giussani, *The Religious Sense*, trans. John Zucchi (Montreal: McGill-Queens University Press, 1997), 130.
26 Giussani, 131.
27 Giussani, 131, citing Gilbert K. Chesterton, *The Man Who Was Thursday* (Middlesex: Penguin Books, 1988), 88.
28 Benedict XVI, *Deus Caritas Est*, 20; Ratzinger, *Called to Communion*, 142.
29 Ratzinger, *Called to Communion*, 142.

therefore, the institution might summarize the above by stating: *Our organization is not merely a provider of x service. We are first and foremost a group of persons gathered in response to Christ's call to love and serve Him and one another. The work we do—healing the sick, feeding the poor, teaching the faith—is in every case a response to His call, even as it is also manifestly a humanitarian service. Our unity relies upon our mutual personal witness and conforming our entire institution to the call of Christ. We cannot, therefore, obey a demand from the state that requires us to disobey Jesus Christ, the source and substance of our unity.*

A COMMUNITY DISPLAYING
THE INBREAKING OF THE KINGDOM

A Catholic institution might also be understood as a group of persons whose lives and interactions are meant to display the inbreaking of the Kingdom of God, God's "new creation," a society whose life in Christ affects everything they do, precisely because He has commanded them to "love one another as I have loved you." The *Catechism* asserts that the Church is the structure Christ initiated to manifest His Kingdom until He comes again.[30] The Congregation for the Doctrine of the Faith's 2000 Declaration *"Dominus Iesus"* refers to the Kingdom as the "realization of God's plan of salvation in all its fullness," and to the Church as its "seed," "beginning," "sign," and "instrument."[31] Ecclesial communities taking part in essential work of the Church—educating and providing health care and social assistance—have a part in this. For this reason, they must be the "visible plan of God's love for humanity,"[32] the "sacrament—a sign and instrument, that is, of communion with God and of unity among all men."[33]

Dominus Iesus cautions that the Kingdom should never be conceived of as a purely human or ideological reality.[34] Concrete

---

30 *Catechism of the Catholic Church,* § 763.
31 Congregation for the Doctrine of the Faith, *Declaration* "Dominus Iesus" *on the Unicity and Salvific Universality of Jesus Christ and the Church,* August 6, 2000, 18, 19.
32 *Catechism of the Catholic Church,* § 776 (citation omitted).
33 *Catechism of the Catholic Church,* § 775 (citation omitted).
34 Congregation for the Doctrine of the Faith, *Declaration* Dominus Iesus, 18.

human activity is rather the response to God's initiative, God's invitation to participate in the Kingdom.

The *Compendium of the Social Doctrine of the Church* likewise states that the Kingdom is not an economic, social, or political order, but the "development of a human social sense which . . . is a leaven for attaining wholeness, justice and solidarity, in openness to the Transcendent, as a point of reference for one's own personal, definitive fulfillment."[35] This highlights, too, that Christ redeems not only the individual, but also the social relations between individuals. Catholic communities must therefore be places where this is manifest. They must be places of "communion, witness and mission," and thus a "catalyst for redeeming and transforming . . . social relations."[36] *Evangelii Gaudium* phrases this demand as a requirement that communities are "called to bear witness to a constantly new way of living together in fidelity to the Gospel."[37]

Note how such communities observe the tie between a vertical relationship with God and horizontal relationships among human beings. The *Catechism* states that the love of neighbor and of God are "inseparable."[38] God's love for each person demands and inspires his or her loving relations with other people, and the community together thus lives in a way that witnesses to Him. This was a great Christian innovation. As the theologian Henri de Lubac concludes: "That God loves us all postulates the brotherhood of all men. He is 'our Father'—no more father to one than to another. What unites us is by definition therefore greater than what divides us."[39] This is reflected in Jesus's prayer: "I pray not only for them, but also for those who will believe in me through their word, so that they may all be one, as you, Father, are in me and I in you" (Jn 17: 20–21).

The Catholic thinker Luigi Giussani uses the marvelous concept of "impossible unity" to describe the relationships that should obtain in a community that calls itself Christian: "The phenomenon that

---

35 Pontifical Council of Justice and Peace, *The Compendium of the Social Doctrine of the Church* (Washington, D.C.: USCCB, 2005), 51.

36 Pontifical Council of Justice and Peace, 52.

37 Francis, *Evangelii Gaudium*, 2.

38 *Catechism of the Catholic Church*, § 1878.

39 Henri de Lubac, *Paradoxes of Faith*, trans. Ernest Beaumont (San Francisco: Ignatius Press, 1987), 10.

best demonstrates God's power is precisely the unity of those who acknowledge Him. The new way of looking at others and of dealing with each other testifies to His Presence in the most convincing way for human reason. In the new way in which I look at others, and in the way I say 'you,' all sense of foreignness is abolished, everything tends towards unity."[40]

The Holy Trinity is a model of a Catholic community living in unity, in loving communion. Like God, who is three persons in an unbroken communion of love, it is the nature of a Catholic community to receive love and to give it both to God and one another.

Jesus's Sermon on the Plain provides a description of how Christian communities are to live together in a radical loving union. Persons observing such a community would be hard-pressed not to see in such behavior evidence of a "new creation":

> But to you who hear I say, love your enemies, do good to those who hate you, bless those who curse you, pray for those who mistreat you.
> To the person who strikes you on one cheek, offer the other one as well, and from the person who takes your cloak, do not withhold even your tunic.
> Give to everyone who asks of you, and from the one who takes what is yours do not demand it back.
> Do to others as you would have them do to you. . . .
> Love your enemies and do good to them, and lend expecting nothing back; then your reward will be great and you will be children of the Most High, for he himself is kind to the ungrateful and the wicked.
> Be merciful, just as [also] your Father is merciful. (Lk 6:27–36)

During His life on earth, Jesus preached on many occasions that "the kingdom of heaven is at hand" (e.g., Mt 4:17). Catholics believe that Jesus inaugurated this Kingdom and left the Church as its "beginning," but required Christians to further it by imitating Jesus's "new way of acting."[41] In the words of Pope Francis, "the Gospel is not

---

40 Luigi Giussani, *Generating Traces in the History of the World* (Montreal: McGill-Queens University Press, 2010), 35; see also 33–36.
41 *Catechism of the Catholic Church*, § 764.

merely about our *personal relationship* with God. Nor should our loving response to God be seen simply as an accumulation of small personal gestures to individuals in need . . . The Gospel is about the *kingdom* of God (cf. *Lk* 4:43)."[42] A 1984 document from the Congregation for the Doctrine of the Faith quoted Paul VI's statement that the "Kingdom of God" begun in the Church does not center upon human progress but "in knowing ever more deeply the unfathomable riches of Christ, to hope ever more strongly in things eternal, to respond ever more ardently to the love of God, to spread ever more widely grace and holiness among men. But it is this very same love which makes the Church constantly concerned for the true temporal good of mankind as well."[43]

Accounts of the lives of the earliest Christian communities show how they understood and lived Christ's exhortations to live in society in a new way in order to imitate Jesus's way of being, to witness to the inbreaking of the Kingdom of God by "put[ting] into action in this world the energies and means received from the Creator to serve justice and peace."[44] For example, the Acts of the Apostles records that they "devoted themselves to the apostles' teaching and fellowship, to the breaking of bread and the prayers" (Acts 2:42). Acts also records that "all who believed were together and had all things in common; they would sell their property and possessions and divide them among all according to each one's need" (Acts 2:44–45). When Jerusalem was suffering material want, early Christians responded with a collection (1 Cor 16:1–4; Rom 15:25–31).

Early Christian communities later pioneered charitable institutions that were at the service of all. In the words of the historian Robert Louis Wilken, "From earliest times Christian leaders had taken to heart the exhortations in the Scriptures to care for the poor."[45] Even by the second century, some Christian churches were purchasing burial land for the poor and by the fourth century were constructing

---

42 Francis, *Evangelii Gaudium*, 180 (italics mine).

43 Congregation for the Doctrine of the Faith, *Instruction on Certain Aspects of the "Theology of Liberation*," August 6, 1984, conclusion, citing Paul VI, *Profession of Faith of the People of God*, June 30, 1968, AAS 60 (1968), 443–44.

44 *Catechism of the Catholic Church*, § 2820 (citation omitted).

45 Robert Louis Wilken, *The First Thousand Years: A Global History of Christianity* (New Haven: Yale University Press, 2012), 156.

hotels, hospices, and other buildings to house them.[46] One of these structures—an important example of Christians' understanding of the implications of their modeling the inbreaking of the Kingdom—was the fourth-century "Basilead." This institution was founded by Saint Basil, a bishop moved by the widespread discussion in the Christian world of Jesus's admonition to the rich young man to give everything to the poor. Basil interpreted this to apply to every person and preached that all Christians should live simply and give generously to the poor.[47] He founded the Basilead as a place offering free shelter, food, and medical treatment for the poor. Both clergy and laypeople co-resided there with the needy. This was not merely a bricks and mortar institution, but, in the words of one Church historian, a kind of "alternative society," a "new set of relationships," and a "sign of [the] presence" of "the Kingdom of God" in humanity's midst.[48]

Early Christians further understood that their family relations should reflect the new reign of God. As chapters 6 and 7 will describe in further detail, they rejected the norms of the surrounding Roman culture that failed to respect—or even abused—women, children, and slaves, in favor of a set of relations reflecting God's way of loving.

Fast forward to contemporary times, and the Catholic Church continues to understand itself as a community of persons charged to "go out of its way" for others, like the Good Samaritan, even in the teeth of the culture's insistence that "choice" is prior to responsibility. In their 1995 statement *Faithful for Life*, the US bishops captured this in a memorable passage following a retelling of the Good Samaritan story: "We are all journeying down from Jerusalem to Jericho, and this story haunts us, for it flatly contradicts the strong persuasion so widely held today that our loyalties and our obligations are owed only to those of our choice. On the contrary, we owe fidelity to those we choose and, beyond them, to others we do not choose. It is we who have been chosen—to go out of our way for them."[49]

---

46 Wilken, 156, 158.

47 St. Basil the Great, *On Social Justice*, introduction and commentary by and trans. C. Paul Schroeder, Popular Patristics Series 38 (Yonkers, N.Y.: St. Vladimir's Seminary Press, 2009), 26–28, 31.

48 C. Paul Schroeder, introduction to St. Basil the Great, *On Social* Justice, 38.

49 US Conference of Catholic Bishops, *Faithful for Life: A Moral Reflection* (September 1995), 1, https://www.usccb.org/issues-and-action/human-life-and-dignity/abortion/upload/Faithful-for-Life-A-Moral-Reflection-Bishops-Statement-09-1995.pdf

Benedict XVI's Motu Proprio concerning Catholic charitable institutions further illustrates how this understanding should permeate every aspect of such an organization.[50] It reflects first upon the necessity of the Church being "called as a whole to the exercise of the *diakonia* of charity," which requires "a variety of institutional expressions." Overall, the institution's "practical activity," must "visibly express[] a love for man, a love nourished by an encounter with Christ." This means that the activity "at all levels must avoid the risk of becoming just another form of organized assistance," but instead should "exercise a valuable educational function," that helps people "to appreciate the importance of sharing, respect and love in the spirit of the Gospel of Christ."[51]

Benedict also notes how every aspect of the institution should reflect its religious origins and goals. Operations must both be "in conformity with the demands of the Church's teaching and the intentions of the faithful," and "likewise respect the legitimate norms laid down by civil authorities."[52] Contributions should not be accepted from sources whose means or ends "are not in conformity with the Church's teaching."[53] Even salaries and operational expenses should testify to "Christian simplicity of life." They must both "respect[] the demands of justice and a necessary level of professionalism," but remain "in due proportion to analogous expenses of [the bishop's] diocesan Curia."[54] Regarding services, the "activities and management of these agencies" must respect the "norms of the Church's universal and particular law."[55] Should this cease to be the case, the bishop is obliged to inform the faithful and to prohibit the organization from using the name "Catholic."[56] And personnel, in order "to ensure an evangelical witness in the service of charity," must demonstrate, "along with due professional competence," "an example of Christian life and witness to a formation of heart which testifies to a

---

50 Benedict XVI, *On the Service of Charity.*
51 Benedict XVI, Introduction.
52 Benedict XVI, Introduction.
53 Benedict XVI, Art. 10, § 3.
54 Benedict XVI, Art. 10, § 4.
55 Benedict XVI, Art. 4, § 3.
56 Benedict XVI, Art. 11.

faith working through charity." To this end, agencies should provide suitable "theological and pastoral formation" for personnel.[57]

The religious freedom consequences of an institution's theological self-understanding as having been charged with manifesting the inbreaking of the Kingdom are clear. They might be articulated as follows by Catholic institutions caught up in a religious freedom struggle: *We must correct a common misperception that we are strictly a humanitarian service provider. Rather, it is our mission to live every aspect of our communal life and work so as to provide onlookers a glimpse of the Kingdom of God/God's reign, which is the kingdom of perfect love, even as we know we will often fail and need to try again and again. For this reason, our employees strive to model their interpersonal relations upon the love of Christ. Our services strive to be an extension of God's love for human beings. Even our operations strive to testify to Christian virtues of material simplicity alongside fairness and integrity. We cannot obey a law that would alter the very nature and way of being of this community, organized as it is in order to witness to God's reign in the world.*

THE PRESENCE OF THE LIVING CHRIST

Another crucial model of Catholic community is that of a group of persons seeking to manifest the *living* Christ to others two thousand years after His physical departure from earth. Paul's letter to the Hebrews puts it succinctly: "Strive for peace with everyone, and *for that holiness without which no one will see the Lord*" (Heb 12:14, emphasis added). Fr. Luigi Giussani also captures this briefly when he writes that the Church is the answer to the question:

> How can those who encounter Jesus Christ a day, a month, a hundred, a thousand, or two thousand years after his disappearance from earthly horizons, be enabled to realize that he corresponds to the truth which he claims? . . . That this really is Something of supreme interest to me, and how can I know this with any reasonable degree of certainty?[58]

---

57 Benedict XVI, Art. 7, § 2.
58 Giussani, *Why the Church?*, 8.

Giussani concludes that this requires Catholics today to communicate the Good News in the same way that Jesus did during His time
on earth: through personal encounters with other human beings.
He elaborates: Jesus is born into a family, invites twelve Apostles to
accompany Him during His public ministry, and moves among towns
and villages where He encounters and speaks with individuals and
groups both large and small. His "method" of evangelization is "come
and see!"[59] The Apostles, Jesus's witnesses, observe Him over time.
They see not only His supernatural powers of healing and forgiving
sins and His "coherent intelligence" and "invincible dialectics," but
also a "gaze that recognize[s] and love[s them]" deeply.[60] The Apostles
eventually conclude:

> It is hard to find a person who is powerful, and yet truly good.
> In Jesus, by contrast, witnesses were able to see that gaze,
> which was not only powerful and prodigious, intelligent and
> captivating, but also good. It seems almost impossible for such
> great power to be contained within the bounds of profound
> goodness, difficult to find such sharp intelligence with such a
> positive simplicity, like a child's instinctive show of affection
> and openness....
> ... By sharing his life, by constantly experiencing the sensa-
> tion that Jesus was exceptional, it became highly reasonable to
> trust in him. With the passage of time, they acquired incom-
> parable certainty about this man.[61]

Giussani compares these interactions to a child's experience of her
parents. The child bonds with her parents not on the basis of empirical
evidence, but by "co-existence" and "companionship."[62]
That Jesus wants His followers to do the same—to bring others
to know Him via personal encounter—is suggested by His example during His lifetime. Jesus delegated to His Apostles the work of
bringing Christ to other human beings even while He remained on

---

59 Giussani, Alberto, and Prades, *Generating Traces*, 5.
60 Luigi Giussani, *At the Origin of the Christian Claim* (Montreal: McGill, Queen's University Press, 1998), 53.
61 Giussani, 54, 58.
62 Giussani, *Why the Church?*, 81.

earth. When He sent out the seventy-two disciples ahead of Him, He told them: "Whoever listens to you listens to me. Whoever rejects you rejects me" (Lk 10:16). When He sent out the twelve apostles to announce the inbreaking of the Kingdom of Heaven, He directed them to "cure the sick, raise the dead, cleanse lepers, drive out demons" (Mt 10:5–8). He said that "whoever receives you, receives me" (Mt 10:40). Jesus promises them that in their work of human encounter, He will be *actually* present: "And behold, I am with you always, until the end of the age" (Mt 28:20).

In sum, Jesus's words and example clearly indicate one important way in which human beings born later can come to know Him: through encounters with those who believe in Him and who can, by the witness of their lives—by their being *"imago Dei"*—reveal Christ to them. This is the method that Catholics are to employ today. This is why the *Catechism* states that the People of God are like the "moon" reflecting Christ, who is the sun.[63] It is why Pope Francis's *Evangelii Gaudium* (The joy of the gospel) exhorts that "all religious teaching ultimately has to be reflected in the teacher's way of life, which awakens the assent of the heart by its nearness, love and witness."[64] And it is why Pope Benedict's 2012 document on Catholic charities requires that all those who work in the Church's charitable apostolate, "along with due professional competence, give an example of Christian life and witness to a formation of heart which testifies to a faith working through charity."[65]

This will strike many as shocking—"scandalous" (a stumbling block) in Catholic theological terms—that frail, sinful human beings have been charged to communicate the divine by way of the human, as God did in a sinless Jesus.[66] But it is a core Catholic tenet. It also makes sense. We come to most of what is crucially important to us about another person not by means of information given, but by encounter. And people are more likely to be persuaded by good example than by words and exhortations, especially today when more and more people are highly resistant to words uttered by traditional institutions and clergy. Paul VI's encyclical on evangelization correctly observed:

---

63 *Catechism of the Catholic Church*, § 748.
64 Francis, *Evangelii Gaudium*, 42.
65 Benedict XVI, *On the Service of Charity*, Art. 7, § 2.
66 *Catechism of the Catholic Church*, §§ 119, 123.

Modern man listens more willingly to witnesses than to teachers, and if he does listen to teachers, it is because they are witnesses. . . . It is therefore primarily by her conduct and by her life that the Church will evangelize the world, in other words, by her living witness of fidelity to the Lord Jesus—the witness of poverty and detachment, of freedom in the face of the powers of this world, in short, the witness of sanctity.[67]

Pope Francis repeated this sentiment in *Evangelii Gaudium*: "Today too, people prefer to listen to witnesses: they 'thirst for authenticity' and 'call for evangelizers to speak of a God whom they themselves know and are familiar with, as if they were seeing him.'"[68] Pope Benedict XVI has used the appealing phrase "dependable company," to summarize what Catholic communities must be. Their members should

help[] one another to enter into a living relationship with Christ and with the Father. This has been from the start the fundamental task of the Church as the community of believers, disciples and friends of Jesus. The Church ... is that dependable company within which we have been brought forth and educated to become, in Christ, sons and heirs of God. . . . It means while walking, helping one another to become truly friends of Jesus Christ and children of God.[69]

I should note here that contrary to the idea that only ordained clergy are tasked with "witnessing to Christ," this is a task for all the laity, too. The *Catechism* charges the laity to "engag[e] in temporal affairs" and to "illuminate and order" them so that they "grow according to Christ."[70] *Lumen Gentium* states that every layperson, "in virtue of the very gifts bestowed upon him, is at the same time a witness and a living instrument of the mission of the Church itself according to the measure of Christ's bestowal."[71]

67 Paul VI, Apostolic Exhortation *Evangelii Nuntiandi* (December 8, 1975), 41.
68 Francis, *Evangelii Gaudium*, 120, citing Paul VI, *Evangelii Nuntiandi*, 76.
69 "Address of His Holiness Benedict XVI to the Participants in the Convention of the Diocese of Rome," June 11, 2007.
70 *Catechism of the Catholic Church*, § 898.
71 Vatican Council II, *Lumen Gentium*, 2, 33.

On a practical level, this makes good sense. Clergy and religious are relatively few, but the laity is everywhere, in every culture and kind of work. Their potential for evangelization is overwhelming. In fact, the *Catechism* specially emphasizes that lay duties are "the more pressing when it is *only* through them that humanity can come to know Christ."[72] This has direct application to the situation we face today, in which laity largely staff and lead most Catholic institutions in the US.

In light of this imperative of witnessing to Jesus Christ, Catholic institutions can insist upon their authority to make decisions about services, operations, and personnel. This self-understanding has the most obvious implications for institutions' right to make their own personnel choices as against laws demanding that they hire or retain persons who reject what Christian witness requires. This includes not only those personnel who undertake obviously theological tasks— liturgies, prayer, retreats, religious education—but all personnel who interact regularly with others in the community.

Thus, when faced with a law or regulation demanding that Catholic institutions incorporate into their communities persons unwilling to be such "dependable company," an institution might state: *We are not the same as secular institutions offering services similar to those that we offer. As a Catholic institution, our personnel are charged to witness to the love of Christ in their lives, including in their interpersonal relations, so as to make Him present among us in the world today, just as He promised He would be. Catholics are charged to manifest Christian love not only to colleagues, clients, students, patients, and all those we meet, but also and of course to those people with whom we are most closely in contact and affect most profoundly—our family and friends. Christian love is indivisible. Not one of us can perfectly manifest the love of Christ, but we can commit ourselves to try again after every fall.*

It should be very easy for courts and the public to understand that laws forcing Catholic institutions to hire or retain employees who reject the Church's mission are a clear violation of the institutions' religious freedom rights. Secular scholars and institutional leaders easily accept and practice the notion that "personnel is policy." But courts and members of the public regularly refuse to acknowledge

---

72 *Catechism of the Catholic Church*, § 900.

this commonplace when Catholic institutions insist upon exercising authority over personnel who publicly oppose Catholic teachings on sexual expression. Because this is such a common problem, even before chapter 5 undertakes a survey of US Catholic institutions' instantiating the models described in this chapter, chapter 4 will briefly summarize the empirical literature supporting the necessity of institutions' retaining final authority over personnel in order to protect their identity and mission.

– 4 –

PERSONAL WITNESS MATTERS: THE SCIENCE OF SOCIAL INFLUENCE

THIS CHAPTER IS DIFFERENT FROM THE OTHERS IN THIS BOOK, but for good reason. It is neither strictly legal nor theological. Rather, it is a compilation of the empirical evidence that may be used to demonstrate to a court of law or public opinion the *practical* necessity of a religious institution's having final authority over its personnel, so that it can further the religious mission that the Supreme Court insists has been committed solely to its authority, and never to the state's.[1] This evidence supports and harmonizes with the material in chapter 3 about how the theological nature of Catholic institutions requires their retaining final authority over personnel decisions.

Recall how each of the three models of Catholic institutions described in chapter 3 involves the presence of Christian witnesses. The first model spoke of their *unity* in Christ, the second of their *communal and interpersonal behaviors* seeking to model His reign, and the third of *"being Christ" to one another*. In short, a religious institution's mission rests in an important way upon the visible choices and behaviors of its personnel. When the state interferes with personnel

---

1 A slightly longer exposition of this literature is found in Helen M. Alvaré, "Church Autonomy After Our Lady of Guadalupe: Too Broad? Or as Broad as It Needs to Be?" *Texas Review of Law & Politics* 25 (2021): 319–75, 354–70. Parts of this article are used here with the permission of the journal.

choices, therefore, it is striking directly at the religious character of the institution. Luigi Giussani expresses this starkly:

> The most ferocious persecution is the modern state's attempt to block the expression of the communital dimension of the religious phenomenon. As far as the state is concerned, a person can, in conscience, believe what he likes, as long as this faith does not imply that all believers are one, and therefore, have the right to live and express this reality. To obstruct communital expression is like cutting off the roots that nourish the plant: the plant soon dies.[2]

Employees who *publicly* reject an institution's Catholic beliefs are, by definition, unable to help it be all that it is called to be. Note here that I refer to employees' *public* or *visible* behaviors—for example, living in a romantic partnership in a cohabiting or same-sex household or sharing racist statements or abortion advocacy on social media. It is certainly possible that employees with *privately* held divergent beliefs or ways of life might detract from a religious institution's achieving one or more of its religious goals and aspirations. But because Catholic institutions (rightly) have no taste for witch-hunting and surveillance and generally react only to publicly known rejections of Church teaching, I limit myself here to the matter of employees' public choices. I also render no personal judgments about others' states of mind and consciences in this chapter, or in the whole book for that matter. I am strictly addressing the harmony or disharmony between an employee's *actions* and what Catholic institutions are and do, as well as the religious freedom implications of these.

It is difficult to understand how judges or the public could doubt a religious institution's need to have the final say over the personnel comprising and personifying the institution. Virtually everyone would agree that a political party or nonprofit or business needs employees who support its mission in order for the institution to be what it is and to be that well. But not a few courts and members of the public ignore this common sense conclusion when a religious institution is in the dock on a matter related to sexual expression. They instead harbor the

---

2   Luigi Giussani, *The Religious Sense* (Montreal: McGill-Queens University Press, 1997), 131.

idea that a publicly dissenting employee who is not employed for the sole purpose of imparting religious teaching is irrelevant to furthering the employer's religious mission. But empirical data indicates otherwise and perfectly complements the theological material in the previous chapter concerning the relationship between personnel and the "being" of a Catholic community. It shows that employees—not only clergy or teachers in academic settings, but *all* those who regularly interact with others in a group setting—can importantly influence others. This material is gathered below. It applies to both secular and religious organizations, but is set forth here in support of the latter's religious freedom claims.

This material is known generally as "Social Influence Theory." When it examines influences affecting religion, it may be published under the headings of the sociology or psychology of religion. It strongly supports the notion that religious enterprises that wish to protect their mission should secure their employees' personal witness to that mission in public word and deed, whether they are speaking to colleagues or clients or students or patients. Beliefs and norms are more successfully maintained and transmitted in group settings in the presence of a majority—or at least some critical, influential mass—of knowledgeable, confident, expert, relatable individuals who speak in favor of, and role-model, the desired beliefs and norms. If, on the other hand, organizations employ public dissenters—especially dissenters who are knowledgeable, confident, relatable, and/or who role-model opposing beliefs and norms—the institution's beliefs and norms, and thus its mission, are significantly undermined.

With respect to religious institutions, these findings do not apply only to clergy or to teachers, but to *all* persons who come into contact with third parties in group settings, whether fellow colleagues, clients, or others. It should not be surprising that these findings apply in religious as well as secular settings; human beings in all kinds of groups are prone to influencing and being influenced by others in their acceptance or rejection of both ideas and norms. Professor Cass Sunstein (a well-known law professor and expert in behavioral economics who also served as President Obama's "regulations czar") summarized the state of this research in his 2019 book, *Conformity: The Power of Social Influences*: "The actions and statements of other people provide information about what is true and what is right";

this applies to the "spread of the world's great religions," as well as to other group phenomena.[3] Insofar, therefore, as a religious institution is intent upon witnessing to its beliefs and norms and transmitting these to others, the words and conduct of those constituting its community—its personnel—matter a great deal.

After a brief introduction to Social Influence Theory, the material below will discuss some of the leading personal traits and dynamics that individuals display in groups that are likely to influence fellow group members. Again, these considerations apply whether or not these individuals play a teaching or ministry role in a religious institution. Their interactions, words, and visible conduct can matter, no matter their role.

Introduction to Social Influence Theory

Social influence scholarship made an important early appearance in a mid-twentieth- century experiment examining whether some people in a group could alter others' beliefs about the truth and falsity of a simple fact: the relative lengths of lines. In this experiment, conducted by Solomon Asch, several students were recruited as "confederates" (subjects who were in private league with the convenor) within a larger group, and instructed to provide deliberately wrong answers to questions about the relative length of lines. After several rounds of questions, and even though the confederates' answers began to be rather obviously incorrect, significant numbers of "innocent" subjects began to agree with the confederates' factually wrong conclusions.[4]

This type of finding has been replicated, according to Professor Sunstein, in 130 sets of results from 17 countries,[5] with additional studies demonstrating that the more confederates there are in a group, the more likely it is that the conclusions of the innocent subject will begin to give way.[6]

3   Cass Sunstein, *Conformity: The Power of Social Influences* (New York: New York University Press, 2019), ix.
4   Solomon Asch, "Opinions and Social Pressure," *Scientific American* 193, no. 5 (November, 1995): 32–34.
5   Sunstein, *Conformity*, 16–17, and citations therein.
6   Robert S. Baron and Norbert L. Kerr, *Group Process, Group Decision, Group Action*, 2nd ed. (Maidenhead, UK: Open University Press, 2003), 75.

Later experiments tested whether some members of a group could influence others' conclusions not only just about facts, but also about *norms*—what is good or bad, right or wrong.[7] The research concluded that the answer is yes. "Expectation[s] about appropriate behavior that occurs in a group context" are also subject to group influence.[8]

Over the years, researchers have investigated which individual traits and group dynamics seem to influence group members. And other researchers have explored whether these operate in religious settings. The leading findings of both of these types of investigations are set out below.

PEOPLE ARE INFLUENCED BY PERSONAL RELATIONSHIPS

People are naturally inclined to seek approval. They are therefore influenced by those with whom they have personal relationships, especially those with whom they associate a great deal.[9] These findings have been explored with respect to religious communities. Belonging to a religious community influences people's religious belief and commitment, in part because socializing leads to mutual influence.[10] This applies not only to those already within a religious community, but also to those who are considering conversion. It appears that not only do affective ties impact a person's evaluation of the credibility of the religion, they also provide a conduit of information about the religion, and even, in some cases, pressure to conform to its beliefs and practices.[11]

Within religious communities, the influences exerted by personal relationships on religious beliefs and practices have been explored by two leading sociologists of religion, Rodney Stark and William Sims

---

7 Payel Kundu and Denise Dellarosa Cummins, "Morality and Conformity: The Asch Paradigm Applied to Moral Decisions," *Social Influence* 8, no. 4 (October, 2013): 268–79; 276 ("Our results clearly show a strong conformity effect, indicating that moral decision making is strongly influenced by social context, thereby replicating Asch's seminal finding in a new domain.").

8 Rachel I. McDonald and Christian S. Crandall, "Social Norms and Social Influence," *Current Opinion in Behavioral Sciences* 3 (2015): 147–51, 147.

9 Sunstein, *Conformity*, 6–7.

10 Marie Cornwall, "The Social Bases of Religion: A Study of Factors Influencing Religious Belief and Commitment," *Review of Religious Research* 29, no. 1 (1987): 44–56, 54.

11 David A. Snow and Richard Machalek, "The Sociology of Conversion," *Annual Review of Sociology* 10, no. 1 (1984): 167–90, 183.

Bainbridge.[12] Their work demonstrates that whether one is considering the dynamics of radical religious cults or mainstream religions, there is "overwhelming support for the crucial role played by social networks in the formation and growth of such groups."[13] Stark and Bainbridge find that this is true even for people in large urban settings exposed to mass media.[14] Stark and Bainbridge show that all faiths, including even less communally focused religions, rest upon "network influences," and that "belief is firmest among those whose social network and religious affiliation are coterminous."[15]

Stark and Bainbridge's findings dovetail with the conclusions of sociologist Richard Lee, who has written about the role of conversational interactions between individuals in religious networks. He asserts that, because developing a relationship with another person is a form of reward, "as interaction increases between individuals, so does influence upon religious affiliation," no matter the "ostensible purpose of their conversations" (e.g., instruction, fun, or other).[16]

One important method by which religious communities appear to influence people to adopt beliefs or commitments is by providing "plausibility structures."[17] An individual's world is built and maintained "in the consciousness of the individual by interactions and conversations with significant others" in one's community.[18] By their words and lives, do these others suggest that the religion is plausible? Is it true? Is it lived out in a way that is possible and attractive?

One of the pioneers of social influence science, Albert Bandura, underscores the above findings by observing that religiosity is ordinarily socially grounded rather than being an "intrapsychic self-engagement with a Supreme Being. Thus, what happens in religious

---

12 See generally Rodney Stark and William Sims Bainbridge, "Networks of Faith: Interpersonal Bonds and Recruitment to Cults and Sects," *American Journal of Sociology* 85, no. 6 (May 1980): 1376–95, 1376.

13 Stark and Bainbridge, 1376.

14 Stark and Bainbridge, 1378–79 (citation omitted).

15 Stark and Bainbridge, 1389–90.

16 Richard R. Lee, "Religious Practice as Social Exchange: An Explanation of the Empirical Findings," *Sociological Analysis* 53, no. 1 (1992): 1–35, 24, https://www.jstor.org/stable/3711625.

17 Cornwall, "The Social Bases of Religion," 44–45.

18 Cornwall, 44.

groups is crucial; these provide multiple models of behavior and reinforce lifestyles patterned on them."[19]

Bandura's observation is affirmed by a qualitative study of religious influences among twenty-eight "highly spiritual youth" ages twelve to twenty-one from six countries and eight different religious traditions.[20] Subjects most frequently cited religious influences as proceeding from persons with whom they had regular contact, first parents (93 percent), then friends (68 percent), then religious groups or organizations (57 percent), and finally religious leaders (43 percent).[21] Family regularly appears in studies to be the most important agent of religious socialization, but the degree of influence of peers and members of religious communities—including those who are *not* officially deemed *leaders*—remains notable.[22]

One potentially important religious community that can influence members may be found in institutions of higher education. For example, a specialized investigation compared the effects of relationships forged in religious versus nonreligious colleges with respect to decisions to enter the Catholic priesthood or religious life.[23] Relationships beyond those that were "instructional" (i.e., teachers), proved important, including those with college staff and others in the community.[24] In this survey, those attending Catholic colleges reported significant encouragement toward their vocation from professors (72 percent)—including professors outside the theology department[25]—while those not attending Catholic college reported far less such encouragement (25 percent). In this same study, priests and priest candidates who had attended religious colleges reported too that *other* members of the

19 Albert Bandura, "On the Psychosocial Impact and Mechanisms of Spiritual Modeling," *International Journal for the Psychology of Religion* 13, no. 3 (2003): 167–73, 171.

20 Pamela Ebstyne King, Mona M. Abo-Zena, and Jonathan Weber, "Varieties of Social Experience: The Religious Cultural Context of Diverse Spiritual Exemplars," *British Journal of Developmental Psychology* 35, no. 1 (March 2017): 127–41, 127.

21 King, Abo-Zena, and Weber, 132.

22 See generally, Cornwall, "The Social Bases of Religion."

23 James Cavendish, Melissa Cidade, and Ryan Muldoon, *The Influence of College Experiences on Vocational Discernment to Priesthood and Religious Life* (Washington D.C.: Center for Applied Research in the Apostolate, Georgetown University), September 2012, https://nrvc.net/ckeditor_assets/attachments/2086/report_only_-_influence_of_college_experiences_on_vocational_discernment_5-10-13.pdf.

24 Cavendish, Cidade, and Muldoon, 5.

25 Cavendish, Cidade, and Muldoon, 55–56.

community also played a significant role in their vocational discernment. For example, of those who attended Catholic colleges, 50 percent reported being encouraged in their vocation by a staff member, as compared to only 14 percent of those who attended non-Catholic colleges.[26] Those attending Catholic colleges also reported that 62 percent of college administrators expressed "some" or "very much" "interest in faith, religion, and prayer, while only 10 percent of those attending non-Catholic colleges reported the same.[27]

There is a substantial literature about the influence of religious social networks on the faith of children and emerging adults that indicates the importance of relationships and the personal witness of others in a community. A study concerning the transmission of faith by sociologists Christian Smith and Justin Bartkus, for example, concluded that "before children need catechism or theology, they require witness."[28] In the authors' words, "it is unimaginable that parents could transmit a religious worldview without exposing their children to outside persons, communities, and experiences which constitute the cultural 'world' in which Catholic belief makes sense."[29]

Another study considering the impact of religious youth groups concluded that these can preserve and transmit faith, in part by "facilitating more conversation and support between young adults and other adults in a parish."[30] And another project evaluating efforts to influence the spirituality of emerging adults in religious communities reported that

> building community and developing friendships need to be incorporated into all ministry and faith formation with emerging adults. Churches that do an exceptional job of attracting

---

26 Cavendish, Cidade, and Muldoon, 6.

27 Cavendish, Cidade, and Muldoon, 35.

28 Justin Bartkus and Christian Smith, *A Report on American Catholic Religious Parenting* (Notre Dame, Ind.: McGrath Institute for Church Life and Center for the Study of Religion and Society, the University of Notre Dame), 2019, 66, https://churchlife-info.nd.edu/thank-you-for-downloading-a-report-on-american-catholic-religious-parenting?submissionGuid=dbf09fec-ce92-451f-a0df-82f a4b080685.

29 Bartkus and Smith, 67.

30 Patricia Snell, "What Difference Does Youth Group Make? A Longitudinal Analysis of Religious Youth Group Participation Outcomes," *Journal for the Scientific Study of Religion* 48, no. 3 (2009): 572–87, 578.

and involving emerging adults find that community is vital to the emerging generations. Emerging adults long to be deeply invested in others and have others deeply invested in them. They desire to be a major part of each other's lives—the day-to-day, big and small "stuff of life." . . . Young adults are trying to connect and will make a lasting connection wherever they can find belonging in a congregation.[31]

Perhaps the leading study of faith transmission between generations, authored by the sociologist Vern Bengtson,[32] focuses primarily on the positive influences wielded by intact families who regularly practice their faith and have "affectual solidarity" with their children.[33] But Bengtson also reports that their community's[34] and their schoolmates' religiosity matter with respect to whether adolescents will practice religion.[35]

If personal relationships influence group members as much as the above research indicates, this strongly counsels for protecting institutions' ability to maintain final authority over the choice of personnel. Students, colleagues, and clients in religious communities will almost certainly form personal relationships with persons serving in a wide variety of roles. This was remarked on by the priest candidates in the survey by Cavendish, Cidade, and Muldooon reported above, who identified not only teachers but also administrators as important sources of encouragement for their vocations. It is even supported by news accounts about employees who have been separated from Catholic institutions, some of which are summarized in chapter 2. Clients, colleagues, parents, or others who engaged with the ex-employee regularly testify to his or her important influence upon their lives or the lives of their children. Furthermore, it is easy to find such

31 John Roberto, *Directions for Faith Formation with Emerging Adults: Insights from the Changing Spirituality of Emerging Adults Project* (Catholic University of America, 2008), 1–2.

32 Vern Bengtson, *Families and Faith: How Religion is Passed Down Across Generations* (Oxford: Oxford University Press, 2013).

33 Bengtson, 61, 63, 73–74, 79.

34 Bengtson, 166.

35 Mark D. Regnerus and Jeremy E. Uecker, "Finding Faith, Losing Faith: The Prevalence and Context of Religious Transformations During Adolescence," *Review of Religious Research* 47, no. 3 (2006): 217–37, 230–31.

claims in popular news stories about employees who are *not* teachers including, for example, a vice-principal,[36] a guidance counselor,[37] a church music director,[38] and dance and sports coaches.[39]

Certainly, it is likely that the relationships forged in more immersive interactions will play a more important role in fostering or undermining religious belief. These may arise, for example, in the daily interactions between students and employees in a religious school, or in the regular help that a religious provider gives to a client or patient with a social or health problem at a Catholic charity or hospital. In other words, a wide array of religious institutions are potential sites for forging regular, personal relationships that can shape both beliefs and norms. And it is clear that a wide array of employees in those institutions engage in those relationships.

ROLE-MODELING MATTERS

In light of the material set forth immediately above, it is not surprising that people in religious communities are influenced by role models. This has been extensively documented by experts in the field of the psychology of religion.

A preliminary matter concerns the role of personal example or "observational learning" *generally* in human beings' acquisition of knowledge and values. Psychologist Albert Bandura likely offers the most often-cited theory of social learning via personal example:

---

36 Steve Kiggins, "Catholic School Vice Principal Forced Out Over Same-Sex Marriage," *South Florida Gay News*, December 20, 2013, https://southfloridagaynews.com/National/catholic-school-vice-principal-forced-out-over-same-sex-marriage.html.

37 Audra Levy, "Roncalli Guidance Counselor Says She Was Asked to Resign After School Learned of Same-Sex Marriage," WRTV (ABC) (Indianapolis) website, August 13, 2018, https://www.wrtv.com/news/local-news/indianapolis/roncalli-guidance-counselor-says-she-was-asked-to-resign-after-school-learned-of-same-sex-marriage.

38 Tresa Baldas, "Catholic Church Fires Lesbian Music Director for Marrying a Woman," *Detroit Free Press*, June 24, 2020, https://www.freep.com/story/news/local/michigan/oakland/2020/06/24/detroit-archdiocese-terry-gonda-catholic-church-same-sex-marriage/3247103001/.

39 Cyd Zeigler, "Lesbian Coach Sues Catholic School That Fired Her for Marrying Her Wife," SB Nation Outsports website, August 22, 2016, https://www.outsports.com/2016/8/22/12598934/gay-basketball-coach-christian-catholic-school; David Gee, "Catholic School Fires Dance Coach for Living with Her Fiancé Before Marriage," *Patheos: Friendly Atheist*, June 12, 2018, https://friendlyatheist.patheos.com/2018/06/12/catholic-school-fires-dance-coach-for-living-with-her-fiance-before-marriage/.

If knowledge, values, and competencies could be acquired only by trial and error, human development would be greatly retarded, not to mention exceedingly tedious and hazardous. Moreover, limited time, resources, and mobility impose severe limits on places and activities that people can directly explore to gain new social perspectives and styles of thinking and behaving. However, humans have evolved an advanced cognitive capacity for observational learning that enables them to shape and structure their lives through the power of modeling.[40]

Bandura goes so far as to claim that "*most* human behavior is learned by observation through modeling."[41] People look to others for learning, "which takes place in a variety of ways: conscious or unconscious, ad hoc or systematically pursued within a community context."[42] Note the mention of "unconscious" learning; Bandura is claiming that people can be influenced even if not consciously aware of it. Put succinctly, "vicarious modeling influences can powerfully operate through consistent repeated exposure without engaging a person's conscious intention."[43]

Doug Oman has further considered Bandura's theory—called "spiritual modeling"—writing that it "expresses the idea that people may grow spiritually by imitating the life or conduct of one or more spiritual exemplars. . . . Central to spiritual modeling phenomena is what we term observational spiritual learning, that is, the learning of spiritually relevant skills or behaviors through observing other persons."[44]

The American Psychological Association's (APA) volume on the psychology of religion and spirituality reports that psychology affirms what religions have continuously believed about role-modeling, or what it calls "the value of keeping company and attending to the

---

40 Bandura, "On the Psychosocial Impact and Mechanisms of Spiritual Modeling," 167.

41 Albert Bandura, *Social Foundations of Thought and Action: A Social Cognitive Theory* (Hoboken, NJ: Prentice Hall, 1986), 47 (emphasis added).

42 Bandura, 51.

43 Doug Oman and Carl E. Thoresen, "Spiritual Modeling: A Key to Spiritual and Religious Growth," *The International Journal for the Psychology of Religion* 13, no. 3 (2003): 149–65, 154 (citations omitted).

44 Oman and Thoresen, 150.

example of good or holy persons."[45] It reports that people "tend to become more like those with whom they associate," and that "the power of example has been recognized in modern scientific psychology, and its ability to activate and channel behavior has been documented abundantly."[46]

The APA volume describes how a wide variety of religions have long believed and acted upon the above-described principles of spiritual modeling:

> Throughout history, religious traditions have emphasized the importance of keeping good company and attending to the example of good or holy persons, arguing that people tend to become more like those with whom they associate. . . .
>
> In Christianity, spiritual modeling is affirmed in the teachings and title of *The Imitation of Christ*, a 15th-century devotional book widely read by Protestants, Catholics, and Orthodox alike, and by slogans in popular culture, such as "What Would Jesus Do?" Islam celebrates Muhammad as a "beautiful exemplar" (*uswa hasana*, Qur'an 33:21). Because of the importance of his example, a central place in Islamic culture is given to hadith, the science of the authenticated narratives of the Prophet's sayings and actions. Ancient Hindu scriptures explicitly affirm the power of spiritual modeling. . . . In some forms of Buddhism, "bodhisattvas and buddhas are humanized figures, more to be emulated as models of behavior, than to be worshipped for miraculous efficacy." . . . In Judaism, the Torah's instruction to "cleave unto God" [Deut. 11:22] can be done, according to interpretations, through cleaving to sages.[47]

Oman and Thoresen conclude that, by recognizing the power of companionship and modeling, traditional religions are acting consistently with "recent psychological theory and practice." Citing Albert

---

45 Doug Oman, "Spiritual Modeling and the Social Learning of Spirituality and Religion," in *The American Psychological Association Handbook of Psychology, Religion, and Spirituality*, vol. 1, *Context, Theory, and Research*, ed. Kenneth I. Pargament, Julie J. Exline, and James W. Jones (Washington, D.C.: American Psychological Association, 2013), 187.

46 Oman, "Spiritual Modeling," 187.

47 Oman, 187, 191 (citations omitted).

Bandura they conclude: "The people with whom one regularly associates, either through preference or imposition, delimit the behavioral patterns that will be repeatedly observed, and hence, learned most thoroughly."[48]

Religious institutions are especially keen to understand how to teach and role-model a faith to adolescents.[49] A substantial body of literature explores this. One study of adolescents indicated that the most important religious role models are likely those experienced in the normal course of daily living.[50] While some religious adolescents report profound mystical experiences, "largely their narratives describe how their spirituality was shaped through the ebb and flow of life and their interactions with those around them. Their stories also reinforce that everyday interactions of offering support and encouragement . . . have the potential to shape and influence a young person's spiritual commitments."[51]

In the qualitative investigation referenced above of twenty-eight spiritually oriented youth ages twelve to twenty-one, 64 percent described observing someone who was an example of spiritual excellence that led them to deepen their religious commitment.[52] And a widely-hailed book on the faith of emerging adults reports their positive experiences of and interactions with adults who "reflect[] their beliefs and priorities" and who "understand them."[53] They seem especially influenced by those who are honest, exhibit integrity, are not phony, elitist, or hypocritical, offer explicit support, and are positive about religion.[54] During emerging adulthood, "while parents may influence the religious and spiritual development of emerging adults in more indirect ways, other adults, peers, and the media may have

---

48 Oman and Thoresen, "Spiritual Modeling," 150, citing Bandura, *Social Foundations of Thought and Action*, 55.

49 See, e.g., Carolyn McNamara Barry et al., "Religiosity and Spirituality during the Transition to Adulthood," *International Journal of Behavioral Development* 34, no. 4 (2010): 311–24, 318.

50 Bandura, "On the Psychosocial Impact and Mechanisms of Spiritual Modeling," 170.

51 King, Abo-Zena, and Weber, "Varieties of Social Experience," 136.

52 King, Abo-Zena, and Weber, 133–34.

53 Lisa Pearce and Melinda Lundquist Denton, *A Faith of their Own: Stability and Change in the Faith of America's Adolescents* (Oxford: Oxford University Press, 2011), 158–59.

54 Pearce and Denton, 161, 164–67, 170.

a more direct influence on them during this time period."[55] In fact, McNamara Barry et al. conclude that "given the apparent decline in influence that parents have, other adults with whom emerging adults interact regularly actually have the potential to impact them more during this time period than do parents."[56]

Any employee in an institution who interacts with others can become a role model for colleagues, students, and members of the public who are clients. The janitor who chats with the children attending aftercare. The secretary who works with multiple vendors and colleagues to organize institutional events. The receptionist at the school who sits with sick children until their parents can pick them up. The math teacher who provides students extra help. The food services director who interacts with the kids in the school cafeteria or with families stopping at the hospital canteen. Certainly, a Catholic institution might decide that some employees are unlikely to have these sorts of opportunities and interactions. But it will almost certainly conclude that many do. In this event, it should explain clearly to a court of law or public opinion that *employee X interacts regularly with clients/colleagues/schoolchildren/patients and thereby has the opportunity to communicate the values and identity of this institution or to undermine them.*

CONFIDENT PEOPLE CAN OVERWHELM

As described above, while many people in a group—especially those who engage in personal relationships and who are likeable and trustworthy—can potentially affect others, the relevant literature highlights that confident people possess heightened potential to influence others, especially people who feel they don't know as much. In fact, people who appear confident can influence others even if they do *not actually possess* relevant expertise or more information than their listeners; their confidence alone can cause others to believe that they are better informed.[57] An important experiment in the social influence literature conducted by Mehdi Moussaïd concluded that if even

55 McNamara Barry et al., "Religiosity and Spirituality During the Transition to Adulthood," 314.

56 McNamara Barry et al., 315.

57 Sunstein, *Conformity*, 6, 11, 23; see also Muzafe Sherif, "An Experimental Approach to the Study of Attitudes," *Sociometry* 1, no. 1/2 (1937): 90–98.

15 percent of a group confidently declare themselves "experts" on a subject, they can change what many members had previously claimed to believe. Moussaïd also observes that low-confidence people have trouble maintaining their opinions in a group.[58]

This matter of the influence exerted by apparently confident people is closely related to the influence that actual or perceived "authority figures" can exert. Many are familiar with Stanley Milgram's studies wherein "expert" scientists pressured test subjects to "shock" confederates—strapped to an electric chair—with increasing strength when they provided incorrect answers to questions (the shock was simulated, not real). The confederates simulated pain at the application of a certain level of voltage, and became completely silent—as if unresponsive—at even higher levels.[59] Most subjects continued to administer "shocks" beyond the level where the victim expressed pain, even though there were no consequences for their refusal. In short, they set aside their moral qualms in the face of expert instructions. Even as many have criticized Milgram's methods, scholars continue to cite these experiments to show how individuals are willing to violate even strongly held norms in order to follow the orders of an authority figure.[60]

Having compatriots, however, can boost an individual's willingness to disagree with even a confident influencer. Research indicates that those who disagree with a confident group member will gain strength to resist his or her influence if they have a sufficient number of peers to go along with them.[61] Interestingly, the physical presence of such peers is important. Even a temporary physical absence of a codissenter appears to weaken a dissenter's strength.[62] And it does not seem to matter whether such compatriots are highly confident; when both a dissenter and a codissenter have a similar opinion, both tend to keep to their initial judgment.[63]

58 Moussaïd et al., "Social Influence and the Collective Dynamics of Opinion Formation," *PLoS ONE* 8, no. 11 (November 2013): 1, 2.

59 See generally Stanley Milgram, *Obedience to Authority: An Experimental View* (New York: Harper Collins, 1974).

60 Sunstein, *Conformity*, 28–34, and citations therein.

61 See Sunstein, *Conformity*, 33, citing Milgram, *Obedience to Authority*, 113–22.

62 See Asch, "Opinions and Social Pressure," 31, 34.

63 See Moussaïd et al., "Social Influence and the Collective Dynamics of Opinion Formation," 3.

The social influence material on confidence and expertise points to the importance of religious institutions' building communities of knowledgeable, confident witnesses to their beliefs and to their avoiding the incorporation of too many confident dissenters within them. At the very least, it appears that such institutions should attempt to employ a critical mass of convinced, confident believers, and *also* take continual steps to boost members' confidence in their beliefs, if they wish individuals and the community to retain widespread support for their faith, doctrine, and mission. That religious institutions likely need to follow such a course is a strong indication either that a substantial group of its employees may be "ministers" in the First Amendment sense, or at least that the institutions need to retain authority over personnel under the broader church autonomy doctrine.

I should note here that it seems very likely today that many people who are convinced of the new sexual expression orthodoxy regularly display high levels of confidence. Elite media, academia, celebrities, corporations, and politicians support them loudly, constantly, and with great fanfare. They are sometimes heralded as heroes. Polls show that a significant majority of the public supports this orthodoxy too, even if only relatively recently and thinly. Those who speak out against the new orthodoxy—no matter how reasonably, how scientifically, or how kindly—are increasingly treated as social pariahs. Religious institutions without the ability to exert final authority over employment are at an obvious and serious disadvantage in such an environment. They should highlight this comparative disadvantage to a court of law or the court of public opinion (e.g., respecting abortion, same-sex unions, etc.) as an introduction to their arguments about their rights, as a matter of religious freedom, to maintain final authority over their own personnel. Otherwise, the result of a contest of ideas with the powers that be will too often be a foregone conclusion.

PEOPLE WITH STATUS CAN OVERWHELM

Closely related to the finding that confident people wield influence is the finding that people with status are more likely to influence others. That is, people who serve as informal social leaders—called "social referents" in the literature—can "powerfully affect behavior."[64] This is

---

64 See McDonald and Crandall, "Social Norms and Social Influence," 149.

related to the rather obvious research finding that people do more of what they receive rewards for (the "success proposition").[65] If a high-status person approves of a person's opinion, this is a kind of reward. These findings obviously apply to the predicament that many religious institutions experience today respecting personnel. Devout religious commitment—especially concerning culturally prominent issues of sexual expression—is more and more criticized as irrational, unintelligent, or even bigoted.[66] Opposing opinions are valorized as enlightened and compassionate. Thus, findings about the influence wielded by high-status persons indicate that it is in the interests of religious institutions to ensure that its staff is comprised of persons who are not only knowledgeable about the faith but who also enjoy respect, authority, and status.

MAJORITIES INFLUENCE DISSENTERS

Scholarship further indicates that opinions commanding majority assent can significantly move the opinions of others in a group. People have a predisposition to imitate a majority position because of an "evolved psychological mechanism that facilitates conformity."[67] In an article providing an "evolutionary perspective" on conformity, one author writes:

> Conformist transmission is a simple mathematical model that leads to clear and testable evolutionary hypotheses about how and when people will imitate the behaviour of others. If we are unsure of ourselves we are more likely to look around at what other people are doing and imitate the most common behaviour. From this perspective the directive "when in Rome, do as the Romans do" can be seen as an adaptive shortcut.[68]

---

65 Lee, "Religious Practice as Social Exchange," 7.

66 See, e.g., The United States Civil Rights Commission, *Peaceful Coexistence: Reconciling Nondiscrimination Principles with Religious Liberties,* Statement of Chairman Martin Castro (2016), 29, https://www.usccr.gov/pubs/docs/Peaceful-Coexistence-09-07-16. PDF. ("The phrases 'religious liberty' and 'religious freedom' will stand for nothing except hypocrisy so long as they remain code words for discrimination, intolerance, racism, sexism, homophobia, Islamophobia, Christian supremacy or any form of intolerance.")

67 Julie C. Coultas, "When in Rome . . . An Evolutionary Perspective on Conformity," *Group Processes & Intergroup Relations* 7, no. 4 (2004): 317–31, 330.

68 Coultas, 330.

One reason why majorities influence the opinions of others is that onlookers often feel uncertain about relevant facts and look to others for information.[69] When a consensus diverges from our own beliefs, we become uncertain, particularly regarding whether others have information that we do not. In this way, conformity can seem to be a rational decision in the face of uncertainty.[70]

Majorities influence others' conclusions about norms also because people want social acceptance and approval.[71] It seems "that pronounced social consensus in a decision-making context signals the creation of a social norm; that is, an explicit or implicit rule concerning what one is permitted, obligated, or forbidden to do in the current context."[72]

Levels of confidence regarding a fact or a norm interact with growth in the size of the cohort taking on a new opinion. One experiment showed, for example, that low-confidence individuals give way in their views after several rounds of opinion-sharing about a topic. After several rounds, "a tipping point occurs at which a critical proportion of people meet up in the same region of the opinion space. This creates a subsequent increase of confidence in this zone, which in turn becomes even more attractive to others. This results in a positive reinforcement loop, leading to a stationary state in which the majority of people end up sharing a similar opinion."[73]

Catholic institutions are operating in an environment today marked by majority opposition to many of their sexual expression norms. Powerful players are fueling these majorities: lawmakers, leading media, the academy, corporations, and highly funded interest groups. Because of the clout of majorities, it will be more than difficult for Catholic institutions to maintain their institutional values and identity without having a final say about the composition of their pool of employees.

---

69 See Sunstein, *Conformity*, 4; Asch, "Opinions and Social Pressure," 32; Sherif, "An Experimental Approach to the Study of Attitudes," 90–98.

70 Abhijit V. Banerjee, "A Simple Model of Herd Behavior," *Quarterly Journal of Economics*, 107, no. 3 (1992): 797–817, 798.

71 Kevin Wren, *Social Influences* (London: Routledge, 1999), 25.

72 Kundu and Cummins, "Morality and Conformity," 276–77.

73 See Moussaïd et al., "Social Influence and the Collective Dynamics of Opinion Formation," 5.

Conclusion

There should be little doubt based not only upon the above empirical evidence, but also upon common sense and life experience, that the employees constituting an institution crucially determine its ability to sustain its mission and identity. This is as true of religious organizations as it is of other organizations, whether corporations, secular charities, state agencies, or others. All are constituted by human beings who behave in groups in somewhat predictable manners, as detailed above.

There is also little doubt that efforts are well underway on the part of the state and private interest groups to wrest more control over employment within religious institutions, using the tool of "nondiscrimination" laws. These same players importantly affect several of the above-described factors driving individuals' opinions about sexual expression away from those held by Catholic institutions. They exude confidence and claim to possess expertise and majority support.

In light of the dynamics of social influence within groups and the current social environment regarding sexual expression, it is crucial that Catholic employers seeking to maintain their religious identity retain final say over their personnel decisions. A few caveats, however, are in order here. First, as already noted above, some religious employers may decide that certain positions do not require staff who support the mission. These positions/persons do not interface with others much or at all, and they are highly unlikely to influence others concerning the mission or identity of the institution.

Second, again as previously noted, none of this material is intended to suggest that Catholic employment is restricted to the spiritually perfect. Were this true, no humans need apply! Instead, all who participate in the "field hospitals" that Catholic communities are, are invited to experience God's mercy and love after they "fall down," repent, and start again. Despite the imperfection of their employees, Catholic educational, health care, and social services institutions in the US have maintained an impressive record of realizing the Church's theological aspirations for Catholic communities. Though founded and staffed by large numbers of diverse and imperfect human beings, they nevertheless continue to love and care for fellow human beings as a response to God's saving action and thus to maintain their religious identity. The next chapter explores these institutions in more detail.

- 5 -

THE RELIGIOUS IDENTITY OF US CATHOLIC INSTITUTIONS

CATHOLIC RELIGIOUS INSTITUTIONS IN THE US ARE SIMILAR in many respects to their secular counterparts engaged in the work of health care, education, and social services. But they are also distinctive precisely because of their Catholic identity. As described in chapter 3, broadly speaking this means that unlike secular entities they were founded by and are regularly staffed by persons responding to a belief in Jesus Christ, and that they seek not only to manifest the living Christ, but also a new model of human community that provides the world a glimpse of the Kingdom of God. They do these things for the same reasons that animate all worshipping communities, even as they also offer particular forms of help to Catholics and others. They are responding to one or more of Jesus's invitations to "heal the sick" (Lk 9:2), to "give to the poor" (Mk 10:21), and to "go into the whole world and proclaim the Gospel to every creature" (Mk 16:15). Thus, as I argued in chapters 3 and 4, they must enjoy a broad right of "church autonomy" concerning all of the elements of their organization—their services, operations, and personnel—in order to continue to be what they are.

This is not to say that every Catholic institution today will continue to operate in accordance with its founding religious aims, nor that it will judge every employee, operation, and service as importantly tied to its religious identity. It is only to claim that institutions wishing to preserve a Catholic identity possess what is legally requisite to make a strong "church autonomy" claim respecting control over their internal affairs. They also have the tools to make an appealing case for retaining this control in the face of problematic sexual expression laws and regulations. Certainly they can do better than many are doing now.

At the same time, however, we should recall that most Catholic institutions will have no difficulty conforming their institutions to a wide variety of applicable laws, even laws concerning personnel choices. Catholic institutions already and often submit to governmental and professional oversight that does not undermine their religious mission. They are subject to legal requirements directed to the usual array of state interests—health, safety, and welfare—and to professional standards set by the relevant, expert accrediting and membership organizations. Catholic institutions regularly and willingly comply with these and uphold and advertise competence in their chosen fields of endeavor. Most of these requirements and standards will not contradict the institution's mission at all, and in fact many will operate very much in concert with their mission to provide excellent services to students, patients, and other clients. This may even be true of the vast majority of laws and regulations affecting Catholic institutions. Conversely, though, various sexual expression laws and regulations *do* contradict the religious identities of Catholic institutions. These will be resisted on religious freedom grounds.

In order to understand in greater detail how such laws and regulations can violate the religious freedom of Catholic educational, health care, and social services organizations, this chapter will take an abbreviated tour of the theology, history, and mission of such institutions as they have arisen in the US. It will explain how they live out the three models of Christian community outlined in chapter 3. My explanations are intended to aid these institutions in making thicker and more religiously specific arguments for retaining authority over their services, operations, and personnel. Painting with a broad brush—as US Catholic institutions have inspired an enormous body of literature—I will show how each type of institution, from its founding to today, has operated as a community gathered in unity around Christ, seeking to witness to His living presence and the inbreaking of His reign. Throughout, I will note that although their religious missions were often originally shaped by the religious sisters, brothers, or priests who founded them, many continue today to choose to be Catholic even as more and more laypersons both work for and even lead them.

I will begin with Catholic education and then discuss social services and health care. In each case, I will begin by summarizing the theology undergirding the particular kind of institution, and thereafter describe its history and mission in the US.

Catholic Education

THE THEOLOGY OF CATHOLIC EDUCATION

Documents of the universal and US Catholic Church emphasize Catholic education's role in keeping the faith alive, especially by transmitting it intergenerationally and forming persons who will witness the living Christ to the wider world. They also treat the subject of Catholic education's benefit to the common good by its participation in the dialogue between faith and reason and by offering the world a Christian perspective on all of reality.

All three models of Catholic community presented in chapter 3 are featured in a leading document of the universal church outlining the theology of Catholic education, *Gravissimum Educationis*, the Declaration on Christian Education that was produced by the Second Vatican Council.[1] Here, Jesus is called the "divine founder" of Catholic schools, which pursue His "mandate of proclaiming the mystery of salvation to all men and of restoring all things in Christ."[2] These schools are aimed at forming students who respond to Christ by coming to know better "the mystery of salvation," "how to worship God the Father in spirit and truth," and how to "be conformed in their personal lives

---

1   Paul VI, Declaration on Christian Education *Gravissimum Educationis* (October 28, 1965).
2   Paul VI, Introduction.

according to the new man created in justice and holiness of truth," in order to become more Christlike.[3]

Students are also to learn "how to bear witness" to the world to the "hope that is in them" and thus "contribute to the good of the whole society,". . . not only by "leading an exemplary apostolic life [so as to] become, as it were, a saving leaven in the human community," but also by helping "order the whole of human culture to the news of salvation."[4] Furthermore, the school community should be a light to the participants themselves and to the wider community: the Catholic school's "proper function is to create for the school community a special atmosphere animated by the Gospel spirit of freedom and charity, to help youth grow according to the new creatures they were made through baptism."[5]

Additional and numerous documents of the universal and US church have continued to sound each of these themes as they apply to every level of Catholic education. For example, the theme of Christ's call to believers to form educational communities united by faith was sounded in Pope Saint John Paul II's *Ex Corde Ecclesiae* (From the heart of the Church), a 1990 document addressed to Catholic universities. In it, John Paul II referred to them as communities "inspir[ed]" by Christ, whose source of "unity springs from a common dedication to the truth, a common vision of the dignity of the human person and, ultimately, the person and message of Christ which gives the institution its distinctive character."[6]

Catholic educational communities as places of witness to Christ is a persistent theme in myriad Church documents and teachings. These highlight the mission of Catholic education to bring a Christian perspective to every field of knowledge. Vatican II's *Gravissimum Educationis* spoke particularly of the fruitful interplay of faith and science.[7] *Ex Corde Ecclesiae* spoke of the "honour and responsibility of a Catholic University to consecrate itself without reserve to *the cause of truth.*" It stated that the Church has "an intimate conviction that truth is [its] real ally . . . and that knowledge and reason are sure ministers to

---

3   Paul VI, 2.
4   Paul VI, 8.
5   Paul VI, 8.
6   John Paul II, Apostolic Constitution *Ex Corde Ecclesiae* (August 15, 1990), 21.
7   Paul VI, *Gravissimum Educationis*, 10.

faith." *Ex Corde* further claimed that Catholic universities could assist the world by "assur[ing] in an institutional manner a Christian presence in the university world confronting the great problems of society and culture."[8] And the 2004 *Compendium of the Social Doctrine of the Church* charged Catholic education with bringing a Gospel perspective to all social problems.[9] In order to pursue this ambitious agenda while remaining a Catholic community, *Ex Corde* teaches that the community itself must be an "authentic human community animated by the spirit of Christ."[10] Furthermore,

> in a Catholic University . . . Catholic ideals, attitudes and principles penetrate and inform university activities in accordance with the proper nature and autonomy of these activities. In a word, being both a University and Catholic, it must be both a community of scholars representing various branches of human knowledge, and an academic institution in which Catholicism is vitally present and operative.[11]

As the following section will demonstrate, many Catholic schools in the US at every level, both at the time of their foundings and today, subscribe to these ideas and norms. Even as some have become more ambivalent about or attenuated their Catholic identity—not infrequently due to disagreements over sexual expression norms—a large number of Catholic schools persistently cultivate their Catholic identity. Their large number and their presence throughout the entire country testifies to the Church's claim that Catholic education is a fundamental expression of the Catholic faith, a direct response to Jesus's "Go therefore and make disciples of all nations" (Mt 28:19).

CATHOLIC SCHOOLS IN THE US

While the first Catholic schools in what is now the US were founded in the seventeenth century by religious missionaries intending to

---

8   John Paul II, *Ex Corde Ecclesiae*, 1, 4, 13 (citations omitted).
9   Pontifical Council of Justice and Peace, *The Compendium of the Social Doctrine of the Church* (Washington, D.C.: USCCB, 2005), 532.
10 John Paul II, *Ex Corde Ecclesiae*, 21.
11 John Paul II, 14.

evangelize residents of the New World,[12] the US Catholic elementary and secondary school system as it appears today is more directly the descendant of the schools formed in response to the migration of large numbers of Catholics to the country in the mid-nineteenth century. Likely in response to the widespread poverty, robust ethnic loyalties, and high rates of legal delinquency found among some Catholic immigrant communities, the public schools considered it their mission to improve and "Americanize" Catholic youth[13] along Protestant lines. Public schools required daily prayers and Protestant Bible reading. Catholics, however, eager to preserve the faith in succeeding generations and rejecting a perceived "godless" America, were disinclined to send their children to such schools.[14] They founded their own institutions, with significant encouragement from both the Vatican and the US bishops. Both urged the formation of a Catholic school system focused on the transmission of faith. This concern characterized the bishops' statements at their First Plenary Council of Baltimore in 1852 and in an 1885 encyclical letter by Pope Leo XIII, *Spectata Fides*.[15] The latter asserted that "for it is in and by these schools that the Catholic faith, our greatest and best inheritance, is preserved whole and entire."[16]

Catholic elementary and secondary school systems grew a great deal over the course of the next century, peaking in the 1960s, when over five million students were enrolled in thirteen thousand Catholic schools.[17] The numbers mostly declined after that time, and with a declining number of vocations to the priesthood and religious life, by

---

12 Richard M. Jacobs OSA, "U.S. Catholic Schools and the Religious Who Served in Them: Contributions in the 18th and 19th Centuries," *Catholic Education: A Journal of Inquiry and Practice* 1, no. 4 (1998): 364–83.

13 See generally, Marvin Lazerson, "Understanding American Catholic Educational History," *History of Education Quarterly* 17, no. 3 (Autumn, 1977), 297–317, and Sean McCarroll, "The Plenary Councils of Baltimore (1852–1884): The Formation of America's Catholic School System Amidst Anti-Catholicism in the U.S.," *The Michigan Journal of History* 8, no. 1 (2011), https://michiganjournalhistory.files.wordpress.com/2014/02/mccarroll.pdf.

14 Lazerson, "Understanding American Catholic Educational History," 298–99.

15 See McCarroll, "The Plenary Councils of Baltimore"; Leo XIII, Encyclical Letter *Spectata Fides* (November 27, 1885).

16 Leo XIII, *Spectata Fides*, 4.

17 Betsy Shirley, "The Era of the Parochial School Is Over. Meet the Catholic Educators Searching for What's Next," *America Magazine*, January 25, 2019, https://www.americamagazine.org/faith/2019/01/25/era-parochial-school-over-meet-catholic-educators-searching-whats-next.

the 2020–2021 school year, Catholic schools employed 143,000 full-time professional staff, only 1.4 percent of which were nuns, and 0.9 percent clergy and other vowed religious men.[18] As Catholic schools in the US began more often to employ and even to be led by laypersons and to welcome more non-Catholic students—some primarily interested in the schools' academic reputations—their religious identities faded. Some began to downplay their confessional identity in favor of highlighting their academic or community-related strengths. Their public marketing materials might, for example, reference their Catholic identity by referring to "vague Christian inspiration or . . . human values," a tendency disparaged by Pope Francis's Congregation for Catholic Education in 2013.[19]

Contrast, for example, the self-description of the US's oldest Catholic university, Georgetown University, with that of one of the newer "classical" Catholic schools just a few miles away in Washington, D.C. Georgetown's website advertises:

> We're a leading research university with a heart. Founded in the decade that the U.S. Constitution was signed, we're the nation's oldest Catholic and Jesuit university. Today we're a forward-looking, diverse community devoted to social justice, restless inquiry and respect for each person's individual needs and talents.[20]

Compare that with the website of a nearby elementary level classical school, St. Jerome's Academy:

> We are pleased to offer an educational program that stresses growth in virtue and intellect. We believe that Jesus Christ—the Logos—is both the foundation and goal of our studies, as

---

18 The National Catholic Education Association, *United States Catholic Elementary and Secondary Schools, 2020–2021: The Annual Statistical Report on Schools, Enrollment, and Staffing* (Arlington, Va.: The National Catholic Education Association, 2021), infographic, https://ncea.org/NCEA/Who_We_Are/About_Catholic_Schools/Catholic_School_Data/NCEA/Who_We_Are/About_Catholic_Schools/Catholic_School_Data/Catholic_School_Data.aspx.

19 Congregation for Catholic Education, *Educating to Intercultural Dialogue in Catholic Schools: Living in Harmony for a Civilization of Love*, October 28, 2013, 56.

20 "Who We Are," Georgetown University (Washington, D.C.) website, https://www.georgetown.edu/who-we-are/.

we survey the history of mankind and develop the skills of observation and analysis.[21]

Beginning in the 1980s, many perceived a "drift" in the religious missions of Catholic elementary and secondary schools. Two reactions ensued: first, a renewed effort among some Catholic schools to reestablish a closer bond with the faith,[22] and second, universal and national Church bodies offering additional guidelines for maintaining a robust Catholic identity.

The contemporary Catholic "classical academies" phenomenon is one result of schools' intentionally reinvigorating their Catholic identity. The classical academies regularly focus intensely on the interplay of faith and reason and expose students to high-level, classical, primary sources.[23] They number at least forty-five in the US, and more are planned.[24] Also growing are new forms of partnerships and management structures among Catholic schools that are designed to foster both Catholic identity and high academic standards while keeping tuitions manageable.[25]

At the level of higher education, more than a few Catholic colleges and universities (hereafter referred to as "colleges") began to advertise their religious mission in a full-throated manner in the late twentieth and early twenty-first centuries. The Catholic University of America, for example, asserts at the very beginning of its "About Us" webpage:

> "The teaching of the University should be faithfully Catholic, conformed in all things to the creed of the Church and the decisions of the Holy See." This was the first principle set down by the founders of The Catholic University of America as the

21 "Welcome to St. Jerome Academy," St. Jerome Academy (Hyattsville, Md.) website, https://stjeromes.org/welcome.

22 Timothy Egan, "The Changing Face of Catholic Education," *New York Times*, August 6, 2000, https://www.nytimes.com/2000/08/06/education/the-changing-face-of-catholic-education.html.

23 Julia Duin, "Embracing a Classical Education," *Washington Post Magazine*, April 10, 2011, https://www.washingtonpost.com/magazine/embracing-a-classical-education/2011/03/09/AFj6amwC_story.html.

24 See "Classical Catholic Liberal Arts Schools Map," Institute for Catholic Liberal Education website, https://catholicliberaleducation.org/map-of-schools/.

25 See Shirley, "The Era of the Parochial School Is Over."

foundation of all our work and guide for all future action. We are still faithfully Catholic today.[26]

At the same time, more than a few Catholic colleges (and some secondary schools as well) are increasingly inclined to embrace publicly only those Catholic teachings likely to meet with applause from the early twenty-first century powers that be. Some distance themselves from currently less popular teachings touching on sexual expression and/or announce more popular initiatives—for example, improvements to their environmental footprints or other kinds of socially aware investment practices.[27]

Official Church bodies have responded to the changes in personnel, focus, and enrollment affecting Catholic schools in the last few decades. Documents issued under the last three papacies and from the US bishops have stressed the close relationship between Catholic schools and the central evangelizing mission of the Catholic Church. A 2022 document from the Vatican's Congregation for Catholic Education, for example, characterized all Catholic schools as "ecclesiastical institutions,"[28] whose mission is evangelization and Christian formation that takes place alongside a high level of training in secular disciplines. The Congregation also wrote that this "ecclesial dimension," should "penetrate[] and inform[] every moment of [the institutions'] educational activity," and constitute "a fundamental part of [their] very identity and the focus of [their] mission."[29] It insisted upon "no separation between time for learning and time for formation."[30] Regarding the schools' personnel, it wrote that the "education mission is carried out in a spirit of cooperation between various parties—students, parents, teachers, non-teaching personnel and the school

26 "About Us," The Catholic University of America, https://www.catholic.edu/about-us/faithfully-catholic/index.html.

27 See, e.g., Arabella Advisors, *Investments in Action: How Catholic Institutions Are Using Their Investments to Counter Climate Change* (2016), https://www.arabellaadvisors.com/wp-content/uploads/2016/10/Assets-in-Action-9.9-final.pdf (reviewing Catholic institutions' investment initiatives designed to counteract climate change).

28 Congregation for Catholic Education, *The Identity of the Catholic School for a Culture of Dialogue*, March 29, 2022, 20.

29 Congregation for Catholic Education, 21, citing Congregation for Catholic Education, *The Catholic School on the Threshold of the Third Millennium*, December 28, 1997, 11.

30 Congregation for Catholic Education, 23, citing *The Catholic School on the Threshold of the Third Millennium*, 14.

management—who form the educational community."[31] It expressed the hope that educators would be "competent, convinced and coherent" and "teachers of learning and of life" who should strive to reflect "albeit imperfect[ly] but still vivid[ly] . . . the one Teacher."[32] Further regarding the importance of personal relationships in the work of faith transmission, it wrote that the educating community "favour[s] interpersonal, real, and lived relationships," involving "bearing witness, knowledge, and dialogue."[33]

A 2005 document by the US bishops reaffirmed these themes, stating that Catholic elementary and secondary schools are "intimately bound up with the whole of the Church's life" and "invaluable instruments in proclaiming the Good News from one generation to the next."[34] Responding to the presence of a growing cohort of lay and even non-Catholic employees at Catholic schools, it stated that

> Catholic school personnel should be grounded in a faith-based Catholic culture, have strong bonds to Christ and the Church, and be witnesses to the faith in both their words and actions. . . . We gratefully acknowledge the contributions of school personnel who are not Catholic, but who support and cooperate in accomplishing the mission of the Catholic school.[35]

Another document from Pope Francis's Congregation for Catholic Education stresses again Catholic schools' "ecclesial and pastoral mission rooted in a relationship with the Church's pastors,"[36] and the importance for faith transmission of the interpersonal relations in the school, stating that "Catholic schools' primary responsibility is one of witness."[37] Like earlier documents from the US bishops and the

---

31 Congregation for Catholic Education, 37, citing Congregation for Catholic Education, *Consecrated Persons and their Mission in Schools: Reflections and Guidelines*, October 28, 2002, 41.

32 Congregation for Catholic Education, 23, citing *The Catholic School on the Threshold of the Third Millennium*, 14.

33 Congregation for Catholic Education, 34.

34 US Conference of Catholic Bishops, *Renewing Our Commitment to Catholic Elementary and Secondary Schools in the Third Millennium* (Washington, D.C.: USCCB, 2005), 2, quoting *Catechism of the Catholic Church*, §§ 5, 7.

35 US Conference of Catholic Bishops, *Renewing Our Commitment*, 10.

36 Congregation for Catholic Education, *Educating to Intercultural Dialogue*, 85.

37 Congregation for Catholic Education, 57 (citation omitted).

Vatican, it added that "Catholic schools . . . are not limited to a vague Christian inspiration or one based on human values. They have the responsibility for offering Catholic students, over and above a sound knowledge of religion, the possibility to grow in personal closeness to Christ in the Church."[38]

Looking more closely at Catholic colleges, these too are a significant presence on the US educational landscape. By the early 1900s, there were already 150 Catholic colleges in the US,[39] often founded by religious orders or dioceses. Today, there are about 260 Catholic institutions of higher education in the US.[40] Their founding missions were clear: to transmit the faith while also fostering the knowledge that would prepare students to take up the employment and other responsibilities of adulthood. From about the middle of the twentieth century to today, however, Catholic colleges' relationships with their founding religious orders and with the institutional Church—bishops, dioceses, and the Vatican—have become more attenuated or, in some cases, even fraught.[41] Financial pressures on Catholic (as on all) institutions of higher education have mounted, and lay employees and leadership, as well as non-Catholic students, have proliferated. Polarization and loss of mission have likely accelerated. Certainly, there are a handful of Catholic colleges—often openly marketing themselves as more conservative—expressly advertising their Catholic identities. But according to American theologian Massimo Faggioli, the "liberal-progressive" Catholic university in the US has

> embraced deconstruction of the neo-Scholastic hegemony since Vatican II so fully that it's now suspicious of any Catholic institutionalism. It has been too accommodating of the identity politics that have taken root since the 1960s. It is perhaps

---

38 Congregation for Catholic Education, 56.

39 Matthew Garrett, "The Identity of American Catholic Higher Education: A Historical Overview," *Catholic Education: A Journal of Inquiry and Practice* 10, no. 2 (2006): 229–47, 232, https://digitalcommons.lmu.edu/cgi/viewcontent.cgi?referer=&httpsredir=1&article=1401&context=ce.

40 "Catholic Higher Education FAQs," The Association of Catholic Colleges and Universities website, https://www.accunet.org/Catholic-Higher-Ed-FAQs#HowMany.

41 See generally, Wilson D. Miscamble, *American Priest: The Ambitious Life and Conflicted Legacy of Notre Dame's Father Ted Hesburgh* (New York: Image, 2019), and James Tunstead Burtchaell, *The Dying of the Light: The Disengagement of Colleges and Universities from their Christian Churches* (Grand Rapids, Mich.: Eerdmans, 1998).

still too closely linked to a vision of Catholic higher education laid out more than fifty years ago in the Land O'Lakes Statement, which is showing its age. And, in a sort of culminating gesture, it adopted a view of 1990's *Ex Corde Ecclesiae* (and also the *Catechism of the Catholic Church* of 1992) based on the belief that John Paul II and the Vatican were imposing an unacceptably unilateral understanding of Catholicism and Catholic education.[42]

Still, many Catholic colleges continue to find ways to manifest a religious mission,[43] even if they do not strongly highlight it. They accomplish this in their mission statements, hiring contracts, and personnel handbooks. They hire professors of Catholic theology and Catholic campus ministry staff and host retreats and training with Catholic content for faculty and administrators. Many also feature discrete programs or institutes devoted specifically to Catholic studies. Catholic campuses offer frequent Masses and other religious services and prayer opportunities, as well as service opportunities that are oriented toward Catholic social teaching. Some arrange dormitory life and rules with an eye to preserving Catholic dating and sexual norms. And today, in response to Catholic social teachings on consumerism, poverty, and the environment, some Catholic universities have also reshaped their investment and environmental practices.[44]

The preservation of the Catholic identity of Catholic higher education remains a continuing concern of both the US Catholic Church and the Vatican. As noted above, in 1990 John Paul II issued *Ex Corde Ecclesiae* on the subject of the Catholic identity of Catholic colleges. The document devoted significant attention to each of the models of Catholic community described in chapter 3. It identified the task of Catholic education as "explor[ing] the mysteries of humanity and

42 Massimo Faggioli, "Identity Crisis: Why We Can't Lose the 'Catholic University,'" *Commonweal*, March 30, 2021, https://www.commonwealmagazine.org/identity-crisis-2.

43 See generally, The Association of Catholic Colleges and Universities, *Institutional Principles for Catholic Identity and Mission Assessment: A Best Practices Guide* (Washington, D.C.: The Association of Catholic Colleges and Universities, 2020).

44 See, e.g., The Catholic University of America, "University Signs Sustainability Pledge, Recognized Green Power Champion," CUA Communications Office Press Release, April 30, 2019, https://communications.catholic.edu/news/2019/04/sustainability-pledge.html; see also Arabella Advisors, *Investments in Action*.

of the world, clarifying them in the light of Revelation,"[45] and urged Catholic colleges to be "a living *institutional* witness to Christ and his message."[46] It exhorted them to witness Christ to the world by "not only . . . preaching the Gospel in ever wider geographic areas or to ever greater numbers of people, but also by affecting and, as it were, upsetting, through the power of the Gospel, humanity's criteria of judgment, determining values, points of interest, lines of thought, sources of inspiration and models of life, which are in contrast with the Word of God and the plan of salvation."[47] *Ex Corde* further urged that a Catholic identity should permeate every aspect of the college:

> Catholic teaching and discipline are to influence all university activities, while the freedom of conscience of each person is to be fully respected. Any official action or commitment of the University is to be in accord with its Catholic identity.[48]

While recognizing that Catholic university communities are largely comprised of laity,[49] it insisted that everyone in the school community, including the "non-academic staff," "contribute[] towards . . . maintaining and strengthening the distinctive Catholic character of the institution." Even non-Catholic members of the community are required to "respect the Catholic character of the University, while the University in turn respects their religious liberty."[50]

In 1999, the US Catholic bishops officially promulgated *Ex Corde* in the US, stating that they "want to maintain, preserve and guarantee the Catholic identity of Catholic higher education."[51] Later, a 2014 document issued by Pope Francis's Congregation for Catholic Education emphasized the importance of interpersonal relations within all Catholic schools, both for personal religious formation and as a

---

45 John Paul II, *Ex Corde Ecclesiae*, 3.

46 John Paul II, 49 (emphasis in original).

47 John Paul II, 48 (citation omitted).

48 John Paul II, Part II, art. 2, § 4 (citation omitted).

49 John Paul II, 25.

50 John Paul II, 21, 24, 27.

51 "Decree of Promulgation: The Application of *Ex Corde Ecclesiae* for the United States," US Conference of Catholic Bishops website (November 17, 1999), Introduction, https://www.usccb.org/committees/catholic-education/application-ex-corde-ecclesiae-united-states.

witness to God's inbreaking Kingdom in the world, stating that "in every environment, whether it is favorable or not, Catholic educators will have to be credible witnesses."[52] It added:

> Catholic schools must be run by individuals and teams who are inspired by the Gospel, who have been formed in Christian pedagogy, in tune with Catholic schools' educational project, and not by people who are prone to being seduced by fashionability, or by what can become an easier sell, to put it bluntly . . . . Therefore our institutions must proclaim the Gospel beyond believers, not only with words, but through the power of our educators' lives, which must be consistent with the Gospel.[53]

In sum, while Catholic schools at the elementary, secondary, and college levels differ in many respects from one another, many and perhaps most are still eager to witness that they exist as a response to the call of Jesus Christ, that they educate students to witness Christ to the world, and that they attempt to live as communities in which His Kingdom is anticipated. Academic success is important to them, but never separated from the search for the whole truth, which includes God's sovereignty and the imperative to engage in dialogue with reason and culture so as to illuminate both with the light of Christ.

Educational institutions pursuing this path can more than credibly claim that their raisons d'être, their personnel, their services, and their internal operations are indispensable elements working *together* to realize the aims of their particular Catholic community. Thus they must enjoy a high degree of religious autonomy respecting each of these elements.

---

52 Congregation for Catholic Education, *Instrumentum Laboris, Educating Today and Tomorrow: A Renewing Passion*, 2014, introduction to Part III.

53 Congregation for Catholic Education, Part III, 1(a).

Catholic Social Services

THE ANCIENT HISTORY AND
THE THEOLOGY OF CATHOLIC SOCIAL SERVICES

Catholic social services—here meant to include all human welfare services save health care and education—are as old as the first Christian communities. Yet perhaps the most compact, complete, and inspiring account of their religious meaning—of their role in the Church and in the world—is contained in Pope Benedict XVI's 2005 encyclical, *Deus Caritas Est*. There, Benedict positioned Catholic charitable services not as a response to a mere ethical command addressed to the individual Catholic, and "not a kind of welfare activity which could equally well be left to others."[54] Instead, they are part of the Church's "nature, an indispensable expression of her very being," "as essential to her as the ministry of the sacraments and preaching of the Gospel."[55] Jesus commanded that they be done, and Catholic communities from the earliest days to the present have understood their importance as nothing less than a response to this command to love God and one another.

Some of Jesus's most direct and inspiring exhortations include His instruction to the "rich young man": "If you wish to be perfect go, sell what you have and give to the poor, and you will have treasure in heaven" (Mt 19:21). When asked by a scholar of the law what he must do to inherit eternal life, Jesus replied: "You shall love the Lord, your God, with all your heart, with all your being, with all your strength, and with all your mind, and your neighbor as yourself" (Lk 10:27). St. Paul echoes this instruction to the new Christian communities, stating that "the one who loves another has fulfilled the law" (Rom 13:8). Jesus also taught that every human being was in some sense a representative of God: "Whatever you did for one of these least brothers of mine, you did for me" (Mt 25:40).

Two additional quotations from *Deus Caritas Est* are in order because they inspiringly describe in more detail the origins and rationale of this fundamental work of the Church:

---

54 Benedict XVI, Encyclical Letter *Deus Caritas Est* (December 25, 2005), 25(a) (citation omitted).
55 Benedict XVI, 22, 25(a).

As a community, the Church must practise love. Love thus needs to be organized if it is to be an ordered service to the community. The awareness of this responsibility has had a constitutive relevance in the Church from the beginning: "All who believed were together and had all things in common; they would sell their property and possessions and divide them among all according to each one's need" (Acts 2:44–45).[56]

And further,

a decisive step in the difficult search for ways of putting this fundamental ecclesial principle into practice is illustrated in the choice of the seven, which with regard to the daily distribution to widows, a disparity had arisen between Hebrew speakers and Greek speakers. The Apostles, who had been entrusted primarily with "prayer" (the Eucharist and the liturgy) and the "ministry of the word," felt over-burdened by "serving tables," so they decided to reserve to themselves the principal duty and to designate for the other task, also necessary in the Church, a group of seven persons. Nor was this group to carry out a purely mechanical work of distribution: they were to be men "full of the Spirit and of wisdom" (cf. Acts 6:1–6). In other words, the social service which they were meant to provide was absolutely concrete, yet at the same time it was also a spiritual service; theirs was a truly spiritual office which carried out an essential responsibility of the Church, namely a well-ordered love of neighbour. With the formation of this group of seven, "*diaconia*"–the ministry of charity exercised in a communitarian, orderly way–became part of the fundamental structure of the Church.

As the years went by . . . charity became established as one of her essential activities, along with the administration of the sacraments and the proclamation of the word: love for widows and orphans, prisoners, and the sick and needy of every kind, is as essential to her as the ministry of the sacraments and preaching of the Gospel. The Church cannot neglect the service of charity any more than she can neglect the Sacraments and the Word. A few references will suffice to demonstrate this. Justin Martyr († c. 155) in speaking of the Christians' celebration of Sunday, also mentions their charitable activity, linked with the Eucharist as such. Those who are able make offerings in accordance with their means, each as he or she wishes; the Bishop in turn makes use of these to support orphans, widows, the sick and those who for other reasons find themselves in need, such as prisoners and foreigners. The great Christian writer Tertullian . . . relates how the pagans were struck by the Christians' concern for the needy of every sort. And when Ignatius of Antioch († c. 117) described the Church of Rome as "presiding in charity (*agape*)," we may assume that with this definition he also intended in some sense to express her concrete charitable activity.[57]

Benedict further describes in *Deus Caritas Est* the "earliest legal structures associated with the service of charity in the Church," including in the fourth century "the '*diaconia*': the institution within each monastery responsible for all works of relief," noting that by the "sixth century this institution had evolved into a corporation with full juridical standing, which the civil authorities themselves entrusted with part of the grain for public distribution." Eventually, in Egypt, each "individual Diocese eventually had its own *diaconia*; this institution then developed in both East and West." In Rome "charitable activity on behalf of the poor and suffering was naturally an essential part of the Church of Rome from the very beginning, based on the principles of Christian life given in the Acts of the Apostles."[58]

Perhaps the most famous example of Christians' early, organized service of charity is the institution first described in chapter 3, the fourth century "Basilead" of Saint Basil. He was a bishop who was convinced that Jesus's admonition to the rich young man to give everything to the poor applied to every person. He urged Christians to live simply and give generously to the poor, given that God provides the resources of this world for the common benefit of humanity.[59] At

---

57 Benedict XVI, 21–22.
58 Benedict XVI, 23.
59 St. Basil the Great, *On Social Justice*, introduction by and trans. C. Paul Schroeder (Yonkers, NY: St. Vladimir's Seminary Press, 2009), 26–28, 31.

the Basilead, the poor received free shelter, food, and medical treatment. Clergy co-resided with the needy.[60]

Other scholars have chronicled Christians' early grasp of the duty of charity. Historian Robert Louis Wilken, for example, writes that "from earliest times Christian leaders had taken to heart the exhortations in the Scriptures to care for the poor."[61] This included at least Jesus's instruction to the rich young man (Mt 19:21), his announcement of the greatest commandment (Lk 10:27), and his insistence that charity to any human being also constitutes love of God (Mt 25:40). And because Jesus proclaimed every person a potential representative of Christ, there could be no exceptions to Christian charity, according to Byzantine scholar Judith Herrin: "Christ [had] identif[ied], and elevat[ed] . . . these unfortunates as persons most worthy and deserving of good works" and left his followers "unmistakable instructions."[62]

Historian Peter Brown highlights how this behavior constituted a signal departure from Roman practices, which generally distributed alms only to citizens.[63] Christian practice was therefore also a new way of conceiving of the relevant community of which Christians were a part: "God's category" for community included *all* fellow humans.[64] As Benedict XVI observes: "On the basis of an intimate encounter with God" one learns "to look on this other person not simply with my eyes and my feelings, but from the perspective of Jesus Christ. His friend is my friend. . . . Here we see the necessary interplay between love of God and love of neighbor."[65]

And who is the neighbor? Benedict writes that the "standard" of Christian charity is set by the Good Samaritan: "*Caritas-agape* extends beyond the frontiers of the Church." The Church must demonstrate

---

60 C. Paul Schroeder, Introduction to St. Basil the Great, *On Social Justice*, 35–38.

61 Robert Louis Wilken, *The First Thousand Years: A Global History of Christianity* (New Haven: Yale University Press, 2012), 156.

62 Judith Herrin, *Margins and Metropolis: Authority Across the Byzantine Empire* (Princeton: Princeton University Press, 2013), 300.

63 Peter Brown, "From *Patriae Amator* to *Amator Pauperum* and Back Again: Social Imagination and Social Change in The West Between Late Antiquity and the Early Middle Ages, Ca. 300–600," in *Cultures in Motion*, ed. Daniel T. Rogers, Bhavani Raman, and Helmut Reimitz (Princeton: Princeton University Press, 2014), 87–106.

64 Brown, 91.

65 Benedict XVI, *Deus Caritas Est*, 18.

"universal love towards the needy whom we encounter 'by chance' (cf. Lk 10:31), whoever they may be."[66]

In surveying US Catholic social services below, it is easy to conclude that they have sought to operate from the beginning as described by *Deus Caritas Est*. They often provided service to co-religionists first, but then extended themselves to all in need. They grew up throughout the US in response to local and even national needs. They were founded by a wide range of Catholic persons and groups—religious orders, clergy, dioceses, and laywomen and men—all of whom understood themselves as charged to respond to Jesus's invitation. Without a doubt, they have expressed and continue to express a fundamental impulse and task of the Church. And they regularly operate as do all Church communities: by gathering believers in unity around Jesus Christ, by witnessing in word and deed to the living Christ, and by providing observers a vision of an alternative society, a "new set of relationships, a new social order that both anticipates and participates in the creation of 'a new heaven and new earth where justice dwells.' . . . The new city is present wherever people live together in this way, waiting for the Kingdom of God even as they constitute a sign of its presence in our midst."[67]

CATHOLIC SOCIAL SERVICES IN THE US

Recognizable Catholic social services institutions likely first began in the US with an orphanage founded in New Orleans in about 1727 by the Ursuline sisters.[68] Like Catholic schools, however, Catholic social services grew tremendously in the nineteenth century in response to the influx of Catholic immigrants.

At first, these institutions provided charitable services at a local level through parishes and voluntary groups comprised of laypersons, clergy, and religious. The Society of Saint Vincent de Paul, for example, imported from France into the US in 1845 and comprised

---

66 Benedict XVI, 25(b).
67 Schroeder, introduction to St. Basil the Great, *On Social Justice*, 38.
68 Heloise Hulse Cruzat, "The Ursulines of Louisiana," *The Louisiana Historical Quarterly* 2, no. 1 (January 1919): 5–23. https://www2.latech.edu/~bmagee/louisiana_anthology/texts/cruzat/cruzat--ursulines.html.

of lay volunteers organized at the parish level,[69] was a particularly important group. It supported, among other things, homes for foster children, youth residences, emergency aid, and youth clubs. According to a leading treatment of the history of US Catholic social services, they focused especially on family services, and their "leading motive was to save the souls of the children and their parents, but the importance of material provision and service was never undervalued."[70]

By 1900 there were more than eight hundred Catholic institutions dedicated to providing charitable services in the US.[71] These were often sponsored by religious congregations, and involved hundreds of lay volunteers under one umbrella in some of the bigger cities. They included orphanages, settlement houses, industrial schools, remedial institutions, and shelters for women. Catholics also began to offer "noninstitutional" services, including employment registries, probation and recreational services for youth, outdoor relief, family casework, and home nursing services.[72]

In the early twentieth century, bishops began to centralize and professionalize hundreds of independent institutions within their dioceses, in response to the increasing professionalization of social work and to the desire to deliver quality services to a large cohort of people.[73] Charitable services offices were created within most dioceses, and were ordinarily called "Catholic Charities" agencies.[74] Currently, Catholic Charities USA (CCUSA) is the national office of over 160 local Catholic Charities agencies sponsoring 2,600 service locations serving over 12 million Americans annually, without regard to creed.[75]

---

69 "The Society of St. Vincent de Paul in the United States," National Council of the United States, Society of St. Vincent de Paul website, https://www.svdpusa.org/About-Us/History.

70 Dorothy M. Brown and Elizabeth McKeown, *The Poor Belong to Us: Catholic Charities and American Welfare* (Cambridge, Mass.: Harvard University Press, 1997), 3.

71 Jack Hansan, "Catholic Charities USA," Virginia Commonwealth University, VCU Libraries Social Welfare History Project, 2010, https://socialwelfare.library.vcu.edu/religious/catholic-charities-usa/.

72 Brown and McKeown, *The Poor Belong to Us*, 3.

73 Brown and McKeown, 5.

74 "Our History," Catholic Charities USA, https://www.catholiccharitiesusa.org/about-us/history/.

75 John Gehring, "'Without Compassion, I Fear We Are Complicit,' an interview with Sister Donna Markham," *Commonweal Magazine*, April 6, 2020, https://www.commonwealmagazine.org/without-compassion-i-fear-we-are-complicit.

In an important account of the work of Catholic Charities, theologian Charles Curran writes that these agencies understand themselves as integral parts of the mission of the Church, carrying out services essential to the Church's solidarity with the needy in the world.[76] In short, they are expressing what Pope Francis called in *Evangelii Gaudium*—echoing Pope Benedict XVI—"a constituent element of the Church's mission and an indispensable expression of her very being."[77]

Like Catholic schools, Catholic social services have grappled with challenges to their Catholic identity. These emerged at least as far back as the Great Depression, when a great deal of care for the poor shifted away from lay Catholic volunteers to large federal and state agencies as well as professional social workers. At this time, some Catholic bishops pleaded for the retention of an evangelizing focus in connection with Catholic charities. At a 1933 meeting of the National Conference of Catholic Charities, for example, Bishop Aloisius Muench of the Fargo diocese "appealed for the charity that engendered the sanctification of client, volunteer, and diocesan worker."[78] The question of Catholic identity also arose because Catholic agencies began to receive a significant portion of their funding from government sources. Today, for example, more than 60 percent of CCUSA's income comes from state and federal sources.[79]

In the midst of these concerns, Popes Benedict XVI and Francis have stressed the necessity of a Catholic identity for Catholic charities, and the particular role of personnel in securing this goal. Benedict XVI wrote in *Deus Caritas Est*, for example, that personnel of charities must "want to work with the Church and therefore with the Bishop. . . . By their sharing in the Church's practice of love, they wish to be witnesses of God and of Christ, and they wish for this very reason

---

76 Charles Curran, "The Catholic Identity of Catholic Institutions," *Theological Studies* 58, no. 1 (1997): 90–108, 101.

77 Francis, Apostolic Exhortation *Evangelii Gaudium* (November 24, 2013), 179, citing Benedict XVI, Motu Proprio *Intima Ecclesiae Natura* (November 11, 2012).

78 Brown and McKeown, *The Poor Belong to Us*, 193, citing Rev. Aloysius J. Hogan, "'The Catholic Church and the Social Order,' Proceedings of the Nineteenth National Conference of Catholic Charities" (1933).

79 Kelly Riddell, "Catholic Church Collects $1.6 Billion in U.S. Contracts, Grants, Since 2012," *Washington Times,* September 24, 2015, https://www.washingtontimes.com/news/2015/sep/24/catholic-church-collects-16-billion-in-us-contract/.

freely to do good to all."[80] He cautioned that the operations themselves must "not become just another form of social assistance," but must themselves reveal "love of neighbour . . . as a consequence deriving from . . . a faith which becomes active through love."[81] On his first day as pope, Francis famously preached on the religious identity of Catholic charitable work, stating that "if we do not confess to Christ, what would we be? We would end up a compassionate NGO [nongovernmental organization]. What would happen would be like when children make sandcastles and then it all falls down."[82]

In recent years, spurred on by the above-described self-reflection of the Church, Catholic social services institutions have undertaken new efforts to maintain their religious identity. In addition to ensuring that their services demonstrate Christlike love for the clients, they also take care that their operations respect Catholic understandings of justice and charity. This means, for example, paying fair but not exorbitant salaries and providing health care benefits to their employees, attending to the environmental effects of their operations, and aligning their investments with Catholic social teaching.

With respect to personnel, many institutions are undertaking visible and significant efforts to hire and train those who will enthusiastically support the Catholic identity of the enterprise. In 2010, for example, CCUSA published a "toolkit" to assist agencies in "living out" their Catholic identity.[83] In addition, its "vision statement" closely reflects the scriptural origins of the earliest Catholic charitable services, with references to the need to witness to "the presence of God in our midst," to the parable of the Good Samaritan, and to the "mission of Jesus given to the church."[84] The vision statement exhorts local and national offices of Catholic Charities to more intentionally adopt Catholic identity tools, such as regional workshops on religious

80 Benedict XVI, *Deus Caritas Est*, 33.

81 Benedict XVI, 31.

82 BBC News, "Pope Francis Warns Church Could Become 'Compassionate NGO,'" *BBC News*, March 14, 2013, https://www.bbc.com/news/world-europe-21793224.

83 Catholic Charities USA, *Catholic in Charity and in Identity: Resources to Enhance the Legacy* (2010), introductory letter from Rev. Larry Snyder, president of Catholic Charities, USA, https://www.catholiccharitiesusa.org/wp-content/uploads/2018/05/CCUSA-Catholic-Identity.pdf.

84 Catholic Charities USA, *Catholic in Charity and in Identity*, "Vision of Catholic Charities" and § 2.

mission and detailed plans for hiring and forming employees and board members according to the needs of the mission. Catholic Charities is also incorporating education about its religious identity into its new-employee orientations and sponsoring staff development days, educational materials, and staff retreats. Catholic identity promotion is also a factor in employee evaluations.[85]

In sum, Catholic social services in the US continue to understand themselves today as a specific response to Jesus's commands to love and to His exhortations to serve the poor. Through the services they offer and the way in which they offer them, they explicitly aim to model Christ to those they encounter. They seek to become a new kind of community, one that provides a glimpse to all who encounter it of a society foreshadowing the reign of God, wherein human beings respond to Christ's invitation by treating one another as the face of Christ. Delivering high-quality services as delineated under the law and by professional associations, and assisting as many persons in need as possible, are important to Catholic social services. But they intend to be far more than another talented NGO. Rather, their entire organizations and their ways of operating are intended as a response to and a manifestation of the living Christ.

Catholic social service institutions pursuing this path can more than credibly claim that their raisons d'être, their personnel, their services, and their internal operations are indispensable elements working *together* to realize the aims of their particular Catholic community. Consequently, they should enjoy a high degree of religious autonomy respecting each of these elements.

Catholic Health Care

THE ANCIENT HISTORY AND THE THEOLOGY OF CATHOLIC HEALTH CARE

Like Catholic social services, Catholic health care has existed since the early days of Christianity. In the words of one Catholic theologian: "We have had church organizations—schools, priories, monasteries, hospitals and social service agencies—that have acted on behalf of

85 Catholic Charities USA, §§ 3.1–3.8.

the church for centuries. They 'gave flesh' to the church's mission by preaching through works of mercy, healing and education."[86] The Basilead of the fourth century, described above, is a perfect example. It provided health care to the poor, as well as other forms of charity.

The US bishops refer to Catholic hospitals as fulfilling the Church's mission "to embody our Savior's concern for the sick," referring to the numerous accounts of Jesus's healings during His ministry on earth.[87] At the same time they note that Catholic health care is never solely about physical health. As did Jesus, Catholic health care should seek people's "physical, mental, and spiritual healing" as well (Jn 6:35, 11:25–27).[88] "Healing" has always been a "major part" of the "mission of evangelization to which Jesus sent his followers" (Lk 10:8–9; and Mt 25:34–40).[89] The bishops urge providers to model this healing on the Gospel parable of the Good Samaritan (Lk 10:25–37).

Pope Francis's Pontifical Council for Pastoral Assistance to Health Care Workers has also weighed in with a 2017 document about the religious identity and mission of Catholic health care. In its *New Charter for Health Care Workers*—addressed to every person participating in providing health care in Catholic institutions (including administrators and even volunteers)[90]—it referred to their services as an expression of "love of neighbor,"[91] which, when performed "in fidelity to the moral law," constitutes both "fidelity to man" and an expression of the "wisdom" of God.[92] The document expressly welcomes science, and advocates for the interplay of faith and reason, stating that the Church "accept[s] everything good that emerges from human works and from various cultural and religious traditions."[93] At the same time,

---

86 Charles E. Bouchard OP, "Health Care as 'Ministry': Common Usage, Confused Theology," *Health Progress* (Journal of the Catholic Health Care Association of the United States), May-June, 2008, https://www.chausa.org/publications/health-progress/article/may-june-2008/health-care-as-%27ministry%27-common-usage-confused-theology.

87 US Conference of Catholic Bishops, *Ethical and Religious Directives for Catholic Health Care Services*, 6th ed. (Washington, D.C.: USCCB, 2018), 6.

88 US Conference of Catholic Bishops, *Ethical and Religious Directives*, 6.

89 US Conference of Catholic Bishops, *Health and Health Care: A Pastoral Letter of the American Catholic Bishops*, November 19, 1981, 4.

90 Pontifical Council for Pastoral Assistance to Health Care Workers, *New Charter for Health Care Workers* (Philadelphia: The National Catholic Bioethics Center, 2016), 3.

91 Pontifical Council for Pastoral Assistance to Health Care Workers, 5.

92 Pontifical Council for Pastoral Assistance to Health Care Workers, 5, 6.

93 Pontifical Council for Pastoral Assistance to Health Care Workers, 6.

it insists that Catholic health care is always a "response to a transcendent call that takes shape in the suffering face of the other," and thus "surpasses the purely human level of service to the suffering person and takes on the character of Christian witness, and therefore of mission."[94] As such, Catholic health care services are a "prolongation and . . . fulfillment of the charity of Christ," and even "directed toward Christ himself," who reminded us that when we assist a brother or sister, "You did it to me" (cf. Mt 25:31–40).[95]

The US Conference of Catholic Bishops regularly updates a document that governs the relationship between Catholic health care institutions and the Catholic faith: *The Ethical and Religious Directives for Catholic Health Care* (ERDs).[96] The ERDs are addressed to every single person comprising the health care institution, including the "sponsors, trustees, administrators, chaplains, physicians, [and] health care personnel."[97] They require that all "employees of a Catholic health care institution must respect and uphold the religious mission of the institution and adhere to these Directives."[98]

The ERDs refer to the provision of health care by Catholic institutions as an "ecclesial mission,"[99] an aspect of the work of the Church itself. The identified theological bases for Catholic health care delivery are scriptural: to continue the "Savior's concern for the sick" during His time on earth and to properly acknowledge that all human beings are an image of God.[100]

On many occasions, the ERDs note the importance of specific collaboration with the diocesan bishop in his role as teacher. He should be consulted to "ensure[] the moral and religious identity"[101] of the hospital, to approve the hiring of the pastoral care staff,[102] and regarding the terms of any proposed merger with a non-Catholic health care entity.[103] The ERDs also provide that Catholic canon law

94 Pontifical Council for Pastoral Assistance to Health Care Workers, 9.
95 Pontifical Council for Pastoral Assistance to Health Care Workers, 10.
96 See US Conference of Catholic Bishops, *Ethical and Religious Directives*.
97 US Conference of Catholic Bishops, *Ethical and Religious Directives*, 4.
98 US Conference of Catholic Bishops, *Ethical and Religious Directives*, 9 (Directive 9).
99 US Conference of Catholic Bishops, *Ethical and Religious Directives*, 4.
100 US Conference of Catholic Bishops, *Ethical and Religious Directives*, 6, 7, 23.
101 US Conference of Catholic Bishops, *Ethical and Religious Directives*, 7.
102 US Conference of Catholic Bishops, *Ethical and Religious Directives*, 12 (Directive 21).
103 US Conference of Catholic Bishops, *Ethical and Religious Directives*, 5 (Directive 67).

must be observed when founding, selling, closing, or substantially revising the mission of a Catholic health care institution.[104]

The ERDs also instruct Catholic health care providers to attend to the spiritual dimensions of the human person, and require, therefore, "cordial and cooperative relationships between the personnel of pastoral care departments and the local clergy and ministers of care."[105] They stress the importance of the ready availability of sacraments such as Holy Communion and Reconciliation, especially given the possibility of death.[106]

The ERDs also contain specific requirements concerning patients and procedures. Catholic hospitals are to attend especially to vulnerable persons: preborn human beings, the poor, and the un- and under-insured.[107] They must refuse medical procedures and research that are contrary to Catholic teachings, including certain assisted reproductive technologies, abortion, sterilization, and euthanasia.[108] They are held to certain safeguards in connection with organ transplants and the treatment of sexual assault victims.[109] They must establish ethics committees to sort out difficult moral questions.[110]

As the next section will show, it is easy to see in today's Catholic health care institutions the Church's ancient and ongoing mission to heal both body and soul in imitation of Christ. This is true even though Catholic health care institutions today can be large and complex, and even though a few have distanced themselves from their religious foundations.[111]

---

104 US Conference of Catholic Bishops, *Ethical and Religious Directives*, 9 (Directive 8).
105 US Conference of Catholic Bishops, *Ethical and Religious Directives*, 10.
106 US Conference of Catholic Bishops, *Ethical and Religious Directives*, 11.
107 US Conference of Catholic Bishops, *Ethical and Religious Directives*, 8, 16.
108 US Conference of Catholic Bishops, *Ethical and Religious Directives*, 18, 19, 20.
109 US Conference of Catholic Bishops, *Ethical and Religious Directives*, 15, 22.
110 US Conference of Catholic Bishops, *Ethical and Religious Directives*, 15.
111 Amanda Lee Myers, "Phoenix Hospital Loses Catholic Status Over Surgery," *The East Valley Tribune*, December 21, 2010 (describing bishop's retracting Catholic status from a hospital that performed a direct abortion), https://www.eastvalleytribune.com/local/the_valley/phoenix-hospital-loses-catholic-status-over-surgery/article_fb8a6996-0d30-11e0-9f38-001cc4c03286.html.

CATHOLIC HEALTH CARE IN THE US

In the US today, Catholic hospitals feature prominently in the overall health care landscape. There are over 660 Catholic hospitals and nearly 1,600 Catholic continuing care and other health facilities that serve about one out of every seven patients in the US.[112] In a detailed history of the early days of US Catholic hospitals, Professor Barbara Mann Wall reports that religious sisters alone founded almost five hundred Catholic hospitals in the US between 1866 and 1926.[113] Often their services and institutions were organized to respond to specific needs, such as those arising from mass immigration, large urban populations, acute diseases, war, and railway and mining accidents.[114] But from the beginning, it was intended that Catholic hospitals would provide care for both body and soul, in imitation of Christ. They did this in numerous ways.

Religious sisters witnessed to their beliefs first with their continuous, comforting presence and care. They also directly exhorted patients to repentance and prayer.[115] Wall concludes that religious beliefs and practices permeated Catholic hospitals, which understood spiritual consolations to be part of healing.[116] These facilities integrated the rosary and other prayers throughout the day, as well as frequent Masses.[117] In fact, they were often designed with chapels located near to patient rooms.[118] Wall writes that the presence of a Catholic hospital in a community was a "powerful means of spreading religious devotion into local and regional communities."[119]

Imitating the practice of ancient Catholic charities of serving all in need, Catholic hospitals accepted a wide array of patients, including those who were outcasts at the time, regularly shunned by other

---

112 Catholic Health Association of the United States, *U.S. Catholic Health Care* (2021), https://www.chausa.org/docs/default-source/default-document-library/2021-the-strategic-profile-_sb_final.pdf?sfvrsn=2.

113 Barbara Mann Wall, *Unlikely Entrepreneurs: Catholic Sisters and the Hospital Marketplace, 1865–1925* (Columbus: The Ohio State University Press, 2005), 4.

114 Wall, 18–22, 76.

115 Wall, 138.

116 Wall, 129–41.

117 Wall, 134–35.

118 Wall, 120–23.

119 Wall, 53.

medical service providers. These included alcoholics, the chronically and contagiously ill, and those suffering from venereal and mental diseases. Additionally, Catholic hospitals offered the poor free services and dignity at the time of death. They further assured the dignified disposal of remains.[120]

The role of the nurse, undertaken often but not exclusively by a religious sister, was deemed especially significant by Catholic hospitals. Their presence at the beds of the sick and dying was intended to be a living example of Christian love and mercy and a crucial spiritual assistance at moments that implicated both the worldly and the divine: birth, illness, and death.[121]

Today, like other Catholic institutions, Catholic hospitals are facing challenges to their religious identity. One prominent legal scholar critical of Catholic hospitals' religious freedom claims refers to some as "zombie religious institutions."[122] There are many reasons for their struggles over identity. They are rarely managed by their founding religious communities. Their boards of trustees and staff include many non-Catholics. They depend significantly upon government programs, and rising costs often lead to mergers with non-Catholic institutions.[123] Furthermore, they are regularly attacked by organizations whose sole focus is stirring up trouble with lawmakers, regulators, and local communities when Catholic hospitals merge with non-Catholic providers and insist upon the continued observation of the ERDs.[124] They are further beset by a stream of laws, regulations, and demands by accrediting agencies to recognize and deliver as "health care," abortion, contraception, sterilization, assisted suicide, and surgeries to remove healthy sexual organs.

Yet, like the Catholic schools described above, many Catholic hospitals and health care systems are working to preserve a specifically Catholic identity. The leading umbrella organization of Catholic

---

120 Wall, 52–53, 139.

121 Wall, 135, 138–39, 191.

122 Elizabeth Sepper, "Zombie Religious Institutions," *Northwestern University Law Review* 112, no. 5 (2018): 929–88.

123 Donald H. J. Hermann, "Religiously Affiliated Health Care Providers: Legal Structures and Transformations," in *Religious Organizations in the United States: A Study of Identity, Liberty, and the Law*, ed. James A. Serritella et al. (Durham, NC: Carolina Academic Press, 2006), 727–58, 730, 736, 745–49.

124 See, e.g., mergerwatch.org.

hospitals in the US, the Catholic Health Association, refers to itself as "a ministry of the Catholic Church continuing Jesus' mission of love and healing in the world today."[125] The Catholic health care system, Ascension, opens its mission statement as follows: "Rooted in the loving ministry of Jesus as healer, we commit ourselves to serving all persons with special attention to those who are poor and vulnerable."[126] There are also new health care efforts springing up regularly in the US that closely model the work of the earliest Christians. In Tennessee, for example, the Sisters of Mercy of Alma initiated a mobile medical clinic for patients without money in one of the poorest areas of Appalachia. They did it because the men and women they serve are "made in the image of God . . . and like all of us, cherished sons and daughters of a loving Father. They ought to be treated as such." As a "picture . . . of the Lord's love," they say, the clinic is always also an "opportunity for evangelization."[127] Finally, and as already described above, all hospitals that wish to be recognized as Catholic in the US agree to abide by the ERDs, which foster a full-bodied expression of Catholic identity.

Thus, despite the many similarities between Catholic and other medical institutions' professional delivery of health care, Catholic institutions remain distinctive. They continue to understand themselves today as a specific response to Jesus Christ. Through their services and the way in which they offer them, they explicitly seek to model Christ to those they encounter. Thus they seek to become a new kind of community, one that provides a glimpse to all who encounter it of a society that foreshadows the Kingdom of God.

Catholic health care institutions are, of course, intent upon delivering high-quality services as delineated under the law and by professional associations. They also wish to assist as many persons in need as possible. But they never aim to be merely "compassionate NGOs." Rather, their entire organizations and their ways of operating are intended to confess Christ. In the words of the Vatican's 2017

---

125 "About," Catholic Health Association of the United States, https://www.chausa.org/about/about.

126 "Mission, Vision and Values," Ascension website, https://ascension.org/our-mission/mission-vision-values.

127 J. D. Flynn, "In Tennessee, Medicine and Mercy Are on the Move," *The Pillar*, May 14, 2021, https://www.pillarcatholic.com/p/in-tennessee-medicine-and-mercy-are.

document on Catholic health care services, they comprise an "integral part" of the mission of the Church.[128] All who are involved—"physicians, pharmacists, nurses, technicians, hospital chaplains, men and women religious, administrative personnel, those who are responsible for national and international policies, and volunteers"[129]—have a role to play in serving that mission.

Catholic hospitals pursuing this path can more than credibly claim that their raisons d'être, their personnel, their services, and their internal operations are indispensable elements that work in concert to realize the faith and doctrine held by these Catholic communities. Consequently, they must enjoy a high degree of religious autonomy respecting each of these elements.

---

128 Pontifical Council for Pastoral Assistance to Health Care Workers, *New Charter for Health Care Workers*, vii (citation omitted).

129 Pontifical Council for Pastoral Assistance to Health Care Workers, 3.

FIXING OUR
SEXUAL EXPRESSION
EXPRESSION

EVEN IF COURTS OF LAW AND PUBLIC OPINION ARE PERSUADED BY THE argument that Catholic institutions are theologically bound to be integrated communities of witness to Christ, they might still struggle to comprehend why these institutions care about observing Catholic sexual responsibility norms. They likely believe instead that an institution can dedicate its people, services, and operations wholeheartedly to delivering, for example, quality health care services, while also cooperating with same-sex unions, contraception, and behaviors and mandates opposed to Christian norms.

The Church should not be surprised at this response. In fact, institutional leadership should vocally empathize with the difficulty of understanding the connection between an institution's apparent "business" (education, health care, social services) and the sexual, marriage, and parenting values reflected in its employees, services, and operations. The law and culture in which we are all swimming today insist that these behaviors are strictly private choices, and fine if consensual. They bear no relationship to a person's ability to be a good administrator, English teacher, or organist! Even if onlookers find it easy to understand the religious freedom violation involved in forcing a Catholic institution to perform problematic services (e.g., abortion or transgender surgery), they will struggle to believe that an institution is harmed by employee sexual behaviors, or by facilitating employees' independent choices to use a government-mandated health insurance benefit for contraception or abortion.

Yet along comes Catholicism with a new perspective. It understands love as indivisible and Christ's command to love as authoritative. It rejects the notion that a person is called to love their "neighbors at work" (e.g., patients, students, clients, colleagues) in a Christian manner, but not their "neighbors at home"—family members or romantic partners. As Benedict XVI observed in *Deus Caritas Est*, the word "love" has a "vast semantic range" within Christianity but is ultimately a "single reality."[1] It "includes love between man and woman, between family members, and love of neighbors outside the family." These various loves point to "God's way of loving," which has become "the measure of human love."[2]

And what is "God's way of loving"? First, it does not resemble constantly shifting and highly imperfect human standards. It is a divine and radically demanding path that we are called to imitate, even as we fail and need healing again and again at the field hospital that is the Church. Second, scripture repeatedly analogizes God's way of loving to the permanent, faithful, fruitful union between a man and a woman in marriage. In the words of Benedict XVI:

> Marriage based on exclusive and definitive love becomes the icon of the relationship between God and his people and vice versa. God's way of loving becomes the measure of human love. This close connection between *eros* and marriage in the Bible has practically no equivalent in extra-biblical literature.[3]

Third, scripture sometimes analogizes God's love to the love of a father for his children. Together, these are powerful scriptural clues for gaining human understanding of how God loves us and thus how we are commanded to love Him and one another.

Scripture insists that God is trying to tell us something of great importance about Christian love through spousal and parenting relationships. Thus Catholic institutions that fail to reflect a commitment

1   Benedict XVI, Encyclical Letter *Deus Caritas Est* (December 25, 2005), 2.
2   Benedict XVI, 11.
3   Benedict XVI, 11.

to Christian love in these spheres manifest an impoverished under-standing of that love. This is true even if these institutions sincerely believe themselves to be motivated by compassion for the human beings involved. They are conforming to transient, popular, worldly standards and thus ultimately denying a fuller understanding of Christian love to the objects of their "compassion," to other members of the Catholic community, and to all those observing the institu-tion. They are falling short of what they *are*: communities united in response to Christ and pledged to witness to His love, even as this is undoubtedly difficult.

Non-Catholics and even many Catholics are unfamiliar with the genuinely radical standards of spousal and parent-child love demanded by Christianity, and thus the necessity, in Francis's words of "our rejection of the evils which endanger that life."[4] Contemporary philosopher Wendell Berry frames the situation similarly, writing that sexual discipline is not for the purpose of reducing pleasure, but for safeguarding what is positive—fecundity, abundance.[5]

Many people are further unfamiliar with the scriptural warrants for Catholic beliefs in these arenas, and with the wealth of Catho-lic history and theology carrying these forward into our own time. Consequently, critics regard Catholic teachings as a set of old rules without any heft or contemporary rhyme or reason—rules unrelated to the fundamental Christian commandment to love God and neigh-bor. They even imagine that contemporary secular sexual expression norms are *more* loving than Catholic prescriptions. For example, they might credit contraception and abortion with preventing the birth of unwanted children and reducing poverty, state-recognized same-sex unions as an expression of love for LGBTQ persons, cohabitation as divorce-avoidance, and transgender surgeries as a way to overcome psychological distress.

In light of these misperceptions, Catholic institutions must find a way to explain confidently, even joyfully, how their fidelity to Cath-olic sexual responsibility norms promotes a Christlike love of every neighbor, even as these institutions have become, understandably, tired of the subject. Sexual responsibility norms are and will continue

---

4   Francis, Apostolic Exhortation *Evangelii Gaudium* (November 24, 2013), 168.
5   Wendell Berry, *Standing by Words: Essays* (Berkeley: Counterpoint, 2011), 126.

to be the focus of sustained attacks upon religious identity by the powers that be. Furthermore, widespread disregard for them is caus-ing profound suffering—especially for already-vulnerable people, including children and adolescents, the poor, and the increasing numbers of people self-identifying as LGBTQ.

Of course, Catholic institutions cannot suggest that observing such norms are the *only* important way in which Catholic commu-nities witness to Christ. *I cannot repeat this enough.* But they are *one* way, and they are increasingly rejected by contemporary soci-ety. Sexual expression unlinked to marriage or children is American culture's current obsession and requires a response; it is likely even an "epochal" preoccupation, as indicated in the Introduction. Long-held Christian norms are under the microscope while we Catholics (and seemingly the world) are asking ourselves about the significance of a two-sexed creation, whose union is complementary, procreative, and apparently crucial for the next generation's freedom, health, happi-ness, and security. While these norms must never provide an excuse for witch-hunting or surveillance, they do constitute a challenge to *every* member of the Catholic community, which, again, is manifestly a field hospital to which every member will eventually repair in search of healing with respect to issues of sex, marriage, and parenting.

This chapter is an attempt to assist institutions with the hard work of thinking and communicating about these fraught matters. It will link Catholic sexual expression norms with an institution's commit-ment to manifest indivisible Christian love, even in the teeth of accu-sations that Catholic norms are "hateful." The chapter following this one will perform this same task with respect to each of the *particular* Catholic teachings ordinarily under fire in contemporary religious freedom contests (i.e., cohabitation, contraception, abortion, same-sex relations, and transgender identity claims), but this chapter will make the general case.

Section I will set forth the scriptural texts linking Jesus's command-ment to love God and neighbor with Catholic sexual and familial norms. Section II will look at the earliest Christians' robust grasp of this link. In other words, it will engage in a *ressourcement*, a review of early Christian material for guidance and inspiration respecting criti-cal questions of our own day at a time when we are profoundly in need of inspiration. Today it is claimed that Catholic sexual responsibility norms are unrelated to Christ's central commands to love God and neighbor. But early Christians' adoption of these norms as an important part of their response to the Good News of Christ strongly indicates otherwise. Like us, these Christians were living in a culture saturated with harmful, exploitative, and misogynistic practices respecting sex, marriage, and parenting. A closer look at why *they* rejected the then prevailing norms and instead embraced a demanding new notion of love applicable both within and outside the family, can teach and inspire *us* today.

Section III discusses how Catholic sexual responsibility norms can make sense of the contemporary human experience of sex, marriage, and parenting. It provides arguments and language to assist Catholic leaders in articulating in broad strokes how Catholic norms better achieve the dignity, happiness, freedom, health, and love desired by the men and women of our time.

Catholic Sexual Expression Norms and Love of God and Neighbor

Scripture often references familial relations—especially spousal and parent-child relations—to teach us about God's love for us and how we are to love Him. Learning how to love God—the infinite, the mysterious, the sovereign—is an intrinsically difficult task. Scripture offers us ways of accomplishing this suited to our human experiences and capacities, including our daily experience of relationships between spouses and between parents and their children. The material immediately following looks at each of these relationships in order.

THE BRIDE-BRIDEGROOM RELATIONSHIP AND HUMAN BEINGS' LOVE OF GOD

Both the Old and New Testaments describe God's relationship with His people using marital imagery. They tell us that He loves us like a bridegroom, and that we are to love Him like a bride. This is a persistent theme, even to the last book of the Bible. Throughout the Old Testament, Israel is reminded that it is the bride to God's bridegroom. For example, the book of Isaiah states: "For your Maker is your husband, the LORD of hosts is his name" (Is 54:5) and Jeremiah prophesies: "Thus says the LORD, 'I remember the devotion of your youth, your love as a bride'" (Jer 2:2). Jeremiah later analogizes an idol-worshipping Israel to an adulterer.

In the New Testament's Gospel of John, John the Baptist refers to Jesus Christ as the bridegroom: "The one who has the bride is the bridegroom; the best man, who stands and listens to him, rejoices greatly at the bridegroom's voice" (Jn 3:29). Jesus does likewise by asking, "Can the wedding guests mourn as long as the bridegroom is with them?" (Mt 9:15).

Perhaps the most well-known passages analogizing God's love to that of a bridegroom and urging Christians to love likewise appear in St. Paul's letter to the Ephesians, where he likens marriage to God's love for His people. He states: "This [marriage] is a great mystery, but I speak in reference to Christ and the church" (Eph 5:32). Shortly afterwards Paul urges: "Husbands, love your wives, even as Christ loved the church and handed himself over for her" (Eph 5:25). In short, God's love looks like Jesus's self-surrender, His death on a cross for us.[6]

The last book of the New Testament is likewise replete with references to marriage. The Book of Revelation characterizes the last judgment as a wedding feast: "For the wedding day of the Lamb has come, his Bride has made herself ready" (Rv 19:7), and it continues: "And the angel said to me, 'Write this: Blessed are those who have been called to the wedding feast of the Lamb'" (Rv 19:9).

And *how* should brides and bridegrooms love one another? Jesus instructs:

> From the beginning of creation, God made them male and female. For this reason a man shall leave his father and mother [and be joined to his wife], and the two shall become one flesh. So they are no longer two but one flesh. Therefore what God has joined together, no human being must separate. In the house the disciples again questioned him about this. He said to them, "Whoever divorces his wife and marries another commits adultery against her; and if she divorces her husband and marries another, she commits adultery." (Mk 10:5–12)

---

6   See Richard B. Hays, *The Moral Vision of the New Testament: A Contemporary Introduction to New Testament Ethics* (San Francisco: HarperSanFrancisco, 1996), 375.

From this it is apparent that God intends us to commit to Him in an extraordinarily close, exclusive, and permanent union. As Joseph Ratzinger eloquently wrote:

> Indissoluble marriage is in fact only comprehensible and feasible on the basis of faith in God's henceforward irrevocable decision, embodied in Christ, in favor of "marriage" with mankind (cf. Eph 5:22–33). It stands or falls with this faith; in the long run, it is just as impossible outside this faith as it is necessary within it.[7]

The Russian philosopher Vladimir Solovyov powerfully captures humans' experience of romantic love as a pathway for understanding God's love in his book, *The Meaning of Love*.[8] He writes that such love requires both the man and the woman to

> acknowledge for another the same absolute central significance which, because of the power of our egoism, we are conscious of only in ourselves. Love is important not as one of our feelings, but as the transfer of all our interest in life from ourselves to another, as the shifting of the very center of our personal lives.[9]

For Solovyov, then, the "shining eyes of an unspoiled boy or girl in love is no mere earthly light. It is a primitive and transient glimpse of the divine image in another human being, and thus of God's love for man."[10] The "idealization of the lower being exists together with an incipient realization of the higher, and in this is the truth of love's intense emotion."[11] In short, human beings come to understand love of God and one another as closely connected phenomena.

My treatment here of marital relations is not meant to idealize spousal love. Clearly, as the book of Genesis details, original sin

---

7   Joseph Cardinal Ratzinger, *Introduction to Christianity*, 2nd ed. (San Francisco: Ignatius Press, 2004), 265–66.

8   Vladimir Solovyov, *The Meaning of Love*, trans. Thomas R. Beyer, Jr. (Herndon, Va.: Lindisfarne Books, 1985).

9   Solovyov, 51.

10   Owen Barfield, Introduction to Solovyov, *The Meaning of Love*, 11.

11   Solovyov, *The Meaning of Love*, 91.

profoundly affects the relations between man and woman. The man blames the woman for his own sin, and God tells the woman, "in pain shall you bring forth children, yet your urge shall be for your husband, and he shall be your master" (Gn 3:15, 16). Anyone paying attention can observe this enmity and oppression on any given day, even as they can also see beautiful examples of spousal mutual regard and self-gift. I mean by this account of spousal relations only to show that the New Testament significantly relies upon bride-bridegroom relations as Christ calls them to be, as a privileged means by which human beings are to understand how God loves us, and how we are to love God and one another, as the Great Commandment instructs. At the very least, this undergirds the special status that the Catholic Church grants marriage and its refusal to equate marriage with same-sex or nonmarital cohabiting partnerships.

CHILD-PARENT IMAGERY AND HUMAN BEINGS' LOVE OF GOD

Jesus also and frequently uses child-parent relations to model human beings' proper relationship with God. He calls us God's "children," and God "Our Father" (Mt 6:9). In the Gospel passage immediately following His above-quoted instruction about marriage, Jesus exhorts us to love Him as a child loves a parent:

> And people were bringing children to him that he might touch them, but the disciples rebuked them. When Jesus saw this he became indignant and said to them, "Let the children come to me; do not prevent them, for the kingdom of God belongs to such as these. Amen, I say to you, whoever does not accept the kingdom of God like a child will not enter it." Then he embraced them and blessed them, placing his hands on them. (Mk 10:13–16)

Jesus's teachings thus charge every earthly parent with attempting to provide his or her child Christlike love, so that the child might begin to understand the Father's love. At the very least, this supports Catholics' practice of welcoming children as divine gifts, their rejection of abortion, their reservation of sexual intercourse for marriage—wherein both parents are available to rear any child conceived—and their avoidance of same-sex parenting, which in every case separates the child from one or both of her natural parents.

In sum, scripture plainly counsels that rightly lived male-female and child-parent relationships are crucial means of comprehending the love between God and humanity. One would have to set scripture aside to conclude that Catholic institutions committed to manifesting the love of God can ignore or repudiate the Church's marital and familial norms.

"WHO IS MY NEIGHBOR?"
CATHOLIC SEXUAL EXPRESSION NORMS
AND LOVE OF NEIGHBOR

One of the most innovative aspects of Christianity was its insistence upon love of neighbor based upon the reasoning that "*because* God loves humanity, Christians may not please God unless they *love one another.*"[12] And how are human beings to love one another? "As I [God] have loved you" (Jn 13:34). Thus, again, they are to love like a bridegroom, like a parent, which immediately imports into the command to love the "neighbor" all of the standards described above: faithfulness, permanence, generosity, fruitfulness, sacrificiality, etc. Clearly this requires Catholic communities to at least seek to observe very high standards of sexual, marital, and parental love.

Respecting love of neighbor, however, Jesus added a new element to the equation: the way of the Good Samaritan. We recall the story:

> He approached the victim, poured oil and wine over his wounds and bandaged them. Then he lifted him up on his own animal, took him to an inn and cared for him.
> The next day he took out two silver coins and gave them to the innkeeper with the instruction, "Take care of him. If you spend more than what I have given you, I shall repay you on my way back." (Lk 10:34–35)

How does this implicate our treatment of romantic partners, spouses, and children? Practically speaking, they are the "neighbors" most frequently strewn on our path over the course of our lives, whose

---

12 Rodney Stark, *The Rise of Christianity: A Sociologist Reconsiders History* (Princeton: Princeton University Press, 1996), 212 (emphasis in original).

well-being we are most likely to impact deeply and even indelibly by our love or failure to love. In the succinct words of a statement by the Irish bishops, "The Church's whole moral teaching about sex is above all the application to sexuality of God's greatest commandment to charity."[13]

In fact, no matter how rightly compassionate most people feel about the plight of convicts on death row, or about the immigrants stranded on our nation's border, only *some* of us will have the beautiful opportunity to directly assist some of them. More will have the opportunity to provide *in*direct assistance, as well as to assist those served by Catholic health care, educational, or social services institutions. But for nearly *all* of us, our primary opportunities to demonstrate Good Samaritan-like love in person will happen within the four walls of our family homes. For most of us, these opportunities are relentless—family members are simply the largest group of "unchosen" objects of most people's care, daily strewn across our paths and requiring considerable help. Yes we choose our spouses, but (as the witty French philosopher Fabrice Hadjadj wisely notes[14]), twenty years into the marriage or so, they are not quite the same person they were at first! Nor are we! Hadjadj also notes that we do not choose our in-laws, but that these persons and the rest of our extended family are, rather, given to us. Likewise, even though we invite children into our lives, we do not know who they will be. Instead, we accept and serve them as they are, when they come.

And not only are family members strewn across the path of *every single person*, presenting each with the human beings she is *most* likely to affect during a lifetime, but these effects are potentially *profound* and likely to persist for a *very long time*, probably the length of an entire life. Common sense and empirical evidence overwhelmingly support the conclusion that it matters to another—deeply and for a long time—whether we have sex with them with or without any intention of maintaining a future relationship, whether we cohabit nonmaritally with them or not, whether together we welcome a child or not, whether we undergo an abortion or allow a child to be born,

---

13 Irish Catholic Bishops Conference, *Love is for Life* (Dublin: Veritas, 1985), 24, https://www.catholicculture.org/culture/library/view.cfm?recnum=5276.

14 Fabrice Hadjaj, *Qu'est-ce que une famille? Transcendence en culottes* (Paris: Salvator, 2014), 39–40.

whether a child is born within or outside of a marriage, and whether we have a same- or opposite-sex sexual encounter.[15] These choices also have spillover and even intergenerational effects within a family. The material in section III of this chapter (as well as in chapter 7) will touch upon the trove of empirical evidence that robustly supports the conclusion that Catholic sexual expression norms promote love of neighbor, beginning with those closest to us and extending more broadly to others in the community. It is important for Catholic institutional leaders to refer to this literature when defending an institution's religious freedom demands in the sexual expression context. After all, the arguments that Catholic teaching is "unloving" toward women and LGBTQ persons powerfully shape the current backlash against Catholic institutions' religious freedom demands. In the words of Benedict XVI, people believe that the Church "blow[s] the whistle just when the joy which is the Creator's gift offers us a happiness which is itself a certain foretaste of the Divine."[16] Confidently demonstrating the opposite matters.

Having described above how the Catholic faith posits a close link between love of God and neighbor and familial relations, it is no surprise that every institution adopting the Catholic mantle—and thus claiming to express Christian love in the world—is called to manifest this link, no matter the professional service the institution provides.

This conclusion is only strengthened by the evidence in the next section that early Christians both understood and lived a close connection between their new faith and the sexual, marriage, and parenting norms we still hold and teach today. As noted above, it is important to recover this material and mine it for wisdom we can currently use, given how often contemporaries deny the link between loving God and neighbor and practicing Christian sexual responsibility.

At the Beginnings of Christianity

It is traditional in Catholic theology to accord special weight to the understandings and practices of the early Christians. As theologian

---

15 The empirical evidence for this conclusion is discussed in chapter 7.
16 Benedict XVI, *Deus Caritas Est*, 3.

Heinz Schürmann observed succinctly in a book co-authored with Joseph Cardinal Ratzinger and Hans Urs von Balthasar, there is arguably a special normativity attached to the "ethical stance of the 'original' Church, which, since she was in the process of becoming, was still receiving revelation (cf. Eph 2:20 and 3:5) and was being molded in an exceptional way by the Spirit of the risen Lord (cf. Acts 11:15)."[17]

In light of this, early Christians' "conspicuous chastity"[18] is worth revisiting. Here, *once again, I want to stress that sexual expression norms are clearly not the only lessons Christians took then, or take today, from the life, death, and resurrection of Jesus Christ!* I am highlighting these because of the subject matter of this book, and because the very "Christian" and "loving" qualities of contemporary Catholic norms are increasingly denied, despite how they support human flourishing and shelter the vulnerable.

There are many excellent accounts of the early Christians' beliefs and practices concerning sex, marriage, and parenting. I recommend them highly both for information and inspiration. Four of the best include Kyle Harper's *From Shame to Sin: The Christian Transformation of Sexual Morality in Late Antiquity,* Rodney Stark's *The Rise of Christianity: A Sociologist Reconsiders History*, Peter Brown's *The Body and Society: Men, Women and Sexual Renunciation in Early Christianity*, and Sarah Ruden's *Paul Among the People: The Apostle Reinterpreted and Reimagined in His Own Time.*

Harper writes that the sex, marriage, and parenting practices of early Christian communities constituted one of their most distinctive markers.[19] Stark documents how these practices likely constituted an important part of Christianity's appeal and therefore its growth. He and others claim, in fact, that women, slaves, and other socially vulnerable persons likely accounted disproportionately for the early growth of Christianity;[20] women particularly appreciated the greater

17 Heinz Schürmann, "How Normative Are the Values and Precepts of the New Testament? A Sketch," in Heinz Schürmann, Joseph Cardinal Ratzinger, and Hans Urs von Balthasar, *Principles of Christian Morality*, trans. Graham Harrison (San Francisco: Ignatius Press, 1986), 9–44, 16.

18 Kyle Harper, *From Shame to Sin: The Christian Transformation of Sexual Morality in Late Antiquity* (Cambridge, Mass.: Harvard University Press, 2013), 100.

19 Harper, 1, 3, 5, 7, 85, 100, 132–33.

20 Stark, *The Rise of Christianity*, 95–107. See also Vishal Mangalwadi, *The Book That Made Your World: How the Bible Created the Soul of Western Civilization* (Nashville: Thomas Nelson, 2012), 283–84.

protection Christianity offered from the social and economic harms caused by divorce, polygamy, and adultery.[21] Women adopting Christianity could also hope more often to avoid the pressure to abort their unborn children or to kill their sick or female newborns. And Christianity decried the "double standard" according to which men could engage in sexual liaisons with male or female slaves and/or with women who were not their wives. Instead, when it came to loving and serving God and one another, Christianity taught that there should no longer be "male or female" but that all would be "one in Christ Jesus" (Gal 3:28). And between spouses there should be mutual subjection "out of reverence to Christ," with husbands called to "love your wives even as Christ loved the Church" (Eph 5:21, 25).

The entire Christian framework for evaluating these practices differed sharply from the framework adopted by the surrounding Greco-Roman culture. According to Harper, the latter assigned variable sexual norms depending upon one's sex and social status.[22] Thus there were different rules for men than for women and for masters than for slaves. For Christians, however, the "cosmos replaced the city as the framework of morality."[23] *All* persons were subject to the same Christian norms. This was due to Christians' understanding of human romantic and familial love as a means of manifesting the nature of all love, including the love of God and of one another. In *Deus Caritas Est*, Pope Benedict XVI succinctly summarized the exploitative sexual culture Christians rejected:

> The Greeks—not unlike other cultures—considered *eros* principally as a kind of intoxication, the overpowering of reason by a "divine madness" which tears man away from his finite existence and enables him, in the very process of being overwhelmed by divine power, to experience supreme happiness. . . . Indeed, the prostitutes in the temple, who had to bestow this divine intoxication, were not treated as human beings and persons, but simply used as a means of arousing "divine

21 Sarah Ruden, *Paul Among the People: The Apostle Reinterpreted and Reimagined in His Own Time* (New York: Image, 2010), 12–14, 72–118.

22 Harper, *From Shame to Sin*, 37–61, 78.

23 Harper, 8.

madness": far from being goddesses, they were human persons being exploited.[24]

For Christians, however, Jesus's Great Commandment required loving faithfully, generously, sacrificially, fruitfully, and with the good of the other first in mind. As these characterized God's love for human beings, they must also shape humanity's love for Him and for one another—no matter whether a person was rich or poor, master or slave, male or female. In this framework, sexual "disorder" became perhaps the "single most powerful symbol of the world's alienation from God."[25] Sexual fidelity, on the other hand "was the corollary of monotheism, while the [Romans'] worship of many gods," like their sexual code, "was in every way, promiscuous."[26] Consequently, acts of the flesh became "burdened with a symbolism they had never known before," as Christians became "intermediaries of an other-worldly order."[27]

This description helps us to see clearly how Christian sexual responsibility is not a man-made moral code to be rightly criticized as "moralism," or "Pelagianism," but rather a *response* to the heart of the Christian message, to the life and words of Jesus Christ. Luigi Giussani captures this succinctly with his observation that "Christ and the Church are the profound inspiration that penetrates the basic structure of all my actions, of everything I do."[28] Pope Francis writes similarly: "Christian morality is not a form of stoicism, or self-denial, or merely a practical philosophy or a catalogue of sins and faults. Before all else, the Gospel invites us to respond to the God of love who saves us, to see God in others and to go forth from ourselves to seek the good of others. Under no circumstance can this invitation be obscured! All of the virtues are at the service of this response of love."[29]

Let us now look a little more closely at four particular traits the early Christians associated with God's love as the model for human love.

---

24 Benedict XVI, *Deus Caritas Est*, 4.

25 Harper, *From Shame to Sin*, 94.

26 Harper, 94.

27 Harper, 2.

28 Luigi Giussani, *Morality: Memory and Desire*, trans. K.D. Whitehead (San Francisco: Ignatius Press, 1986), 17.

29 Francis, *Evangelii Gaudium*, 39.

GOD'S LOVE IS RADICAL

First, Christians understood God's love to be radically demanding. To quote Heinz Schürmann again, Jesus's love was not mere human self-renunciation or "humility" but "qualitatively different";[30] it was complete and utter self-surrender: Jesus came down to our level and allowed Himself to be unjustly put to death in the cruelest possible manner.

> In the New Testament writings, moral exhortation . . . concentrates on the values and precepts . . . that call for a total, loving self-surrender in response to the eschatological love of God in Christ. They are . . . summed up in the twofold command of love of God (i.e., of Christ) and intimately connected with it, love of neighbor. Conduct . . . must be situated at the intersection of this vertical love and its horizontal response.[31]

Schürmann concludes that the call and challenge to Christians to imitate this love, to "join the company of the Crucified and become like Him, must be a distinctive element of New Testament ethics."[32] Christians' radical responses included everything from martyrdom to love of their enemies, poverty, and celibacy,[33] to widowhood without remarriage.[34] Note that this love found expression both within and outside of the familial sphere. Illustrating early Christians' grasp of the indivisibility of Christian love, historian Peter Brown writes that there was

> A need to place in society itself a series of concrete, unmistakable—even shocking—"markers" that served to remind believers and outsiders of the unimaginably wide horizons opened up to humanity by the Christian message. For this reason, fourth-century Christianity fostered attention to extreme states of the human condition. It is no accident that the torrent of Christian preaching on outreach to the poor coincided with a sharp elevation of forms of total sexual renunciation—of

---

30 Schürmann, "How Normative are the Values and Precepts of the New Testament?" 22.
31 Schürmann, 31 (citations omitted).
32 Schürmann, 22.
33 Schürmann, 22–23
34 Stark, *The Rise of Christianity*, 104–5.

virginity, of monastic withdrawal, and even, in certain circles, of clerical celibacy. Indeed, the preachers, writers, and organizers who advocated most vehemently the care of the poor were often the same persons who spoke out most passionately in favor of virginity and celibacy.

These palpable markers brought the "incommensurable" into society. Both outreach to the poor and the adoption of virginity and celibacy were held, by their advocates, to go against the grain of human nature. Both were tinged with a sense of heroic *démesure* that bordered on the supernatural.[35]

The theologian Hans Urs von Balthasar also highlights the far-reaching and intense quality of early Christians' code of conduct, which he acknowledges seems "hard and legalistic to those who are imperfect."[36] He advises us that their code should not surprise us, however, given their convictions that Jesus must be the "norm" in every ethical relationship,[37] such that their behavior could "lead the believer out of the alienation of sin to his true identity and freedom."[38]

GOD AS THE PRIORITY

A second basis for early Christians' sexual responsibility norms was Jesus's repeated instructions to put allegiance to God first, before everything in the world, including family connections. This teaching assumed heightened importance in light of their common expectation of Christ's imminent return. It informed St. Paul's advice to remain celibate in order to testify to the primary importance of one's relationship with God (1 Cor 7:7, 38). Pope Benedict XVI and others have acknowledged how this belief has led not infrequently to an inordinate suspicion of sex and even marriage within Catholic theology. In *Deus Caritas Est*, for example, Benedict XVI acknowledges:

---

35 Peter Brown, "From *Patriae Amator* to *Amator Pauperum* and Back Again: Social Imagination and Social Change in The West Between Late Antiquity and the Early Middle Ages, Ca. 300–600," in *Cultures in Motion*, ed. Daniel T. Rogers, Bhavani Raman, and Helmut Reimitz (Princeton: Princeton University Press, 2014), 87–106, 93–94.

36 Hans Urs von Balthasar, "Nine Propositions on Christian Ethics," in Schürmann, Ratzinger, and Balthasar, *Principles of Christian Morality*, 75–104, 81.

37 Balthasar, 86.

38 Balthasar, 81.

"Nowadays Christianity of the past is often criticized as having been opposed to the body; and it is quite true that tendencies of this sort have always existed."[39] But this tendency is largely overcome in the works of contemporary popes, especially in John Paul II in his "Theology of the Body" and in his 1960 volume *Love and Responsibility*,[40] and by Pope Francis, especially in his apostolic exhortation *Amoris Laetitia*.[41]

Scriptural references making God the priority are plain. During His ministry, Christ says that "if anyone comes to me without hating his father and mother, wife and children, brothers and sisters, and even his own life, he cannot be my disciple" (Lk 14:26). In the Gospel of Matthew, when Jesus is told that His mother and brothers are waiting for Him, He replies: "Here are my mother and my brothers. For whoever does the will of my heavenly Father is my brother, and sister, and mother" (Mt 12:49–50). In short, all "natural affections" must be ordered to "eternal realities."[42] Behavior that demonstrated too great an attachment to worldly things and human will—as distinguished from the necessity of always "straining forward to what lies ahead" (Phil 3:13), toward God—was even sometimes equated with idolatry. This shaped St. Paul's most famous rejection of same-sex relations, characterizing it as a kind of punishment for humanity's putting themselves before God:

> For although they knew God they did not accord him glory as God or give him thanks. Instead, they became vain in their reasoning, and their senseless minds were darkened. While claiming to be wise, they became fools and exchanged the glory of the immortal God for the likeness of an image of mortal man or of birds or of four-legged animals or of snakes.

---

39 Benedict XVI, *Deus Caritas Est*, 5.

40 See John Paul II, *Man and Woman He Created Them: A Theology of the Body*, trans. Michael Waldstein (Boston: Pauline Books & Media, 2006), e.g., 185–90 (the General Audience of January 16, 1980), 194–98 (the General Audience of February 6, 1990), and 548–93 (the entire set of reflections on the Song of Songs). See also Karol Wojtyla, *Love and Responsibility*, rev. ed. (San Francisco: Ignatius Press, 1993).

41 See Francis, Post-Synodal Apostolic Exhortation *Amoris Laetitia* (March 19, 2016), 10–14.

42 Patricia Snow, "Dismantling the Cross: A Call for a Renewed Emphasis on the Celibate Vocation," *First Things*, April 2015, https://www.firstthings.com/article/2015/04/dismantling-the-cross.

> Therefore, God handed them over to impurity through the lusts of their hearts for the mutual degradation of their bodies. *They exchanged the truth of God for a lie and revered and worshiped the creature rather than the creator, who is blessed forever.* Amen. Therefore, God handed them over to degrading passions. Their females exchanged natural relations for unnatural, and the males likewise gave up natural relations with females and burned with lust for one another. Males did shameful things with males and thus received in their own persons the due penalty for their perversity. *And since they did not see fit to acknowledge God,* God handed them over to their undiscerning mind to do what is improper. (Rom 1:21-28, emphases added)

Kyle Harper also concludes that the teaching about the priority of God powerfully informed Christians' thinking about sex. In the context of Roman beliefs about sex as the product of external compulsion and Roman society's overt sexuality and promiscuity, sex became a prominent symbol of the things of this world. Resisting it therefore became a powerful tool for demonstrating attachment, instead, to things above.[43]

Methodist theologian Richard Hays comes to a similar conclusion about the ethics of sex in the New Testament, with the observation that Jesus's words making God the priority "demythologize[] . . . sex. Alongside Jesus' example, they announce that free and joyful lives without sex are possible. Devotion to God comes first."[44]

Peter Brown also observes how early Christians' codes of sexual behavior "bore much of the weight" of Paul's demand to Christians to first attend to the will of God, given the association at the time between the physical world, animal behaviors, and human sexuality.[45] And theologian Wayne Meeks observes that both martyrdom and celibacy were viewed as "prising the body away from the world and the empire while rather visibly prioritizing God."[46]

---

43 Harper, *From Shame to Sin*, 80–117, 132–33.

44 Hays, *The Moral Vision of the New Testament*, 390–91.

45 Peter Brown, *The Body and Society: Men, Women and Sexual Renunciation in Early Christianity* (New York: Columbia University Press, 1988), 51–52, 432–33.

46 Wayne Meeks, *The Origins of Christian Morality: The First Two Centuries* (New Haven: Yale University Press, 1995), 144–45.

THE SACRED BODY

Third, Christians believed that the body is not mere matter to be manipulated, but "consecrated space, a point of mediation between the individual and the divine."[47] They worshiped a God who fashioned all human bodies, became human with a body, suffered, died, and was raised bodily, and ascended into heaven as both human and divine. His body was an inextricable element of His salvation of the human race. During His ministry, His care for others' bodies was an important means of communicating His love. He instructed us to do likewise to one another. Clearly, then, what Christians do with their bodies carries significant ethical weight.

St. Paul applied this specifically to sexual morality in his letters to the Corinthians and Thessalonians:

> The body, however, is not for immorality, but for the Lord, and the Lord is for the body; God raised the Lord and will also raise us by his power. Do you not know that your bodies are members of Christ? Shall I then take Christ's members and make them the members of a prostitute? Of course not! [Or] do you not know that anyone who joins himself to a prostitute becomes one body with her? For "the two," it says, "will become one flesh." But whoever is joined to the Lord becomes one spirit with him. Avoid immorality. Every other sin a person commits is outside the body, but the immoral person sins against his own body. Do you not know that your body is a temple of the Holy Spirit within you, whom you have from God, and that you are not your own? For you have been purchased at a price. Therefore, glorify God in your body. (1 Cor 6:13–20)
>
> This is the will of God, your holiness: that you refrain from immorality, that each of you know how to acquire a wife for himself in holiness and honor, not in lustful passion as do the Gentiles who do not know God; not to take advantage of or exploit a brother in this matter, for the Lord is an avenger in all these things, as we told you before and solemnly affirmed. For God did not call us to impurity but to holiness. (1 Thes 4:3–7)

---

47 Harper, *From Shame to Sin*, 92.

Thus for Christians, there are sexual relations that demonstrate love toward the neighbor because they understand the sacredness of the body, and those that do not. Christ's example is quite radical in this regard; not only are we to avoid exploiting another human body for our own desires, but we must be willing to sacrifice our bodies for the other. He subjected His body to outrageous suffering for our sake. Thus Paul's counsel: "Husbands, love your wives, even as Christ loved the church and handed himself over for her" (Eph 5:25). There simply could not be, in the words of classics scholar Sarah Ruden, any greater contrast with Christ than to use another's body for selfish ends or a show of power.[48] Ruden recalls that many Roman practices regularly featured exploitation by the stronger of the weaker: the young, slaves, the poor, and females. Christianity, instead, offered a "new way of thinking that must have been quite exciting, a hope for something beyond exploitation, materialism, and violence—a plan not for competing in purity and the denial of life, but for the sharing of life in full."[49] It offered a chance not to be treated as a thing.[50]

GOD'S CREATIVE DESIGN

A final theme characterizing early Christians' approach to loving sexual responsibility concerns respect for God's sovereign will, as this might be discerned from creation. St. Paul expresses this in his letter to the Romans, just before his touching upon same-sex relations: "What can be known about God is evident to them, because God made it evident to them. Ever since the creation of the world, his invisible attributes of eternal power and divinity have been able to be understood and perceived in what he has made" (Rom 1:19–20).

As several theologians have observed, God's creation of a two-sexed humanity suited to a one-flesh union and scripturally referred to the love between God and humanity, must have important implications for human love. Love must involve a going out from oneself to another;

---

48 Ruden, *Paul Among the People*, 71.
49 Ruden, 11.
50 Ruden, 18 ("If I had been one of Paul's typical early readers, whatever else I understood from his use of the word [*porneia*], I would have picked up that treating another human being as a thing was no longer ok.")

neither sex can be sufficient unto itself.[51] Relations rejecting God's order of creation turn their back on this divine design and distance the person from God.[52] For early Christians, homosexual sex "vivid[ly]" enacted this.[53]

Contemporary Communication of Indivisible Christian Love

The first two sections of this chapter demonstrate that early Christians' translation of Jesus commandment to love into a set of sexual norms, among other things, is quite convincing on its face. They assure us that the Christian code of sexual responsibility was not merely plucked from a reigning set of social norms. Just the opposite in fact; it was an innovative response to something, *Someone*, who was entirely new in history. It also showed that the Christian code of sexual responsibility relied upon the interplay of faith and reason. What it pronounced as "loving" corresponded with positive, freeing, dignifying outcomes in the world.

Consequently, this account can assist our contemporary need to present the Christian code as a full-throated manifestation of love for the neighbor. It can inform the way we express these teachings in dialogue with what contemporary people want from human love. The following material illustrates several possibilities.

THE ORDINARY HUMAN EXPERIENCE OF LOVE

The Catholic embrace of radical love speaks to Americans' fervent desire for strong family bonds, even as they are not always able to achieve them. Americans are unsurprised to read headlines like this one inspired by the 2018 findings of the Pew Research Center: "Family

---

51 See, e.g., Vigen Guroian, "Saint John Chrysostom," chap. 5 in *Christianity and Family Law: An Introduction*, ed. John Witte, Jr. and Gary S. Hauk, Cambridge Studies in Law and Christianity (Cambridge: Cambridge University Press, 2017), 92–93.

52 Hays, *The Moral Vision of the New Testament*, 386, 387–88, 396–97.

53 Hays, 386.

Ranks First in Pew Study on Personal Fulfillment."[54] Nearly 70 percent of the study's 4,700 respondents answering an open-ended question about how they found meaning in life identified their family. The next closest response was "career," at less than half that rate.

For nearly all people, familial love vigorously informs our lifetime understanding of what love is and how to live it. Beginning with romantic attraction between a man and a woman, it requires acceptance of the coexistence of diversity alongside equality. It requires each person to learn how to build and maintain bridges to an "other." This was particularly well-expressed in a popular and moving account by President Barack Obama regarding his marriage to Michelle:

> What sustains our relationship is I'm extremely happy with her, and part of it has to do with the fact that she is at once completely familiar to me, so that I can be myself and she knows me very well and I trust her completely, but at the same time she is also a complete mystery to me in some ways. And there are times when we are lying in bed and I look over and sort of have a start. Because I realize here is this other person who is separate and different and has different memories and backgrounds and thoughts and feelings. It's that tension between familiarity and mystery that makes for something strong, because, even as you build a life of trust and comfort and mutual support, you retain some sense of surprise or wonder about the other person.[55]

Like God's love, spousal love is also generative, and regularly involves passion, steadfastness, sacrifice, and putting the other's needs before one's own. The birth of children then deepens and expands the epiphany first experienced by the romantic couple, due to the parents' intense love for their children and because of a realization that children often provoke in their parents: everyone is someone's precious child. The experiences of parental and spousal love shape people for a lifetime, either because the couple and the

---

54 Zack Huffman, "Family Ranks First in Pew Study on Personal Fulfillment," *Courthouse News Service*, November 20, 2018, https://www.courthousenews.com/family-ranks-first-in-pew-study-on-personal-fulfillment/.

55 Mariana Cook, "A Couple in Chicago," *New Yorker*, January 19, 2009, https://www.newyorker.com/magazine/2009/01/19/a-couple-in-chicago.

family constitute a true school of love, or because they do not, and thus wound or even "break" the lives of family members.

Common human experience further aids our understanding of what people desire in positive child-parent relationships. At the very least, these include the child's ongoing relationship with both of his or her parents, who are committed to one another in a way that facilitates their ongoing and mutual care for the child. Loving parents foster in the child a profound sense of dependence upon and gratitude to the parent, to whom she owes her very life as well as ongoing care. A child's positive relationship to the parent also includes obedience, as well as simple trust and faith that the parents are acting in the child's best interests, and out of a lifelong willingness to love the child.

Lessons learned in families also generate communal effects. John Paul II referred to this dynamic as families behaving as schools of love and social virtues and of a "deeper humanity."[56] Practically speaking, it is in families that we receive our first and often most formative lessons in how to love "the other," despite differences of age, personality, interests, and talents. We learn how to understand that equality exists alongside diversity—of age, talents, capacities, and personalities. In families we learn to forgive, to make peace, and to preserve relationships over the very long term. We observe the constant interdependence of human life and the continual need to both give and receive aid, including but not limited to during childhood and old age and in circumstances involving disability, sickness, unemployment, loneliness, and addiction, among many others.

Scholars in myriad disciplines agree that family life is a crucible in which human beings form important interpersonal skills, which affect not only members' happiness but also the quality of their relations with others who are later encountered in the wider world. In the words of psychologist Urie Bronfenbrenner, who was instrumental in the formation of the Head Start program to assist poor children in the US: "The family is the most powerful, the most humane and, by far, the most economical system known for building competence and character."[57] The Quaker theologian and peace activist Elise Boulding

---

56 John Paul II, Apostolic Exhortation *Familiaris Consortio* (November 22, 1981), 21, 36. (citation omitted).

57 Urie Bronfenbrenner, "A Generation in Jeopardy: America's Hidden Family Policy," testimony presented at a hearing of the Senate Committee on Rules and Administration

adds that interpersonal skills and experiences arising within family life eventually affect the wider society. This is due, she writes, to the ways in which familial interpersonal relations teach conflict management.[58] And good family life can help people ultimately conclude that we are "kin with all persons," because of its "experience of the social bonds of kinship and intergroup alliances and the need for mutual aid systems in order to survive."[59] From family we can come to understand everyone as somebody's child. This is the insight famously achieved, for example, by the misanthropic grandmother at the conclusion of Flannery O'Connor's "A Good Man is Hard to Find," when, right before her death at the hands of a killer, she cries out to him: "Why you're one of my babies. You're one of my own children!"[60]

Catholic sex, marriage, and parenting norms are clearly directed toward achieving strong family bonds of the kinds Americans deeply desire. Yes, securing these also entails rejecting behaviors that undermine such bonds, even behaviors that are currently valorized. But today, just as in the early days of Christianity, it is easily observable that these norms strengthen the spousal and parenting relations that give life meaning and freedom in the long run.

THE DESIRE AND NEED FOR RADICAL LOVE

Americans usually want radical love, especially in their romantic and spousal relationships. They hope to love and be loved permanently, without betrayal, and in a relationship honoring the norm of "loving the other as you would be loved." Despite our divorce rate, a majority of Americans continue to report that they hope to marry and stay married forever.[61] Conversely, studies considering the leading

---

on a resolution to establish a Select Committee on Families, Youth, and Children, 99th Cong. (July 23, 1986), 4.

58 Elis Boulding, *Cultures of Peace: The Hidden Side of History* (Syracuse, N.Y.: Syracuse University Press, 2000), 101, 102.

59 Boulding, 90.

60 Flannery O'Connor, *A Good Man is Hard to Find and Other Stories* (New York: Harcourt, 1976), 42.

61 See, e.g., United States Congress Joint Economic Committee Social Capital Project, "Is Marriage Still Popular?" February 8, 2019, 3, https://www.jec.senate.gov/public/index.cfm/republicans/analysis?ID=733E5D3C-2FCD-4C23-B542-1C0213A8BDED; see also Alan J. Hawkins and The National Divorce Decision Making Project, *What Are They Thinking? A National Survey of Married Individuals Who Are Thinking about Divorce*

causes of unhappiness among Americans regularly point to missing or broken relationships, often relationships with romantic partners.[62] Children too want and need a radical sort of love. They often fail to thrive without parents willing to make huge sacrifices for them around the clock, at least for a few decades. Radical love is practically a "hygiene factor" in children's lives, so badly do they need it for even normal growth and development.[63] And of course, the class of "children" includes all of us.

Christian sexual norms incorporate all of these radical notions of love. They mirror the radicality of the love of Christ on the cross.[64] Ironically, it is a large part of the rap against Catholic love that it is so demanding! We ought to respond that it is only as demanding as human needs and desires require. It is only as demanding as what is needed by the immigrant, the poor, the imprisoned, the outcast too . . . but exercised in the spheres of sex, marriage, and parenting. Reserving sex for a spouse. Remaining faithful until death. Welcoming children instead of resorting to contraception and abortion. These are not equivalent to Christ's sacrifice on the cross, but they are our human attempts to follow Him in the ordinary circumstances of our human lives. And in the contemporary sexual environment, they easily qualify as radical manifestations of love.

This is the vision of love that attracted the early Christians, who were living in an environment characterized by the careless or even brutal treatment of women and slaves and the poor. It remains attractive today, especially in contrast to messages insisting that human beings are *in*capable of faithful, sacrificial love. And it should be stressed that Catholicism is neither naïve nor blind to human weakness in this arena. Our bishops, priests, and religious also fall down! All of us are affected by original sin!

(Provo, UT: Brigham Young University Family Studies Center, 2015), 1, 4, https://www.researchgate.net/publication/283329227_What_Are_They_Thinking_A_National_Survey_of_Married_Individuals_Who_Are_Thinking_About_Divorce.

62 See, e.g., Alan R. Teo, Hwa-Jung Choi, and Marcia Valenstein, "Social Relationships and Depression: Ten-Year Follow-Up from a Nationally Representative Study," *PLoS One* 8, no. 4, (April 30, 2013), https://doi.org/10.1371/journal.pone.0062396.

63 Helen M. Alvaré, *Putting Children's Interests First in American Family Law and Policy: With Power Comes Responsibility* (Cambridge: Cambridge University Press, 2018), 58–65, 103–34.

64 Hays, *The Moral Vision of the New Testament*, 375, 393.

But our faith bends toward hope. In stirring exhortations, especially to young people, popes John Paul II and Francis underscore human beings' capacity to commit to love. Francis exhorts us that the "important thing is to discover what God wants from us and to be brave enough to say 'yes.'"[65] In John Paul II's 1985 apostolic letter to young people, *Dilecti Amici*, he urged them not to "be afraid of the love that places clear demands on people. These demands—as you find them in the constant teaching of the Church—are precisely capable of making your love a true love."[66]

This level of inspiration and support for the kind of love humans crave is rarely forthcoming from other sources. Catholic institutions can offer it.

AN AWARENESS OF EXPLOITATION: THE SACRED BODY

After one gets past the seemingly endless loop of media content promoting weightless sex, there is evidence of a robust market for faithful, committed, generous, and even sacrificial romantic love, and a hatred of exploitation. The #MeToo movement makes this particularly evident. So too do the dozens of books chronicling the perils of "hookup culture,"[67] and revealing younger Americans' serious misgivings about or even depression in response to our "brave new world" of sex unlinked to tomorrow.

The entire "#MeToo" movement is in fact a stunning and public testament to the truth of a Catholic perspective on the human body. #MeToo victims are responding precisely to bodily, sexual—not nonsexual—violations. The complaints that have brought down dozens of formerly powerful men are about the impact of unwanted sexual touching. It turns out that people viscerally understand the violation perpetrated by an act intended to signal the deepest love

---

65 Elise Harris, "Pope Tells Young People to 'Be Brave' and Answer God's Call," *Cruxnow*, November 21, 2018, https://cruxnow.com/world-youth-day-panama/2018/11/pope-tells-young-people-to-be-brave-and-answer-gods-call/.

66 John Paul II, Apostolic Letter *Dilecti Amici* to the Youth of the World on the Occasion of the International Youth Year, March 31, 1985, 10.

67 See, e.g., Christian Smith, *Lost in Transition: The Dark Side of Emerging Adulthood* (Oxford: Oxford University Press, 2011); Miriam Grossman, *Unprotected: A Campus Psychiatrist Reveals How Political Correctness Endangers Every Student* (New York: Sentinel, 2007); and Debora L. Spar, *Wonder Woman: Sex, Power, and the Quest for Perfection* (New York: Sarah Crichton Books, 2013).

between a man and a woman—an act fraught with consequences for tomorrow—that instead only expresses a man's power over and disdain for a woman and his willingness to use her for the impulses of the moment.

When Catholics say, therefore, that what we do with our bodies sexually affects our minds and hearts and souls—that our bodies are "sacred spaces" where the divine and human come together—our message has traction, especially in a hypersexualized world with similarities to the early Christians' milieu. A world where—in the immortal (and brutal) words of pop star Miley Cyrus: "You can find someone to f--k in five seconds. We want to find someone we can talk to. And be ourselves with. That's fairly slim pickings."[68]

As then Karol Wojtyla wrote in *Love and Responsibility*, human sexual intercourse is particularly prone to exploitation or "use" of the other, when in fact, God intends the sexual expression of love—like all love—to serve the good of the other, and the common good of the couple.[69] This Catholic prescription for love can help the women and men of today to experience the same relief felt by women and other less-powerful human beings living at the time of the origins of Christianity. To repeat a previously quoted observation by Sarah Ruden, in such a world Christianity offered a "new way of thinking that must have been quite exciting, a hope for something beyond exploitation, materialism, and violence—a plan not for competing in purity and the denial of life, but for the sharing of life in full."[70] It offered a chance not to be treated as a thing.[71] It can offer this again.

Conclusion

I conclude by repeating the words of the Irish bishops: "The Church's whole moral teaching about sex is above all the application to

---

68 Bruna Nessif, "Miley Cyrus Talks Dating Men & Women, Difference Between Sex and Friendship: F—king Is Easy. Finding Someone to Talk to Is Hard," *EOnline*, June 15, 2015, https://www.eonline.com/news/666911/miley-cyrus-talks-dating-men-women-difference-between-sex-friendship-f-king-is-easy-finding-someone-to-talk-to-is-hard.

69 Wojtyla, *Love and Responsibility*, 51–57, 66–69, 82–100, 104–9.

70 Ruden, *Paul Among the People*, 11.

71 Ruden, 18

sexuality of God's greatest commandment to charity."[72] Contemporary theologian William Mattison frames the matter similarly: sex is a crucial aspect of the human capacity to express "self-giving love."[73]

At a minimum, this chapter demonstrates that Catholic sexual responsibility norms are not external to the faith, but rather authoritative and integrated elements of Christ's command to love. They are not part of a man-made moral code, against which unpleasant Catholic institutions like to measure their sanctity and the sanctity of their employees, but rather an original and positive insight derived from a faith that calls for loving God and neighbor as God loves us. In fact, the realizations achieved by the early Christians about sex, marriage, and parenting are as salient today as they were nearly two thousand years ago. We are made for faithful, permanent, creative, sacrificial love. Anything less is not enough for human beings, and anything opposed to this love can be deeply destructive.

Of course, my descriptions of early and contemporary Christian beliefs about sex, marriage, and parenting are not intended as claims that, then or now, Christians observed these to the letter! Then and now, Christians sin and repent of their failings in this domain, again and again (and again). At the same time, this recounting has the potential to inspire Catholics and others today and to inform Catholic institutions' explanations to courts of law and public opinion about why the state cannot countermand the Church's sexual expression norms.

When challenged, these institutions can summarize the material in this long chapter by replying: *The observance of Catholic sexual expression norms is an intrinsic element of being a Catholic institution because Christlike love is indivisible and authoritative. For two thousand years, Christians have understood these norms to be a necessary response to Jesus's command to love God and neighbor as He loves us. They are an application of the Good Samaritan principle of charity to the neighbor strewn in one's path—the romantic partner, the spouse, the child—whose lives the vast majority of us will affect by our choices most often, most profoundly, and for the longest time. They treat the*

---

72 The Irish Catholic Bishops Conference, *Love is for Life*, 24.
73 William C. Mattison III, *Introducing Moral Theology: True Happiness and the Virtues* (Grand Rapids, MI: Brazos, 2008), 204.

human body with the respect it is owed. They offer the kind of love humans crave. The proof is in the pudding: experience and even empirical evidence indicate that if people were to treat one another according to Catholic norms, then women, men, children, and vulnerable persons would be far better off.

Are these norms radical, out of step with the world? Yes. But Christians are instructed to love God as He loved us, and to love our neighbor in the same way. What is that way? He came down from heaven, became man, and allowed himself to be put to death in a ghastly manner, in order to atone for our sins. What is the proportionate, loving, Christian response to this? Radical love of the immigrant? Yes. The poor? Yes. The sick? Yes. The romantic partner, the spouse, the child? Yes. Yes. Yes.

A community in which Christians are exhorted to demonstrate such love—even as they need myriad opportunities to repent when they fail—is a community that fully understands and displays the breadth and depth of Christian love. It is the kind of place about which observers could say (as they did of the early Christian communities), "See how those Christians love one another!" In a world of myriad impermanent, unhealthy relationships, such a community would be something of a miracle, or at least a very bright light. It would be a living witness to Christ, a glimpse of the inbreaking of His "new creation." In short, it would be a Catholic community.

It is not only American society that needs this witness, but the members of Catholic communities themselves. Individuals, couples, and families need role models. They need exhortation, social pressure, support, and inspiration from one another in order to persist in a social environment that increasingly demeans these Catholic ideas. Every Catholic institution needs to show that it is a "community that understands itself as the bearer of a distinct and peculiar vocation within the world . . . and . . . embod[ies] the surprising hope of the new creation."[74] Obviously, this vocation is not realized solely by way of our romantic and familial relations—a wide variety of loving actions manifest the new way of life that the Kingdom of God inaugurates. But good familial relations constitute a remarkably important kind of witness to Christ's love, as is clear not only from scripture and tradition, but also from data and from human experience.

---

74 Hays, *The Moral Vision of the New Testament*, 376.

The next chapter will further support this argument by engaging with empirical material affirming that Catholic teachings on particularly hot-button topics that are repeatedly the subject of lawsuits— contraception, nonmarital sex and cohabitation, abortion, same-sex relations, and transgender identity—are, in fact, a loving response to the God who loves us first and an exercise of charity toward the neighbor. In other words, as then Cardinal Ratzinger once wrote, they "correlate with basic insights of human reason, albeit these insights have been purified, deepened and broadened through contact with the way of faith."[75]

---

75 Joseph Cardinal Ratzinger, "The Church's Teaching Authority—Faith—Morals," in Schürmann, Ratzinger, and Balthasar, *Principles of Christian Morality*, 45–73, 72.

- 7 -

TALKING ABOUT SEXUAL RESPONSIBILITY AS LOVE OF GOD AND NEIGHBOR

AS CHAPTERS 3–5 ARGUED, BECAUSE OF WHAT A CATHOLIC INSTITUTION *IS*, the behavior of its employees and the institution's choices respecting operations and services matter to the preservation of its religious mission and identity. All of these institutions have the potential to be or fail to be a genuine response to Christ's invitation to love God and one another. All can witness or fail to witness the living Christ to others. All can contribute to or derogate from the formation of a community whose life together reflects our new creation, the Kingdom of God initiated by Jesus Christ.

Furthermore, as chapter 6 showed, norms related to sex, marriage, and parenting are an important way for Catholics to demonstrate love of God and one another—a Christlike love of the kind by which Catholic communities distinguish themselves generally.

But these norms are precisely what onlookers sometimes call "unloving," or even "hateful." Therefore, whether or not a Catholic institution has a meritorious legal claim to religious freedom in a case involving one of these norms, if it fails to illuminate the positive, loving nature of its substantive position, it may foster disrespect for religious freedom and for its teachings about sexual responsibility.

This chapter is intended to help Catholic institutions avoid this fate. It will clarify how Catholic teachings on the five hot-button sexual issues preoccupying law and culture today enact the Great Commandment to love the neighbor in response to the love of God. These five issues are cohabitation/premarital sex, contraception, abortion, same-sex marriage, and transgender identity claims.

This chapter will not rehearse the accusation rebutted in chapters 3–6 that these five areas are irrelevant to an institution's mission and identity. Nor will it fully canvas the theological debates raging around each of them. This book aims at providing deeply informed communications advice grounded in reason and faith, not full-blown moral theology. Of course, criticisms of Catholic institutions' religious freedom demands do sometimes include an explicit rejection of Catholic theology. But their overriding and most damaging claim is that Catholic sexual responsibility teachings are unloving and therefore un-Christlike. This charge might also figure into a court's inclination to characterize an institution's response as harmful and "discriminatory." Consequently, this is the charge that receives the lion's share of my attention.

A Catholic institution's response has to strike the following balance. It should include enough about the substance of the teaching to indicate that the Church sincerely holds it and that it emerges out of love of God and neighbor. At the same time, there is no point in overloading judicial ears with theology that a court has no legal right to judge or obstruct. A heated religious freedom contest is not the place for *extended* evangelization about sexual responsibility, but it *is* the place for *some* instruction on the subject. Members of the Catholic community involved in the lawsuit need it. They are not fully convinced, and as a practical matter, the teaching is challenging. The public at large will also benefit from it; this is because Catholic norms are not arcane theological points, but universally applicable guides grounded in faith and reason for the attainment of love and freedom. They are also hugely controverted matters attracting enormous attention both within and outside the institution. In sum, the institution should teach! And its teaching might benefit the common good! But it should only supply what can reasonably be received in the context involved.

In order to assist Catholic institutions in threading this needle, I first provide below responses to several criticisms that can be conversation stoppers and are regularly launched in all kinds of sexual expression clashes. They are not criticisms of the "your teaching is hateful" variety, but they can prevent people from listening to anything further the Church might say in support of its norms.

Next, I offer language for Catholic institutions to use in religious freedom contests in response to a charge that a *particular* sexual responsibility teaching is unloving. I begin by describing the cultural situation and the typically raised legal question or questions setting up the clash. Then I describe the criticism that the sexual norm is unloving and therefore un-Christlike. Finally, I propose responses rebutting this criticism. The responses are relatively brief considering all that might be theologically and empirically said about each matter, but they are not "sound-bytey." Rather, they are as long as they need to be in my view in order to correctly, positively, and credibly convey the way in which the particular Catholic teaching seeks to promote love of neighbor as a response to the love of God. Neither courts of law nor public opinion are interested in thousand-word responses about the good of the norm. But they do need to hear more than what is currently offered.

General Accusations and Responses

There are four generalized criticisms launched at Catholic institutions' refusals to facilitate the government's preferred sexual norms. They are intended to broadly undercut a Catholic right to speak. None directly eviscerates the institution's *legal* claim but all can reduce its *moral* credibility before Catholics and the entire court of public opinion, though perhaps at the margins a court might be more willing to believe that a Catholic institution has a discriminatory animus or is insincere about its teachings if it is unable to rebut some of the accusations described here.

The first criticism states that the Church is unfit to speak about its sexual norms considering its own sex-abuse scandals and cover-ups. The second charges that the Church is obsessed with sexual sins and illogically focused more on some of these (e.g., same-sex marriage) than others (e.g., contraception). Third, it is frequently claimed that Catholic institutions treat dissenting sexual behaviors differently from dissent about other Catholic teachings, such as those concerning immigration and poverty. And fourth, critics claim that most Catholics don't believe what the Church teaches and that this fatally undercuts its authority.

THE SEX-ABUSE CRISIS

Regarding Catholics' sex-abuse and cover-up scandals, this is rightly an enormous hurdle to effective Church teaching. No matter that the Church has taken substantial steps toward restitution and prevention and that the overwhelming majority of clergy and religious still enjoy respect, thousands of innocent people were abused, and bishops and other leaders covered up or ignored ghastly wrongs. When this topic arises, it is absolutely necessary to first acknowledge the Church's deep faults—and the credibility hurdle these create. If the Church is what she says she is, she has a long, long way to go before she can responsibly claim that all her employees and institutions are adequately manifesting the inbreaking of the Kingdom in our day.

Following this, if the institution involved has its own strong policies safeguarding against sexual abuse and cover-up going forward, these can referenced. Then it might state that even while it continues working toward its goal of putting victims first in its every response to sexual abuse, it cannot abandon its work of teaching sexual responsibility. It would be happy for listeners to receive such teachings from any source because it is confident that these will conduce to greater happiness, freedom, dignity, and equality. But it feels duty-bound to offer its teachings about the fullness of human love to any who will listen, and is still confident that it has intelligent and inspiring gifts to share in this regard. For some potential listeners, the sex-abuse crisis will remain an impenetrable barrier against Catholic efforts to teach sexual responsibility. But this does not relieve the Church of the obligation to try.

THE CHURCH IS OBSESSED WITH SEX

The second claim insists that the Church is driving an obsession with sex, particularly with its rejection of same-sex marriage. This claim should be firmly dispatched. First, without a doubt, our era's sexual obsessions are brought to all of us not by the Church but by the powers that be in the US and elsewhere—by corporations, law, and politics, and in the entertainment, media, and academic establishments. Has the Church profited from products, advertisements, programs, and rhetoric feting certain sexual desires, images, identities, and behaviors for over half a century? Did the Church write the Supreme Court opinions characterizing sexual expression unlinked to marriage and children as being atop the pantheon of human rights? Did the Church write and fund the sex-education programs encouraging even the youngest students to think about themselves as sexual actors? Did the Church invent the Bratz doll, the toddler bikini, sexually demeaning and violent videos, games, and music, or the mechanical sex doll?

Today's obsession with sex began with powerful secular voices, many of whom are now demanding entrance into religious institutions, while these institutions are struggling to retain their freedom to be what they are, including by fostering stable, loving family relations. It is insulting to have the world's disproportionate preoccupation with sex laid at the Church's door, on the grounds that she has had the temerity to respond to the continual, formidable pressure created by this preoccupation. This is especially true when this also means that her "deepest nature"—"expressed in her three-fold responsibility: of proclaiming the word of God . . . celebrating the sacraments . . . and exercising the ministry of charity"[1]—is thereby obscured.

SELECTIVE OUTRAGE

The second general objection flows neatly into the third. Some observers complain that a given Catholic institution will act against same-sex or cohabiting couples while other employees and members go unscathed, even as they blithely use birth control (a facet of the fourth objection) or resist the Catholic perspective on a non-sexual-expression issue, such as immigration.

---

1   Benedict XVI, Encyclical Letter *Deus Caritas Est* (December 25, 2005), 25(a).

A few brief replies are available. First, the institution should state flatly that it does not pry into people's private lives, but rather responds to public information regarding an employee. Cohabitation, same-sex marriage, and transgender identification are regularly public acts. Resorting to contraception, abortion, and nonmarital sex generally are not.

What about the related claim that sexual responsibility dissent is treated differently from dissent on other subjects? Several responses are useful here. The institutions should observe initially that most dissent is expressed privately, not publicly, and is therefore not at all engaged by Catholic institutions. Again, no witch-hunting is involved.

Next, the institution might point out that regarding the wide variety of issues touched on by the Church's social teaching (e.g., immigration, poverty, health care, the environment, labor), it teaches general, albeit demanding, principles, but not as many clear rules, such as "no nonmarital cohabitation," "no abortion," etc. Furthermore, when the Church takes a position on legislation regarding a social justice issue, it usually constitutes a prudential judgment about how to advance the good in that area; it is not a doctrinal statement. For example, the Church may support amnesty for a class of persons presently without an acknowledged legal right to be in the US if those persons have lived in the country for a certain number of years without committing a crime. This is not a statement of doctrine, but a prudential application of the Church's core teachings on immigration, which include at least respecting people's right to migrate in order to sustain their lives and the lives of their families, and a nation's right to regulate its borders, albeit always with a primary attention to justice and mercy.[2]

How does this difference between the application of a principle and a clear rule apply to employees' public behaviors? Public statements opposing a clear rule are ordinarily problematic for the institution's maintenance and transmission of its identity. But statements constituting a disagreement about a prudential, political judgment—often about *how to effect* a particular Catholic social teaching—ordinarily are not. On its face, the Church's set of teachings on immigration bends *acutely* toward justice, mercy, and welcome, in imitation

---

2 Pontifical Council of Justice and Peace, *The Compendium of the Social Doctrine of the Church* (Washington, D.C.: USCCB, 2005), 297–98.

of Christ's radical love; at the same time, it leaves room for discussion and disagreement regarding the precise shape of a nation's regulatory framework.

Still, some employees' public statements *are* judged by bishops to violate Church teaching about the necessity of mercy and justice respecting immigration and are treated as a rejection of the teaching per se. These *are* treated similarly to public dissent from clear Catholic sexual responsibility principles. Thus, for example, in 2021 a bishop removed a pastor who had, among other things, publicly characterized persons who had entered the US as children and without recognized legal process as "criminal illegal aliens" in the course of his opposing a law to regularize their citizenship.[3]

Social media posts by members of Catholic communities involving another area touched on by Catholic social teaching—race—have also been deemed to transgress clear moral lines. Two different Catholic institutions made news in 2021, for example, for their decisions to separate from an employee and a pair of students who had posted remarks or pictures on social media that the institutions judged to be racist.[4]

In short, Catholic institutions do not deal with public, sex-related violations of love of neighbor differently from other public violations of love of neighbor. They treat them similarly. The average citizen is perhaps less likely to hear about the latter types of cases, though, because the former more often generate coast-to-coast news coverage, while the latter do not.

3 Christopher White, "U.S. Priest Who's Posted Anti-Immigrant, Racist Videos Is Forced to Resign as Pastor," *La Croix*, May 25, 2021, https://international.la-croix.com/news/religion/us-priest-whos-posted-anti-immigrant-racist-videos-is-forced-to-resign-as-pastor/14364.

4 Krystal Nurse, "Lansing Catholic Employee Fired for Posting Racist Photo on School's Social Media Pages," *Lansing State Journal*, March 3, 2021, https://www.lansingstatejournal.com/story/news/local/2021/03/03/lansing-catholic-employee-fired-racist-photo-kkk-nazi-salute/6902189002/; Rebecca Everett, "Girls in Racist Video No Longer Students at N.J. Catholic School. Alums of Color Demand More Change," *N.J.com*, February 23, 2021, https://www.nj.com/bergen/2021/02/girls-in-racist-video-no-longer-students-at-nj-catholic-school-alums-of-color-demand-more-change.html.

GET YOUR OWN PEOPLE ON BOARD FIRST

The fourth and final general objection suggests that a Catholic institution has no right to require observance of sexual teachings with which a majority of Catholics disagree. Of course, such disagreement does not make the teaching any less "held and taught" by the institution, which is really what a court of law needs and wants to know. And there is no scenario under which a court of law is empowered by our laws or Constitution to determine the contents of a religion's teaching or how to measure acquiescence with a teaching (by a percentage agreeing or not agreeing with it). Still, to speak appealingly to both courts of law and public opinion, the institution may choose to highlight, first, that in this case "familiarity breeds *content*." In other words, Catholics who remain actively engaged with their faith—by, for example, attending Mass and practicing other devotions—are far more likely to accept the Church's teachings than those who no longer practice their faith. (News reports of polls regularly fail to acknowledge the difference.) Second, the institution might stress its socially useful, prophetic function. In other words, it does not stop teaching about difficult but socially important subjects—whether immigration or the environment or sexual responsibility—simply because it does not yet enjoy widespread agreement. Third and finally, the institution might offer humbly that it has not taught as well as it would like in this area, but is committed to finding better ways to communicate in the future. This is precisely what the material below is designed to assist with.

I now turn to the five sexual expression issues regularly provoking church-state clashes and offer suggested responses respecting each. Remember, my recommendations are not intended to engage every theological or practical criticism launched at Catholic teachings on these topics. Rather, they respond only to those usually aired in the context of religious freedom cases. My suggested responses show that these teachings enact the love of neighbor, as understood from both Christian and empirical perspectives. They should help foster greater respect for religious freedom and for Catholic sexual expression norms, in no small part because they give evidence of *better* promoting the very values and outcomes that citizens admire and governments (incorrectly) assure citizens that *their* rules promote: equality, dignity, freedom, happiness, and health.

Cohabitation/Premarital Sex

THE CURRENT SITUATION

Cohabitation is widely practiced in the US, including among Catholics, though less among practicing Catholics.[5] There is a growing, firm, and erroneous belief that it is an essential step before entering into marriage. A declining number of Americans believe that it is immoral. The poor engage in it the most,[6] largely because they more often feel that successful marriage is difficult to attain in their communities, which suffer a deficit of stable families. They also more often believe that they cannot attain the level of financial stability they believe to be a prerequisite for marriage.

Cohabitation legally affects Catholic institutions through employment nondiscrimination laws. When it becomes known that an employee is cohabiting, some Catholic institutions ask the employee either to separate from or marry their partner, or alternatively, to leave their employment. This is the result of the Church's teaching about nonmarital sex. Such employees sometimes sue their employer under a state nondiscrimination law banning termination based on "marital status."

Of course, Catholic employers are not terminating employees based on marital *status*—that is, for *being* single, married, divorced, or widowed. They are rather responding to the employee's *conduct*, not their *status*—the conduct of cohabiting while in a sexual relationship, without marriage.

When marital status nondiscrimination laws were passed beginning in the 1970s, no one doubted that they were intended for the limited purpose of protecting women who suffered discrimination in securing mortgages, leases, or credit simply because they were single or divorced.[7] No one believed at the time that they were enacted to

5   David Masci and Gregory A. Smith, "Pope's Proclamation, Like Views of U.S. Catholics, Indicates Openness to Nontraditional Families," *Pew Research Center Fact-Tank*, April 8, 2016, https://www.pewresearch.org/fact-tank/2016/04/08/popes-proclamation-like-views-of-u-s-catholics-indicates-openness-to-nontraditional-families/.

6   W. Bradford Wilcox and Wendy Wang, "The Marriage Divide: How and Why Working-Class Families Are More Fragile Today," Institute for Family Studies website (blog), September 25, 2017, https://ifstudies.org/blog/the-marriage-divide-how-and-why-working-class-families-are-more-fragile-today.

7   See Helen M. Alvaré, "Is This Any Way to Make Civil Rights Law? Judicial Extension of 'Marital Status' Nondiscrimination to Protect Cohabitants," *Georgetown Journal of Law and Public Policy* 17, no. 1 (2019): 247–86, 261.

protect cohabitation, which was in any event still illegal in many states. But judges in several states (not all) today interpret such laws to protect cohabitation anyway.[8] In short, it remains possible that a Catholic institution will find itself in a jurisdiction protecting cohabiting employees under the legal concept of "marital status nondiscrimination." Catholic institutions are not seeking to legally ban cohabitation in any jurisdiction, but only the freedom to be a religious institution that maintains religious sexual responsibility norms among its employees. They also hope to be a light to onlookers. While mainstream sources do query the wisdom of cohabitation from time to time,[9] still the world hears too little wisdom about its risks and consequences.

THE RAP AGAINST THE CHURCH AND PROPOSED RESPONSES

There is not a great deal of substantive criticism of the Catholic stance on cohabitation/premarital sex. Likely many would consider debate about the issue too outdated to merit any attention at all! To the extent one hears complaints about Catholic institutions' separation from cohabiting employees, however, they are generally two. First, that cohabitation is a positive good because it helps people discern whether or not they should marry, and thus helps prevent divorce. Second, one occasionally hears that firing an employee for cohabiting is sexist because the firing sometimes occurs after a single female becomes pregnant, and only females get pregnant.

Beginning with the latter charge, an institution should state that it would, absolutely, treat identically any public information about a cohabiting male or female employee. It should also note that it has no control over the fact that women's motherhood becomes visible earlier. At the same time, it knows that a cohabiting man's becoming a father will likely become visible at some point—whether via his health insurance plan, or employee gatherings and conversation, and/or social media voluntarily shared with other members of the community. In

---

8   For a full discussion of the treatment of marital status nondiscrimination in different jurisdictions, see Alvaré, "Is This Any Way?"

9   See, e.g., Meg Jay, "The Downside of Cohabiting Before Marriage," *New York Times*, April 14, 2012, https://www.nytimes.com/2012/04/15/opinion/sunday/the-downside-of-cohabiting-before-marriage.html.

any event, the institution's response will pertain always to the chosen behavior, and not to the sex of the employee involved.

Regarding the charge that cohabitation helps couples, the Church will want to plainly state that this is untrue. Cohabitation does not communicate or engender the love that God intends human beings to enjoy, a fact that is reflected in decades of empirical investigation. Catholics believe that human beings were made to enjoy and exchange love of the kind Christ has for the human race. Jesus spoke positively about what this means for romantic couples when He recalled the Genesis creation account (Mk 10:6–12) of God's creating male and female for a "one-flesh" union which "no human being must separate." Sexual love therefore is positively intended to communicate fidelity and permanence. Further and myriad New Testament passages approach this, but from the negative perspective: Ephesians 5:5 and Galatians 5:21 refer to fornicators having "no inheritance" in the Kingdom. Revelation 21:8 speaks similarly. Jesus strongly denounces lustful looks at women (Mt 5:27) and calls fornication a choice that comes from inside a person and causes impurity (Mt 15:20). Paul is especially strong about the need to refrain from nonmarital sex in order to demonstrate that God takes priority over earthly things, as well as to demonstrate the sacredness of the human body (1 Cor 6:9–11, 15–20, and 1 Thes 4:1–8). It is worth noting here, again, that early Christians known for their charity to the poor and outcast were convinced of the need to demonstrate similarly radical love in the arena of sexual expression.[10]

It is also important to the Church's stance on nonmarital sex and cohabitation that these actions regularly lead to children, who are then disadvantaged by their parents' choices. Jesus spoke strongly about the love owed to children, which can also be deduced from God's creative design. He exhorted His listeners, "See that you do not despise one of these little ones, for I say to you that their angels in heaven always look upon the face of my heavenly Father" (Mt 18:10). He also indicates the divine import of properly receiving a child. "Taking a child he placed it in their midst, and putting his arms around it he said to them, 'Whoever receives one child such as this in my name, receives me'" (Mk 9:36–37).

---

10 See chapter 6, Part II.

God's creative design further points to what properly receiving children involves. We can grasp this best by contrasting the means God chose for procreation with those He did not. He could have brought about new life from one sex or the other. There could have been no sexual intercourse involved. Any sexual interaction involved could have been unrelated to "love" or "making love." Each human life could have been handed down from heaven, grown in a field, or manufactured! Each child could have had genes unrelated to mother or father, and thus be an entirely new, separate creature without a shared lineage. Each could have been capable of independent action from birth. Instead, however, God places new life at the loving intersection of the man and the woman, via an action nearly universally called "love" or "making love." He makes children a "one flesh" representation of the parents who move into eternity. And He makes them dependent upon their parents for a very long time, for physical as well as psychic and social survival.

One can clearly reason from these scriptural and anthropological bases to the conclusion that cohabitation cannot meet the high standards God has established for love between a man and a woman and between parents and their children. It is lacking in too many ways. Again, making distinctions helps. By design and intention, neither cohabiting adult offers or obtains permanent or complete union with the other. Each has accepted the other's body and sex, but not who the other will become over time—not for "better or worse," "in sickness and in health," "until death do us part." Instead of union, the partners enact distance from one another; they engage in mutual surveillance and testing to determine whether the relationship will work out. Sometimes they cohabit more for reasons of economy or convenience.

Cohabitation is opposed to union also because it undermines a later marriage, with the exception of those relatively rare cohabitating couples who move in together only after a formal engagement with a wedding date in mind.[11] Those who have cohabited are at a higher

---

11   Scott Stanley, "Citations for Tests of the Inertia Hypothesis about the Timing of Cohabitation and Marital Outcomes," *Sliding v. Deciding: Scott Stanley's Blog*, March 26, 2018, http://slidingvsdeciding.blogspot.com/2018/03/citations-for-tests-of-inertia_26.html ; Mariah Sanders, "Cohabitation: Safety Net? Or Stability Threat?" Institute for Family Studies website (blog), February 3, 2020, https://ifstudies.org/blog/cohabitation-safety-net-or-stability-threat#:~:text=An%20analysis%20of%20the%20ever,or%20sexual%20infidelity%20while%20married.

risk of divorce, not only because of the "selection effect" (people who cohabit are often less commitment-minded), but also due to "causal effects" (cohabitation fosters the acceptance of breakups).[12] Serial cohabitation undermines later marriage even more, but is becoming increasingly common.[13]

Cohabitation is further opposed to union because of the amount of infidelity and violence that takes place within it. Studies find from 57 percent to 400 percent more infidelity by men in cohabiting relationships as compared to in marriage, and up to 800 percent more by women.[14] Violence is also far more prevalent in cohabitation than in marriage.[15] Not surprisingly, cohabitants report themselves to be less happy than married couples on average.[16]

Cohabitation also fails to promote the stable love children need. Over 50 percent of the nearly 40 percent of children born outside of marriage in the US today are born into cohabiting households.[17] These children are dramatically more likely to see their parents' relationship dissolve than children born into a marriage. This is true not only in the US, but also in countries with longer experience and social acceptance of cohabitation.[18] These children furthermore suffer a far higher

12 Laurie DeRose and Rebecca Oldroyd, "Cohabitation Changes People: Contemporary European Evidence," Institute for Family Studies website (blog), August 19, 2021, https://ifstudies.org/blog/cohabitation-changes-people-contemporary-european-evidence.

13 Scott Stanley and Galena Rhoades, "Cohabitation is Pervasive," Institute for Family Studies website (blog), June 20, 2018, https://ifstudies.org/blog/cohabitation-is-pervasive; Michael J. Rosenfeld and Katharina Roesler, "Cohabitation Experience and Cohabitation's Association with Marital Dissolution," *Journal of Marriage and Family* 81, no. 1 (2019): 42–58.

14 Camille B. Lalasz and Daniel J. Weigel, "Understanding the Relationship Between Gender and Extradyadic Relations: The Mediating Role of Sensation Seeking on Intentions to Engage in Sexual Infidelity," *Personality and Individual Differences* 50, no. 7 (2011): 1079–83, https://doi.org/10.1016/j.paid.2011.01.029; Brandon G. Wagner, "Marriage, Cohabitation, and Sexual Exclusivity, Unpacking the Effect of Marriage," *Social Forces* 97, no. 3 (2019): 1231–56, 1241.

15 See, e.g., Wendy D. Manning, Monica A. Longmore, and Peggy C. Giordano, "Cohabitation and Intimate Partner Violence during Emerging Adulthood: High Constraints and Low Commitment," *Journal of Family Issues* 39, no. 4 (2018): 1030–55.

16 Juliana Menasce Horowitz, Nikki Graf, and Gretchen Livingstone, "Marriage and Cohabitation in the U.S.," *Pew Research Center* website, November 6, 2019, https://www.pewresearch.org/social-trends/2019/11/06/marriage-and-cohabitation-in-the-u-s/.

17 Alysse ElHage, "For Kids, Parental Cohabitation and Marriage are Not Interchangeable," Institute for Family Studies website (blog), May 7, 2015, https://ifstudies.org/blog/for-kids-parental-cohabitation-and-marriage-are-not-interchangeable.

18 See Laurie F. DeRose and W. Bradford Wilcox, "The Cohabitation-Go-Round: Cohabitation and Family Instability Across the Globe" in *World Family Map 2017: Mapping*

likelihood of being subjected to violence. This is because cohabitation regularly involves men living with women who have children from prior relationships. According to official US records, as compared with married families, the rates of physical abuse in cohabiting households are over ten times higher than in married households, the rates of sexual abuse are about thirteen times higher, and the rates of emotional abuse more than seven times higher.[19] Children from cohabiting households—even those with plentiful state support bringing their standard of living very close to married households, and even those living with their unmarried *biological parents*—also experience worse outcomes respecting safety, family stability, and emotional and educational attainment, on average, than children from stably married biological-parent households.[20]

In sum, a Catholic institution facing a lawsuit concerning a cohabiting employee who has refused to remedy the situation might say to courts of law and public opinion that *its decision is a function of its conviction about the quality of love for which God made every human being. He made us for love which is faithful, permanent, sacrificial, and able to welcome children with all the stability and security their vulnerability requires. This is what adults and children deserve. Cohabitation doesn't reflect God's design for love, and instead regularly harms both the adults and any children involved. These conclusions are based not only upon the words and life of Jesus, but also upon the robust consensus of empirical investigations performed in the US and around the*

Family Change and Child Well-Being Outcomes (New York: Social Trends Institute, 2017), 1-21, http://worldfamilymap.ifstudies.org/2017/files/WFM-2017-FullReport.pdf; see also W. Bradford Wilcox and Laurie F. DeRose, "In Europe, Cohabitation Is Stable...Right?" *The Brookings Institution Social Mobility Memos* (blog), March 27, 2017, https://www.brookings.edu/blog/social-mobility-memos/2017/03/27/in-europe-cohabitation-is-stable-right/.

19 See A.J. Sedlak et al., Department of Health and Human Services, Office of Planning, Research & Evaluation, *Fourth National Incidence Study of Child Abuse and Neglect (NIS-4): Report to Congress, Executive Summary* (Washington, D.C.: U.S. Department of Health and Human Services, Administration for Children and Families, 2010), 5-18–5-30, https://www.acf.hhs.gov/sites/default/files/documents/opre/nis4_report_congress_full_pdf_jan2010.pdf.

20 Nicholas Zill, "Even in Unsafe Neighborhoods, Kids Are Safer in Married Families," Institute for Family Studies website (blog), February 23, 2015, https://ifstudies.org/blog/even-in-unsafe-neighborhoods-kids-are-safer-in-married-families/; H. Brevy Cannon, "Cohabitation Has Superseded Divorce as Key Risk Factor to Children in America," *UVA Today*, August 16, 2011, https://news.virginia.edu/content/new-report-cohabitation-has-superseded-divorce-key-risk-factor-children-america.

world. The Church knows that it is swimming hard against the tide on this subject despite the scientific affirmation of its position, but it will continue to press the case for marriage as the best place to give and receive the quality of love for which human beings are made. The institution is not seeking a legal ban on cohabitation, but only respect for its freedom to live out its beliefs. Its public witness on this matter is a brave and positive contribution to the common good.

Contraception

THE CURRENT SITUATION

Contraception is used by about 99 percent of Americans who have ever been sexually active, including 99 percent of self-described Catholics,[21] though 13 percent of weekly-Mass-attending Catholics believe contraception to be a moral wrong.[22]

Interestingly, though, more than sixty years after the invention of "the pill," there is something of a backlash against contraception. This is due to women's dissatisfaction with its side effects and evidence that the ingestion of synthetic hormones has multiple negative consequences for women's health.[23] Additionally, secular economic and sociological investigations have suggested a causal link between the widespread use of contraception and troubled male-female relations.[24] Still, very loud political and interest-group voices equate unfettered access to cheap or free contraception with women's freedom. The vast

21 Rachel K. Jones, "People of All Religions Use Birth Control and Have Abortions," Guttmacher Institute website (blog), October 2020, https://www.guttmacher.org/article/2020/10/people-all-religions-use-birth-control-and-have-abortions.

22 Michael J. O'Loughlin, "Poll Finds Many U.S. Catholics Breaking with Church over Contraception, Abortion and L.G.B.T. Rights," *America*, September 28, 2016, https://www.americamagazine.org/faith/2016/09/28/poll-finds-many-us-catholics-breaking-church-over-contraception-abortion-and-lgbt.

23 See generally, Holly Griggs-Spall, *Sweetening the Pill: Or How We Got Hooked on Hormonal Birth Control* (Winchester, UK: Zero Books, 2013); Helen M. Alvaré, "Should Government Talk More about the Risks of Hormonal Contraception?" Institute for Family Studies website (blog), November 8, 2016, https://ifstudies.org/blog/should-government-talk-more-about-the-risks-of-hormonal-contraception.

24 See, e.g., Timothy Reichert, "Bitter Pill," *First Things* (May 2010), 25–34; George A. Akerlof, Janet L. Yellen, and Michael L. Katz, "An Analysis of Out-of-Wedlock Childbearing in the United States," *Quarterly Journal of Economics* 111, no. 2 (1996): 277–317.

majority of health insurance policies already provide it cheaply or for free, and federal and state governments together provide over two billion dollars per year of free contraception to those near, at, or below the poverty line.[25]

Catholic health care institutions can experience religious-freedom problems related to contraception because an employee or interest group publicly demands that such institutions provide it, or because a federal or state law or regulation mandates its inclusion in employee or student health insurance plans. When such laws or regulations specify coverage of abortifacient drugs or devices (those sold as "contraception," but potentially acting to destroy embryos), this would be discussed as an abortion problem. Today, religious institutions are regularly protected respecting both contraception and abortion by state and federal conscience-protection laws. But these exemptions are facing increasing opposition, and it is uncertain how many will survive in the future.

The insurance mandate problem has famously plagued the religious order the Little Sisters of the Poor from 2012 until the time of this writing. Thus far, and thanks to many trips to the Supreme Court by the Little Sisters, at the present moment it appears that the state is not likely to successfully argue that it has a compelling interest—realized by means least restrictive of religion—to force Catholic institutions to provide contraception. This is not yet certain because the Court's recent cases on this subject do not address the subject head on,[26] but they have left existing conscience protections in place.

THE RAP AGAINST THE CHURCH AND PROPOSED RESPONSES

Most people are baffled by the Catholic Church's stance on contraception. They believe that in a world awash with nonmarital sex, poverty, and the desire for two-child families, contraceptive use is simply a practical and responsible behavior.

---

25 Guttmacher Institute website, "Fact Sheet: Publicly Supported Family Planning Services in the United States," October 2019, https://www.guttmacher.org/fact-sheet/publicly-supported-FP-services-US.

26 See, e.g., Little Sisters of the Poor Saints Peter and Paul Home v. Pennsylvania, 140 S. Ct. 2367 (2020).

Critics' objections in the context of religious freedom cases, however, are a bit more focused. Often, they dwell upon claims that women's health will be harmed without ready access to contraception as part of employer-provided health insurance. "Health" includes everything from the psychic freedom to have nonprocreative sex to particular medical conditions they claim that contraception ameliorates.

Sometimes critics swing for the fences and claim that women's employment, educational attainment, and emotional well-being (in addition to their physical health) are all highly dependent upon access to contraception. For this reason, they charge that the Church's refusal communicates that it has no regard for women. Contraception advocates will claim, in fact, that its benefits to women are sufficiently overriding to give the state a "compelling interest" in forcing Catholic employers and educators to provide contraception in their health insurance plans.

Before addressing the substance of these accusations, it is important to remember what Catholic institutions are actually demanding when they refuse to cooperate with contraception mandates: they are seeking only to *avoid facilitating* its provision. They are not seeking legal restrictions on its availability. Employees will have ready access to contraception outside of their employee-provided benefits. Contraception is both ubiquitous and cheap. For those with low incomes, the government enthusiastically supplies it in a wide array of federal programs. Women earning at below, and even twice, the official poverty level can obtain it free or on a sliding scale from Medicaid, Title X programs, community health centers, and many other state and federally subsidized programs.[27]

With respect to employed and/or middle-class women wanting contraception, Planned Parenthood claims that the average cost of the pill is between ten and fifty dollars per month. Even one of the most expensive forms of contraception, the intrauterine device (IUD), while it costs over $1,000 initially, is ultimately cheaper than the pill because it lasts from 36 to over 140 months. In short, contraception

27 See Guttmacher Institute, "Fact Sheet: Publicly Supported Family Planning Services." See also Congressional Research Service, *Federal Support for Reproductive Health Services: Frequently Asked Questions*, R46785, May 14, 2021, https://sgp.fas.org/crs/misc/R46785.pdf.

is free for the poor or near-poor and quite affordable for the non-poor women who want it.

Let us now take a look at the claim that contraception provides women with health benefits that Catholics should support. This is not a theological challenge requiring a theological response, but may raise a moral question about how a Church claiming that it loves the neighbor can refuse to supply women contraception if they really need it for their health!

There are three elements to a complete response to the "health" claim. First, when birth control is prescribed not for use as a contraceptive, but as a treatment for a health problem—for example to counteract ovarian cysts—Catholic institutions will insure for such a use as with any other health care treatment.[28]

Second, what about the claim that contraception is important to prevent pregnancy in women with underlying medical conditions making pregnancy dangerous? Some conditions regularly mentioned in support of federal contraception mandates include Marfan Syndrome, congenital heart disease, and pulmonary hypertension. The best response to this claim will surprise you. It turns out that introducing hormonal drugs or devices into the bodies of women experiencing these grave conditions poses significant health threats. Instead, the doctors and medical associations specializing in these sicknesses recommend that afflicted women use inexpensive barrier or even (wait for it. . .) *natural* methods of family planning like those regularly pioneered by Catholic medical professionals.[29] The methods of contraception that mandates usually include are not recommended.

There is one other important point about contraception and women's health that should be made. Without crying that "the sky is falling," it is appropriate to communicate in an accurate and nuanced fashion that hormonal contraception is increasingly acknowledged to pose health risks even to ordinarily healthy women. In 2019 a citizens' petition was filed with the Food and Drug Administration collecting

28 See Rev. Tadeusz Pacholczyk, "Making Sense of Bioethics: Column 129: Catholics and Acceptable Uses of Contraceptives," *The National Catholic Bioethics Center* website, March 30, 2016, https://www.ncbcenter.org/making-sense-of-bioethics-cms/column-129-catholics-and-acceptable-uses-of-contraceptives.

29 See Helen M. Alvaré, "No Compelling Interest: The 'Birth Control Mandate' and Religious Freedom," *Villanova Law Review* 58, no. 3 (2013): 379–436, 417.

data on the negative health and side effects of many forms of contraception and recommending that some forms be removed from the market or accompanied with stronger warning labels.[30] Its empirical argument was lengthy, scientifically well-sourced, and impressive. Over the last fifty years, contraception has been strongly associated with depression, alteration of brain function, cancers, osteoporosis, weight gain, and strokes in a not-insignificant number of women. Similarly troubling side effects of experimental contraception for men are among the leading reasons there is no male hormonal contraceptive on the market today![31]

A telling "request for proposal" issued in 2013 by the federal National Institutes of Health put the matter plainly. It stated that "hormonal contraceptives have the disadvantage of having many undesirable side effects," are "associated with adverse events," and are particularly threatening to obese women (36 percent of the population) and smokers (12 percent of the population).[32]

In sum, the "birth control and women's health" argument is not difficult for the Church to overcome. When such drugs or devices are used directly to support health, Church employers will insure for them. Regarding women whose underlying health conditions would significantly worsen if they were pregnant, the medical establishment recommends cheap barrier or even natural methods of pregnancy prevention, not the drugs and devices that contraceptive mandates cover. And finally, birth control poses its own health risks, which are increasingly well-documented and affect a surprisingly large segment of the female population.

But what about the broader argument that depriving women of their interest in securely avoiding pregnancy—even their "autonomy"—is disrespectful at least and hateful at worst? In response to this, Catholic institutions need to speak using the same blend of faith and reason that shapes all Catholic teachings on sex, love, and contraception.

---

30 William W. Williams et al. (Contraceptive Study Group), "Petition on Hormonal Contraceptives," May 9, 2019, https://www.cathmed.org/wp-content/uploads/2019/05/Citizens-petition-Hormonal-Contraceptives-2019May9-submitted.pdf.

31 See Alvaré, "No Compelling Interest," 417–20.

32 Department of Health and Human Services, National Institutes of Health, "Female Contraceptive Development Program (U01)," grant application, November 5, 2013, https://grants.nih.gov/grants/guide/rfa-files/RFA-HD-14-024.html.

A first response is to remind the critic that the Catholic Church understands many couples' need and desire to plan childbearing so they can manage all of their responsibilities. It offers couples natural family planning (NFP) as part of a responsible and generous way of proceeding; it safeguards both the couple's true union and the procreative meaning of sex. Modern NFP methods, sometimes called Fertility Awareness Based Methods (FABMs) "meet the criteria of modern methods of contraception developed by the World Health Organization, which classifies modern methods as those with a 'sound basis in reproductive biology, a precise protocol for correct use and the evidence of efficacy under various conditions based on appropriately designed studies.'"[33] Efficacy rates for perfect and typical use of NFP compare favorably with, and sometimes exceed, comparable rates for nonnatural contraceptive drugs and devices[34] without any of the side effects of the latter.

NFP both relies upon and strengthens a couple's union. It requires ongoing communication about all aspects of their future, their plans, and their hopes. It requires the man to know about and respect the woman's natural ecology. It preserves the woman's health by avoiding all of the side effects of synthetic birth control and intrusive devices. At the same time, NFP's reliance upon the woman's fertility cycle, and the conversations it requires about the number and spacing of children, ensure that the creative powers of sex are always on the couple's horizon.

Second, a Catholic institution might briefly summarize the faith and reason that together underlie its teaching as follows: *The Church teaches that human beings should not impair the Creator's design for love between a man and a woman.*[35] *God could have designed sex and procreation anyway He wanted. But He put sex together with love*

33 Rebecca G. Simmons and Victoria Jennings, "Fertility-Awareness Based Methods of Family Planning," *Best Practice and Research Clinical Obstetrics and Gynaecology* 66 (2020): 68–82, 75, citing Mario Philip R. Festin et al., "Moving toward the Goals of FP2020—Classifying Contraceptives," *Contraception* 94, no. 4 (2016): 289–94.

34 Simmons and Jennings, "Fertility-Awareness Based Methods," 77 (Figure 2: "% of women in the United States experiencing an unintended pregnancy within the first year of use"). See also Michael Manhart et al., "Fertility Awareness-Based Methods of Family Planning: A Review of Effectiveness for Avoiding Pregnancy Using SORT," *Osteopathic Family Physician* 5, no. 1 (2013): 2–8.

35 *Catechism of the Catholic Church* (Vatican City: Libreria Editrice Vaticana, 1993), §§ 1643, 1652, 2366–70.

between the couple and the possible creation of new human life. By eradicating even the thought of children in relation to sex, contraception removes one of the natural elements of human romantic love; thus it changes love, and not for the better. Ironically, by eliminating the thought of procreation from sex, the couple's union is impaired. This is not to say that Catholics are expected to desire procreation for every act of intercourse, but rather to emphasize that they are called to accept the fullness of the divine creation—the capacity of sex both to unite them and to potentially create new life. Empirical and experiential accounts strongly confirm the Church's teaching on this point. In short, with this teaching, as with its teaching regarding cohabitation/premarital sex, the Church is saying that a certain behavior detracts from the high quality of love men and women were meant to exchange.

Conclusions drawn from experience and empirical evidence bring these simple theological statements to life in our own time. Since the beginning of the widespread use and availability of contraception, relations between men and women have suffered significantly. When sex is separated from "tomorrow"—the possibility or even *thought* of a future commitment or a new life that physically and practically unites the man and the woman—it is reduced to its fleeting characteristics; it easily becomes performance and pleasure. This is not a religious point, but a matter of human experience. Disappointment or worse more likely follows the false enactment of union. Children are envisioned as threats rather than gifts.

Predictions that contraception would lead to the opposite—to closer male-female relations in which the couple could focus on their "love" without "fear" of pregnancy—have been objectively disproved. Onlookers also expected fewer nonmarital pregnancies and abortions. *But the opposite has happened, and happened most often to those with the highest levels of access to free contraception—the poor.* Since the widespread use of contraception began there are *fewer* stable male-female unions in our nation. And there is *more* of all of the following: uncommitted nonmarital sex, sexually transmitted infections, nonmarital pregnancy, abortion, cohabitation, single parenting, and divorce. There is also less and later marriage. Poor women, who receive the largest amount of free contraception, experience the worst consequences arising from every one of these categories.

Economists trace these outcomes to risk compensation[36] (people having sex they might otherwise not have when it seems "insured against" by contraceptives, despite the latter's failure rates) or to the "prisoners' dilemma" (*individual* women choosing uncommitted sexual relations to obtain a relationship though it would advantage *all* women to refrain),[37] but the result is the same: more uncommitted sexual encounters and less long-term love and stability.

Children have been especially victimized with the rise of nonmarital parenting coinciding with the rise in contraceptive use and in public funding for contraception. In the early 1960s about 5 percent of children were born outside of marriage; today, sixty years after "the pill" hit the scene, the figure is around 40 percent.[38] And it is well accepted today among academics both liberal and conservative that children reared without the support of their stably married parents on average suffer in the academic, emotional, cognitive, and employment spheres.[39]

In sum, a Catholic institution embroiled in a controversy concerning contraception could say: *The Church's teachings on contraception are part of its efforts to protect human love so that it is more Christlike. Experience and empirical science support the Catholic approach. Removing "tomorrow" from sex by removing even the thought of its procreative potential tends strongly to undermine the couple's union. And the children conceived in today's more frequently uncommitted sexual encounters fare worse.*

Like all efforts to safeguard the norms of Christian love, this one is difficult. The Church understands why many people have trouble accepting it in a world that often uses the word "love" to mean something far less than a faithful, permanent, self-sacrificing, creative, and other-focused relationship. But experience and data robustly support Catholic insights. More and more people are coming to understand how Catholic teaching on contraception is pro-woman and pro-love. Finally,

---

36 See Akerlof, Yellen, and Katz, "An Analysis of Out-of-Wedlock Childbearing," 290–97.

37 See Reichert, "Bitter Pill," 25.

38 Robert VerBruggen, "How We Ended Up with Forty Percent of Children Born Out of Wedlock," Institute of Family Studies website (blog), December 18, 2017, https://ifstudies.org/blog/how-we-ended-up-with-40-percent-of-children-born-out-of-wedlock.

39 W. Bradford Wilcox, "The Good and Bad News about Family Life in America," Institute of Family Studies website (blog), February 26, 2020, https://ifstudies.org/blog/the-good-and-bad-news-about-family-life-in-america.

the Church does not seek to instantiate its beliefs into law. But it does demand respect for its freedom to live its own beliefs in its own community, which might also promote the common good by shedding light in the surrounding community on these matters, a light that the world sorely needs at this time.

Abortion

THE CURRENT SITUATION

Abortion has been broadly legal in every state in the US since 1973's *Roe v. Wade* decision.[40] As of this writing, it seems possible that the US Supreme Court may use its future opinion in *Jackson Women's Health Organization v. Dobbs* to allow states to restrict abortion more if they wish,[41] although those states that wish to would also remain free to allow abortions up until birth so long as their state constitutions did not protect unborn children against such a rule.

Stunningly, the pro-life movement has retained a very strong following despite opposition from every influential social institution and from powerful members of every branch of government at both the state and federal levels. Interest groups advocating abortion are extremely well-funded and connected. The majority of Catholics who regularly attend Mass are pro-life by a two-to-one margin, while those who do not attend Mass favor legal abortion by a slight majority.[42] Young people under thirty are more pro-life than many expected, with a majority favoring some or far more restrictions on abortion than the law currently allows.[43]

Rates, ratios (abortions per total number of pregnancies), and total numbers of abortions have generally been declining since the 1990s, according to the Centers for Disease Control. At the same time, it is

---

40 410 U.S. 113 (1973).

41 The opinion of the Court of Appeals in this case may be found at 945 F. 3d 265 (5th Cir., 2019).

42 Dalia Fahmy, "8 Key Findings about Catholics and Abortion," *Pew Research Center Fact-Tank*, October 20, 2020, https://www.pewresearch.org/fact-tank/ 2020/10/20/8-key-findings-about-catholics-and-abortion/.

43 The Gallup Organization website, "Abortion Trends by Age" (first graph: "18-to-29-Year-Olds' Views on Legality of Abortion, 1975–2020"), https://news.gallup.com/ poll/246206/abortion-trends-age.aspx.

acknowledged by both pro-life and pro-legal-abortion sources that state and federal abortion reporting systems are inadequate, and that better reporting would likely yield higher numbers but would still show a declining trend. Poor women and women of color suffer from abortion most.[44]

Abortion affects Catholic institutions when state or federal lawmakers attempt to require their cooperation with the procedure by mandating coverage of it in their health care plans, equating refusal to insure for abortion with "sex discrimination" against women, and forcing Catholic health care institutions to perform abortions. Government grants or contacts might also include a requirement to cooperate with abortion.

There are more than a few federal and state laws providing religious "conscience protection" respecting abortion, but some state legislators and some groups like the American Civil Liberties Union continually attempt to pass laws mandating abortion as part of religious institutions' health insurance or hospital care. Such campaigns are particularly harsh with respect to Catholic hospitals that serve more remote populations, and when a Catholic hospital is contemplating a merger with a non-Catholic hospital while requiring the new entity to observe the Ethical and Religious Directives for Catholic Health Care (ERDs).

THE RAP AGAINST THE CHURCH
AND PROPOSED RESPONSES

The rap on the Catholic Church's teaching on abortion is simple and relentless. It takes the form of a syllogism: abortion is the sine qua non of women's freedom; the Catholic Church opposes abortion; therefore, the Church is the enemy of women's freedom. Sometimes the Church is also called the enemy of women's health.

The debate over abortion is long and deep, and often ugly. Advocates for legal abortion deceptively twist together negative caricatures of the Church, total silence about the unborn child and about women's

---

44 For a review of abortion reporting requirements in the United States, declining rates and ratios of abortion since 1990, and the socioeconomic situation of abortion patients, see Helen M. Alvaré, "Nearly 50 Years Post–*Roe v. Wade* and Nearing its End: What *is* the Evidence That Abortion Advances Women's Health and Equality?," *Regent Law Review* 34, no. 2 (2022): 165–217; 187, 204, 205–6, 208.

health and distress after abortion, and unreal, simplistic visions of women's freedom. This has not changed in fifty years.

This is what I found even in 2020 and 2021 when I reviewed in detail the entire legislative histories of recent state laws securing abortion on demand in the states of Rhode Island, Vermont, New York, and Illinois. These states, among others, are "preparing themselves" for a possible Supreme Court reversal of *Roe v. Wade*. They want to have unlimited legal abortion on the books for their *own* states if the day should come when the US Constitution no longer mandates it in *every* state. A review of every intervention by every legislator or interest group supporting unlimited abortion revealed nothing more than endless conclusory statements about "women's health," "women's lives," "women's equality," and the occasional slamming of the Catholic Church. But they did not produce a shred of credible empirical data to support any of it, and demonstrated a stunning lack of curiosity about the mental and emotional effects on women of one of the most frequent surgeries US women experience.

How should a Catholic institution respond to this toxic stew in a way that is sufficiently brief? I would begin by noting that the Catholic position on abortion is really based on a combination of scripture, two thousand years of tradition, and natural law, which together reach the important but also unremarkable conclusion that human beings must not kill one another. Scripture instructs us not to kill human beings and reminds us of God's love and designs for us even in our mothers' wombs. Christians have maintained this view since the earliest days of the Church.[45] And scientific research confirms that the life of human beings begins at conception.

The norm that we should reject killing takes on strength and becomes even more poignant in the case of vulnerable, defenseless human life, such as the elderly, the sick, the disabled, and the life growing in a mother's womb and dependent upon her for survival. Because of this, the Catholic Church is one of the nation's, and even the world's, top providers of charitable assistance to women—as well as men. For the same reasons it is among the most prominent

---

45 US Conference of Catholic Bishops Committee on Pro-Life Activities, Fact Sheet, "Respect for Unborn Human Life: The Church's Constant Teaching," https://www.usccb.org/issues-and-action/human-life-and-dignity/abortion/respect -for-unborn-human-life.

defenders of the immigrant and the prisoner on death row, it is *also* a great defender of the unborn.

At the same time, the Church protects the frightened pregnant mother before and after her child's birth. Women and girls in some situations fear parenting and need help. This is obvious. The pro-life movement, including myriad groups beyond the Church, have devoted literally thousands of centers, homes, services, funding sources, and whole parishes and other churches to assist these women and their children. In fact, largely thanks to female leadership in the Church, the Church is unequaled in the services it provides to women who are seeking to understand and regulate their fertility, to find alternatives to abortion, to receive care and material support for themselves and their children, and to find healing and peace after an abortion. Governments also have myriad income, food, shelter, and other programs to assist pregnant women and mothers. Ironically, despite their "pro-woman" slogans—and their slandering of pro-lifers as inattentive to "born" humans—abortion-advocacy organizations have none of the above.

On the matter of abortion and women's health, it is first important to note that today, abortions are likely never or almost never necessary to save the life of the mother, according to leading experts from Planned Parenthood.[46] Pro-life doctors agree.[47] Claims that abortions are necessary for women's health are also highly suspect. Because the Supreme Court has defined health to include all factors associated with a woman's physical or emotional or psychological health, or with her desires for family, or with her age, every abortion might be deemed a "health"-related abortion.[48] Neither leading abortion providers such as Planned Parenthood nor the federal government try to count "health abortions" with precision. Planned Parenthood's former research arm, the Guttmacher Institute, reported that 8 percent of women in 2004 mentioned a health reason for pursuing an abortion,

---

46 See, e.g., Mary S. Calderone, "Illegal Abortion as a Public Health Problem," *American Journal of Public Health* 50, no. 7 (July 1, 1960): 948–54, 948–49; Alan F. Guttmacher, "Abortion—Yesterday, Today and Tomorrow," in *The Case for Legalized Abortion Now* (Berkeley: Diablo, 1967), 3.

47 Donna Harrison et al., "It Is Never Necessary to Intentionally Kill a Fetal Human Being to Save a Woman's Life: In Support of the Born-Alive Abortion Survivors Protection Act," *Public Discourse*, February 17, 2019, https://www.thepublicdiscourse.com/2019/02/49619/#_ftn3.

48 Doe v. Bolton, 410 U.S. 179, 192 (1973).

but failed to specify whether the women interviewed were referring to a health problem involving themselves or the child, and further failed to specify whether—if the problem involved the woman—a doctor had recommended an abortion as a health measure.[49] Furthermore, when it comes to the question of women's health and abortion, it is necessary to consider the harm that abortion *causes* women. While state and federal governments do not care enough to mandate collection of this information, a review of articles in leading medical journals—including some authored by "pro-choice" researchers—concludes that, on average, abortion psychologically harms women.[50] Abortion advocates deny this information, but without credible studies to refute it. They seem uncurious to say the least. The leading federal health care institution in the nation also seems uncurious. The National Institutes of Health, which bills itself as "the steward of medical and behavioral research for the Nation," designed "to advance significantly the Nation's capacity to protect and improve health,"[51] has *never* commissioned a long-term study to evaluate the health of women postabortion, despite women in the US having undergone over sixty million abortions since 1973.[52]

Abortion is also not linked to women's equality. In the Supreme Court's *Casey* opinion, a plurality of the justices claimed that "the ability of women to participate equally in the economic and social life of the Nation has been facilitated by the availability of abortion in the event that contraception should fail."[53] Abortion advocates continue to lean heavily on this claim, but like the Court, have no empirical data

49 Lawrence B. Finer et al., "Reasons U.S. Women Have Abortions: Quantitative and Qualitative Perspectives," *Perspectives on Sexual and Reproductive Health* 37, no. 3 (September 2005): 110–18, 110, 113.

50 See Expert Report of Dr. Aaron Kheriaty, M.D., in Whole Women's Health Alliance v. Hill, 2019 WL 8223143 (S.D. Ind., Nov. 9, 2019), ¶¶ 67–94; see also David M. Fergusson, John Horwood, and Joseph M. Boden, "Does Abortion Reduce the Mental Health Risks of Unwanted Or Unintended Pregnancy? A Re-Appraisal of the Evidence," *Australian and New Zealand Journal of Psychiatry* 47, no. 9 (2013): 819–27, https://journals.sagepub.com/doi/epub/10.1177/0004867413484597.

51 "About the NIH," National Institutes of Health website, July 7, 2015, https://www.nih.gov/about-nih/what-we-do/nih-almanac/about-nih.

52 Email communication from the National Institutes of Child Health and Human Development Information Resource Center to my research assistant on June 16, 2021: "You requested information about induced abortion and women's health. Although the NICHD currently supports a number of research areas, we regret that we do not have any material relevant to your topic." Copy on file with the author.

53 Planned Parenthood v. Casey, 505 U.S. 833, 856 (1992).

to support it. They rather rely on listeners' simplistic intuition that women can do more when they are unimpaired by children.

But women's advances are far more likely tied to their taking advantage of the opportunities opened up over recent decades not only by the culture, but also by dozens of laws that have enshrined women's rights to equal opportunities in politics, the economy, housing, education, the military, and a myriad of other domains.[54] Furthermore, it is statistically impossible to sustain the claim that women's current successes in these and other domains are *causally* tied to the availability of abortion. There are simply too many factors that have unfolded over too many decades, and that have intersected with too many other phenomena (e.g., the economy generally, developments in technology affecting the labor force, health advancements) to allow for a reliable conclusion in this regard. Furthermore, there is important evidence to the contrary.

First, as noted above, meta-analyses of the credible scientific literature about abortion's effects on women indicate that, on average, it has negative physical and psychological effects. Even were there some economic advantage to obtaining an abortion, the negative effects of these harms would have to be netted out.

Second, empirical data shows that abortion rates (numbers per one thousand women of childbearing age) and ratios (abortions per total number of pregnancies) *declined* at the same time that women's academic, employment, income, entrepreneurial, and political accomplishments *all soared* from the 1990s onward. In short, there isn't even a *correlation* between women having abortions and their achievements in these domains. The correlation goes in the *opposite* direction. So how could abortion have *caused* improvements?[55]

Third, the women having the *most* abortions are also the *least* likely to achieve the higher levels of education, income, and employment that abortion proponents associate with equality. Poorer women

54 Brief of 240 Women Scholars and Professionals, and Prolife Feminist Organizations as Amici Curiae in Support of Petitioners in Dobbs v. Jackson Women's Health Org., No. 19–1392, U.S. Supreme Court, 13–21, 19a-22a, https://www.supremecourt.gov/DocketPDF/19/19-1392/185366/20210804180314919_19-1392%20Brief%20of%20240%20Women%20Scholars%20et%20al%20In%20Support%20of%20Petitioners.pdf.

55 For a detailed exposition of this data accompanied by helpful charts and primary-source footnotes, see Brief of 240 Women Scholars and Professionals in *Dobbs*, 29–35, 23a–34a.

and women of color in fact undergo highly disproportionate rates of abortion. This strongly indicates that abortion advocates have the direction of causation exactly backwards—it is deprivation and tragedy that lead to abortion; abortion does not *cause* higher levels of education and wealth.

In fact, legal abortion has likely held women back from making even greater gains by disincentivizing lawmakers and corporations from more generously accommodating women with children. After all, *only* women bear children, and also often choose to devote extraordinary amounts of time to rearing them as well. If the whole world—including advocates of legal abortion—proclaims that the "ideal worker" is like a man without parenting responsibilities, then why should public and private policies accommodate mothers? Or why else is it only *now*, in the early twenty-first century, that US corporations and lawmakers are seriously considering significant financial assistance for parents, as well as laws and policies mandating greater flexibility for parents and paid leave from work with a job guaranteed upon return?

In conclusion, Catholic institutions might say: *We oppose abortion because of the established fact that it destroys human life, which violates human rights norms as well as sacred scripture. The Church's commitment to defending life—both its existence and its flourishing—extends equally to women, for whom the Church and others have provided unparalleled resources at every stage of life, including while pregnant, parenting, and postabortion. Proponents of abortion offer no credible argument that abortion advances women's health or equality. Instead, there is copious data indicating that women's advancement is due to their taking advantage of the myriad legal and social opportunities afforded, especially since the 1970s. It is also likely that there is less corporate and governmental accommodation of mothers and children due to the wrongheaded message legal abortion communicates: that childlessness is an important ingredient of economic and educational success. The Church demands respect for its ability to live out its own beliefs, which it believes will also promote the common good by shedding light to the surrounding community on this matter, a light the world sorely needs at this time.*

Same-Sex Behavior

THE CURRENT SITUATION

Same-sex attraction is the subject of enormous attention today. It is discussed under the banner of civil rights. Unlike traditional civil rights categories, however, which rely upon who and what people "are"—female, nonwhite, etc.—the campaign for "gay rights" in the context of religious freedom is mostly about what people "do," their entering into state-recognized marriages with persons of the same sex. That is, religious institutions are refusing to cooperate with the *conduct* of members or personnel entering into a state-recognized same-sex marriage, *not* refusing membership or other affiliation to persons experiencing same-sex attraction.

According to the Gallup polling organization, about 5.6 percent of Americans identify as LGBTQ, a 1.1 percent increase from its 2017 update.[56] But the movement for LGBTQ rights is disproportionately visible as well as culturally and legally powerful, especially after its mobilization during the AIDS crisis of the 1980s and 1990s. State and federal governments, the most powerful corporations on earth, and nearly all of the nation's prestige media, entertainment, sports, and academic institutions, continually promote policies, images, and social and political messages and projects initiated by this movement.

In light of this, it hardly seems necessary to discuss at any length the plight of a dissenter. Suffice it to say that disdain for the Catholic Church's position on same-sex relations is common. Among self-described Catholics, a majority (61 percent) support legalized same-sex marriage. Among Catholics who attend Mass regularly, a slight majority (53 percent) oppose it.[57]

---

56 Jeffrey M. Jones, "LGBT Identification Rises to 5.6% in Latest U.S. Estimate," *Gallup: Politics*, February 24, 2021, https://news.gallup.com/poll/329708/lgbt-identi-fication-rises-latest-estimate.aspx.

57 Jeff Diamant, "How Catholics around the World See Same-Sex Marriage, Homosexuality," *Pew Research Center Fact-Tank*, November 2, 2020, https://www.pewresearch.org/fact-tank/2020/11/02/how-catholics-around-the-world-see-same-sex-marriage-homosexuality/; Pew Research Center, "Religious Landscape Study: Views about Same-Sex Marriage among Catholics," 2014, https://www.pewforum.org/religious-landscape-study/religious-tradition/catholic/views-about-same-sex-marriage/.

The current fixation on same-sex attraction has brought legal pressure to bear on the Church in several ways, especially following the Supreme Court's *Obergefell* decision, which interpreted the Constitution to require states to recognize same-sex marriage. Catholic institutions are regularly pressured to structure their services or employee benefits to affirm the validity of same-sex marriages or suffer the penalties imposed by relevant nondiscrimination laws in employment, health care, housing, or public accommodations. The law frequently attempts to require Catholic institutions to extend spousal health care benefits to a same-sex partner, to allow same-sex couples admission to housing that is reserved for married graduate students at Catholic universities, to require Catholic social service agencies to place children with same-sex couples, to allow same-sex marriage celebrations in halls owned by religious groups, and to require Catholic counselors to provide marriage counseling to same-sex couples. Catholic institutions are also pressured by employment nondiscrimination laws to hire and keep employees who enter into a same-sex marriage. This last group of cases constitute the lion's share of the news about the Catholic Church's stance on same-sex relations.

More litigation against Catholic institutions is likely in the future. Without restating all of the law outlined in chapter 2, it is important to remember that federal employment nondiscrimination law has recently been reinterpreted in the Supreme Court's *Bostock* decision to ban discrimination on the basis of sexual orientation and gender identity.[58] The Court's interpretation may be extended in the future to statutes concerning discrimination in housing and public accommodations. Additionally, more states and locales are adding "sexual orientation" to their list of categories of forbidden discrimination across domains. This is problematic for Catholic institutions because they are wrongly charged with sexual orientation discrimination when they have *not* discriminated against a *person*, but rather refuse to cooperate with same-sex *conduct*, like entering into a marriage.

To repeat the explanation in chapter 2, even though nondiscrimination laws were intended to ban unfavorable actions based upon a person's "status,"—that is, *being* a particular race or sex, or *being* same-sex attracted—they are now regularly being interpreted to

---

58 Bostock v. Clayton Cty., 140 S. Ct. 1731 (2020).

protect "*conduct*," such as choosing to enter into a same-sex marriage. Not all courts conflate status and conduct, but many do, and thereby charge Catholic institutions with "sexual orientation" *status* discrimination when they refuse to cooperate with or facilitate another's *conduct* of entering into a same-sex marriage. The US Supreme Court has in the past gone along with this problematic practice,[59] although it is not certain they will continue to do so in the future.

Same-sex marriage is likely here to stay in the US, despite the fact that the *Obergefell* opinion is not legally well reasoned, to put it nicely. But the politics are white-hot and will likely affect even the majority of Supreme Court justices (as of this writing) who *do* understand that the Constitution does not provide for the right of two people of the same sex to obtain a state marriage license. Also, the momentum to expand LGBTQ rights in the law is presently strong and culturally supported. Recently, lawmakers seem more and more reluctant to grant exemptions allowing religious individuals and institutions to decline to cooperate with same-sex behavior.[60]

Again, Catholic institutions do not seek to disadvantage or discriminate against same-sex- attracted persons in their institutions. Such persons are employees, students, clients, and patients of these institutions. But Catholic institutions do seek respect for their ability to live out their own beliefs and refrain from cooperating with same-sex *behavior*, like entering into same-sex marriage.

The Catholic faith also maintains the position that same-sex marriage should not be legally recognized. This position is a function of the Church's religious understanding of marriage, and its recognition of the natural rights and interests of vulnerable parties—children especially—and the harmful consequences of excising children from the public and legal meaning of marriage. To wit, a constitutional right to enter into same-sex marriage suggests that marriage is not ordered to the bearing and education of children; it also forbids every state from asserting that procreation is specially valuable or that children have a right to know and be known by the parents who brought them into this world. Instead, it communicates that procreation is of

---

59 See, e.g., Lawrence v. Texas, 539 U.S. 558, 575 (2003).

60 See, e.g., The Equality Act, H.R. 5, 116th Cong. (2019–20) (providing in §1107 that the act's mandates are not subject to the religious freedom protections of the Religious Freedom Restoration Act).

no greater value than its impossibility, and that it is equally good for children and society for children to be reared by their natural parents, or alternatively, *without* one or both natural parents—which is the situation obtaining in every same-sex household.

THE RAP AGAINST THE CHURCH
AND SUGGESTED RESPONSES

Anger at Catholic institutions' refusal to cooperate with same-sex behavior seems comprised of equal parts rejection of Catholic teaching, dislike of wounding the already-wounded—who regularly believe that criticism of their acts constitutes rejection of their persons—a general distaste for "judgmentalism," and disagreement that same-sex behavior or its recognition would interfere with an institution's central "business" of health care, education, or social services. The anger is exacerbated by the belief that a religion based on love should *doubly* avoid wounding the already-wounded, and instead affirm people's loving one another according to whatever understanding of love they possess.

The last two objections are covered in chapter 6's discussion of the indivisibility and quality of Christian love, and in the material within chapters 3–5 about the theological nature of Catholic institutions. But the other objections together require a response demonstrating how Catholic teaching on same-sex relations is in fact loving.

This is the hardest thing this book attempts to do. Not only because of the cultural maelstrom around this issue, but because both author and readers love our same-sex-attracted friends and family, who are not likely to be easily convinced by even thoughtful, well-sourced arguments. Many readers would likely be emotionally relieved if there existed a theologically sound basis to welcome the news that a same-sex-attracted friend or family member has found a partner. Everyone needs to love and be loved by other human beings. Everyone wants all of his or her friends and relatives to experience faithful, reciprocal love.

But there is not a way within the Catholic tradition to affirm homosexual behavior. And a significant body of experiential and empirical literature indicates that this behavior regularly harms persons in the ways Christian insights portend. The Catholic position is thus a function of its love and compassion for human beings.

In what follows, I will first describe how Catholic teaching on same-sex behavior is a function of the Church's adherence to Christian love. That is, the Church says no as a means of safeguarding a yes to the love God intends for us. I will also reference a fair amount of early Christian material as a source of help for answering contemporary questions, but not to the point of undertaking a full theological explication of the Church's position. I referenced less of this early material in my above discussions of nonmarital sex, contraception, and abortion because contemporary Catholic communications on these subjects are better developed and more convincing. On the matter of same-sex relations, however, Catholic communications today are too thin and unpersuasive in my view. Furthermore, the rejection of Catholic teaching on same-sex relations is regularly vehement, not only because the teaching is considered unloving, but often also because it is claimed to be a misreading of scripture and nature. Consequently, this subject requires more discussion of scripture and early Church sources than the other subjects taken up in this chapter.

I should note here that this chapter does not contain pastoral advice for dialoguing with persons experiencing same-sex attraction, or their families, or members of a particular Catholic community passionately interested in the issue. This is not because pastoral skills and encounters are not absolutely crucial. They are. It is, rather, because the book focuses on Catholic institutions' meeting the legal and communications challenges arising when sexual expression laws burden their religious freedom. Consequently, my advice can seem "cold." But please bear in mind that this advice is no substitute for "warm" pastoral encounters and dialogue. It serves a different purpose, even as some of my thoughts might well be helpful in the context of such a personal dialogue.

For those seeking guidance about pastoral conversations, I cannot do better than to recommend a book that has been an invaluable guide to me in the course of this difficult work: Rev. Louis J. Cameli's *Catholic Teaching on Homosexuality: New Paths to Understanding*.[61] I believe

---

61 Rev. Louis J. Cameli, *Catholic Teaching on Homosexuality: New Paths to Understanding* (Notre Dame, Ind.: Ave Maria Press, 2012).

his work is unparalleled in this regard. At the same time, Father Cameli's work also informed this book's central thrust with his wisdom that Catholic teaching about homosexuality is inseparable from its thinking about human sexuality in toto, and with his conclusion that all of the Church's teaching about the latter is not about preserving "purity" for its own sake, but rather about affirming and fathoming the deeper meaning of our human lives and the identity of God, in whose image we are made. Thus, he writes that the "dynamics of sexuality . . . are co-extensive with our humanity,"[62] and "embedded in human sexuality is the image of God."[63] These "dynamics" include connection, claiming and being claimed, and giving life. This is the pattern of the life, ministry, death, and resurrection of Jesus Christ.[64] It is also, therefore, the pattern of our own lives. All Church teachings about human sexuality seek to preserve this full complement of dynamics in every sexual choice. Father Cameli explains how this informs not only Catholic teaching concerning homosexuality, but also Catholic teaching about masturbation, pornography, nonmarital sex, and so forth. Each lacks some necessary element that would express and strengthen our own humanity and understanding of God. In sum, Father Cameli writes, the Church's teachings about sex, including about homosexuality, should not be understood as a purity code, but as protection against "the substitution of the sexual for the spiritual, a form of idolatry combined with egoism."[65] This perspective sets the table for a drastically improved understanding of everything the Church has said about same-sex relations, especially in connection with St. Paul's letter to the Romans.

I turn now to the matter of how Catholic teaching concerning homosexuality is a function of the Church's understanding of the demands of Christian love. I would urge a Catholic institution to begin any public explanation by reminding listeners that the pattern of adult, romantic love scripture repeatedly proposes is the male-female relationship, capable of one-flesh union and the procreation of children. As described in chapter 6, the Old and New Testaments state

---

62 Cameli, 60.
63 Cameli, 55.
64 Cameli, 52.
65 Cameli, 47.

that this is the relationship—bride-bridegroom—that best reveals not only God's love for us, but how we are to love Him and one another. Catholic theology also sees in marriage a means of glimpsing God's trinitarian existence: in the permanent, interpenetrating bond of life-giving love between the three Persons; in the procession of the Holy Spirit from both the Father and the Son; in the simultaneous union and distinctiveness of the three; and in the essentially relational "being" of each of the three Persons. To wit, the Father is the Father in His relation to the Son, and so forth.[66]

It is only in this context—God's design for love—that one can understand the Church's rejection of sexual relations that do not pursue that design. God fashions human love to involve a going out to an other, and a receiving of an other, in an exchange of gifts that leads to a new life demanding mutual care and exceptional sacrifice. Sexual acts lacking this pattern will lead to a different understanding of love and of the human person herself. They will foster a different relationship with God. The Congregation for the Doctrine of the Faith (CDF) refers to same-sex relations, therefore, as "thwart[ing] the call to a life of that form of self-giving which the Gospel says is the essence of Christian living," while noting also that same-sex-attracted persons can obviously be "generous and giving of themselves" in other ways.[67] This echoes Cameli's observations about the relationship between sexual acts, God's intentions for the human person, and God's own identity.

Pope Francis's Congregation for Catholic Education,[68] as well as several contemporary theologians, further unpack what the CDF has written. The CDF stated that denying God's fundamental, two-sexed structure of love, wherein each person is "completed by the one who is *other than self*," easily impairs our understanding of "being" as intrinsically relational and creative.[69] The theologian Livio Melina writes

---

66 See Marc Cardinal Ouellet, *Divine Likeness: Toward a Trinitarian Anthropology of the Family* (Grand Rapids: Eerdmans, 2006), 31–34; Margaret McCarthy, "'Something Not to Be Grasped': Notes on Equality on the Occasion of the Twentieth Anniversary of *Mulieris Dignitatem*," *Ave Maria Law Review* 8, no. 1 (Fall 2009): 121–52.

67 Congregation for the Doctrine of the Faith, *Letter to the Bishops of the Catholic Church on the Pastoral Care of Homosexual Persons*, October 1, 1986, 7.

68 Congregation for Catholic Education, *"Male and Female He Created Them": Towards a Path of Dialogue on the Question of Gender Theory in Education* (2019), http://www.educatio.va/content/dam/cec/Documenti/19_0997_INGLESE.pdf.

69 Congregation for Catholic Education, 31.

that same-sex relations tend to obscure human understanding of the person as primarily receptive vis-à-vis God, including receptive of his or her own nature and of children.[70] According to the theologian Deborah Savage in her consideration of John Paul II's "spousal meaning of the body," the man-woman relationship and their union and creativity reveal that "our sexuality exists more for the sake of others than for ourselves. . . . We are meant to live lives of self-giving."[71] The Congregation for Catholic Education observes similarly that the human being "becomes himself only with the other" in "dialogue," and through the "authentic gift of []self."[72] And Melina adds that opposite-sex relations teach us that every person is limited and has a vocation to go out of himself or herself to love another, who is in some important respect different from him or her.[73]

Same-sex pairings, however, obscure these aspects of created human nature and even suggest the opposite due to the absence of difference, union, and the possibility of children as a definitive, embodied future. Louis Cameli observes that rejecting the normativity and significance of opposite-sex relations can boost our ego's existing inclination to hate the loss of self that is implied by unity with another person, and it can encourage instead valuing erotic pleasure for oneself. This countermands God's design of human sexuality to bring about connection, claiming and being claimed, and the creation of new life.[74]

In short, the overriding Catholic message on same-sex behaviors is the same as that concerning cohabitation and contraception: such behaviors are prohibited in order to safeguard the love, freedom, happiness, dignity, self-knowledge, and grasp of God's identity that God intended humans to experience. The 1986 statement of the CDF

---

70 Msgr. Livio Melina, "Homosexual Inclination as an 'Objective Disorder': Reflections of Theological Anthropology," in *Living the Truth in Love: Pastoral Approaches to Same-Sex Attraction*, ed. Janet E. Smith and Rev. Paul Check (San Francisco: Ignatius Press, 2015), 138–39.

71 Deborah Savage, "At the Heart of the Matter: Lived Experience in St. John Paul II's Integral Account of the Person," in Smith and Check, *Living the Truth in Love*, 96.

72 Congregation for Catholic Education, *"Male and Female He Created Them,"* 32–33.

73 Melina, "Homosexual Inclination as an 'Objective Disorder,'" 135.

74 Rev. Louis J. Cameli, *The Bible on the Question of Homosexuality* (Notre Dame, Ind.: Ave Maria Press, 2012), 47, citing Gerald G. May, *Will and Spirit: A Contemplative Psychology* (San Francisco: Harper & Row, 1982), 158–59; see also Melina, "Homosexual Inclination as an 'Objective Disorder,'" 136.

says this explicitly. It concludes that sexual behaviors that do not accord with the "creative wisdom of God" prevent persons from attaining their "own fulfillment and happiness," their "personal freedom and dignity realistically and authentically understood."[75] Thus the "Church can never be so callous" respecting what humans deserve, as to affirm same-sex relations.[76]

Before looking at scripture and early Christianity, I offer a few brief notes about *tone* in the context of the most frequent explosive clashes over same-sex relations: employment disputes. While no one should assume naively that even the most careful attention to tone will surely avoid an ugly backlash, there are some practices that constitute a good faith effort to demonstrate love and fairness. First, Catholic institutions should continue a practice they have rightly shown themselves very willing to engage in: offering personal words of thanks for the past service of an employee who has been let go from the institution and the assurance that the institution affirms God's love of, and invitation to, every single human being. Second, before the institution speaks about the sexual responsibility norm at issue and how its application manifests the love of Christ, it should say two things: one, that the Christian pattern of adult romantic love applies to and is challenging for *everyone*, both for same- and opposite-sex-attracted persons; and two, that even the New Testament's clearest rejection of homosexuality occurs in the context of a reminder that all of us are sinners and must avoid "self-righteous" condemnation of others (Romans 2:1).[77]

Turning now to Catholic teaching as it comes to us from the New Testament and early Christianity, one first notes that despite the remarkable diversity between the epochs in which different parts of scripture were authored, it has demonstrated "clear consistency" on the issue of homosexual behavior.[78] The Church's position is not based upon "isolated phrases or facile theological argument, but on the solid foundation of a constant Biblical testimony."[79] The theologian

---

75 Congregation for the Doctrine of the Faith, *Pastoral Care of Homosexual Persons*, 7 (emphasis added).

76 Congregation for the Doctrine of the Faith, 9.

77 Richard B. Hays, *The Moral Vision of the New Testament: A Contemporary Introduction to New Testament Ethics* (San Francisco: HarperSanFrancisco, 1996), 388–89.

78 Congregation for the Doctrine of the Faith, *Pastoral Care of Homosexual Persons*, 5.

79 Congregation for the Doctrine of the Faith, 5.

Richard Hays adds that there is not a "single early Christian text" that approves homosexual activity.[80] Rather, "though only a few biblical texts speak of homoerotic activity, all that do mention it express unqualified disapproval."[81]

New Testament and early Christian texts continued Judaism's rejection of same-sex relations, but also introduced innovative elements. Regarding continuity, Richard Hays interprets Paul's references to "nature" in Romans 1:16–32 as an application of a "commonplace feature" of the rejection of homosexual relations as not being in accord with God's design, a feature included by Greek and Hellenistic Jewish philosophers like Philo and Josephus.[82] Paul's writing is also in harmony with the references to same-sex behaviors in Leviticus 18:22 and 20:13 and with the story of Sodom and Gomorrah at Genesis 19:1–29. While the latter story was first interpreted as depicting corruption and the refusal of hospitality to strangers, by the second century BC, it was understood in Judaism as referring to sexual corruption.[83] The CDF's 1986 document on homosexuality also understands the story as a moral judgment against same-sex relations.[84]

During Jesus's ministry, He described God's creative intentions for sexual relations by articulating the norm of opposite-sex relations intended for a permanent, faithful, procreative, one-flesh union (Mt 10:6 and 19:4). Later, Paul addressed same-sex relations directly in his letters to the Romans and the Corinthians, and to Timothy. It is also possible that the author of Acts included a rejection of same-sex relations as part of the "minimum" rules under which Christianity was to be extended to the Gentiles (Acts 15:20). When the Gentiles are instructed to "avoid pollution from idols, unlawful marriage, the meat of strangled animals, and blood," the reference to avoiding *"porneia"* may have been inclusive of all Christian sexual norms.[85]

---

80 Richard B. Hays, "Relations Natural and Unnatural: A Response to John Boswell's Exegesis of Romans 1," *The Journal of Religious Ethics* 14, no. 1 (1986): 184–215, 202.

81 Hays, *The Moral Vision of the New Testament*, 389.

82 Hays, "Relations Natural and Unnatural," 194.

83 Innocent Himbaza, Adren Schenker, and Jean-Baptiste Edart, *The Bible on the Question of Homosexuality*, trans. Benedict M. Guevin OSB (Washington, D.C.: The Catholic University of America Press, 2011), 12–13.

84 Congregation for the Doctrine of the Faith, *Pastoral Care of Homosexual Persons*, 6.

85 Hays, *The Moral Vision of the New Testament*, 383.

In his first letter to the Corinthians, Paul stated that, among other persons (i.e., fornicators, idolaters, adulterers, boy prostitutes, thieves, the greedy, drunkards, slanderers, and robbers), practicing homosexuals would not "inherit the kingdom" (1 Cor 6:9–10). In Timothy (1 Tm 1:9–10), while considering the need to apply law to the "lawless and unruly," Paul included the "godless and sinful, the unholy and profane, those who kill their fathers or mothers, murderers, the unchaste, sodomites, kidnapers, liars, perjurers, and whatever else is opposed to sound teaching."

Paul's letter to the Romans, however, contains the New Testament's most extensive treatment of the subject. According to the US Conference of Catholic Bishops, it denounces homosexual sex in the context of "Paul's aims to show that all humanity is in a desperate plight and requires God's special intervention if it is to be saved."[86] Paul's letter states:

> The wrath of God is indeed being revealed from heaven against every impiety and wickedness of those who suppress the truth by their wickedness. For what can be known about God is evident to them, because God made it evident to them. Ever since the creation of the world, his invisible attributes of eternal power and divinity have been able to be understood and perceived in what he has made. As a result, they have no excuse; for although they knew God they did not accord him glory as God or give him thanks. Instead, they became vain in their reasoning, and their senseless minds were darkened. While claiming to be wise, they became fools and exchanged the glory of the immortal God for the likeness of an image of mortal man or of birds or of four-legged animals or of snakes. Therefore, God handed them over to impurity through the lusts of their hearts for the mutual degradation of their bodies. They exchanged the truth of God for a lie and revered and worshiped the creature rather than the creator, who is blessed forever. Amen. Therefore, God handed them over to degrading passions. Their females exchanged natural relations for unnatural, and the males likewise gave up natural relations

---

86   US Conference of Catholic Bishops, Commentary on Romans 1:18–3:20, https://bible.usccb.org/bible/romans/1.

with females and burned with lust for one another. Males did shameful things with males and thus received in their own persons the due penalty for their perversity. And since they did not see fit to acknowledge God, God handed them over to their undiscerning mind to do what is improper. (Rom 1:18–32)

There are innumerable books and scholarly articles devoted to this passage. Because, however, my focus remains on communicating the essence of Catholic teaching to courts of law and public opinion during religious freedom disputes, I will concentrate narrowly upon how it understands homosexual relations in the context of God's design for human love.

In this passage of Romans, Paul writes that same-sex relations *follow* a refusal to acknowledge God as creator. This refusal then obscures humans' understanding and leads to people debasing themselves, even as they intend to glorify themselves. God "hands over" these persons to their own inclinations, which do not lead to freedom, but rather to a kind of slavery to their desires.[87]

While Paul names many sins that flow from denying God's creative sovereignty, same-sex relations are highlighted as a particularly apt image of this denial. Richard Hays calls them a particularly "vivid *image* of humanity's primal rejection of the sovereignty of God the creator."[88] The CDF writes that Paul is "at a loss" to find a clearer example of humanity's "disharmony" with God.[89]

Paul's teaching was not a cultural artifact of his world. Romans ridiculed passive homosexual partners and disapproved of pedophiles, but they approved some homosexual relations depending upon the participants' social status. Paul, however, makes *no* distinctions according to social status and explicitly uses terms showing a rejection not only of pedophilia or prostitution or playing the passive role, but of the entire activity of *arsenokoitai* for men, which literally means "sleeping with a man."[90] Paul also rejects same-sex relations between

---

87 Hays, *The Moral Vision of the New Testament*, 383–85; Himbaza, Schenker, and Edart, *The Bible on the Question of Homosexuality*, 98–103.

88 Hays, "Relations Natural and Unnatural," 191 (emphasis in original).

89 Congregation for the Doctrine of the Faith, *Pastoral Care of Homosexual Persons*, 6.

90 Himbaza, Schenker, and Edart, *The Bible on the Question of Homosexuality*, 77. See also Sarah Ruden, *Paul Among the People: The Apostle Reinterpreted and Reimagined in His Own Time* (New York: Image, 2010), 66–67.

women, a subject never before addressed in Roman literature.[91] In short, the Christian standard was not about social hierarchy or even the protection of children from pedophiles, but about God's divine plan for a permanent, faithful, fruitful union of a man and a woman in order to communicate the *imago Dei* and the meaning of love.

For critics of the Catholic position, all of the above remains insufficient. They will suggest that same-sex relations based upon consent—especially longer-term relationships—require a reevaluation of the Catholic position. This is an important question that deserves an answer, especially because—as then Cardinal Ratzinger frequently noted—Catholics hold that their beliefs will have a "correspondence with basic insights of human reason, albeit these insights have been purified, deepened and broadened through contact with the way of faith."[92]

The following discussion asks whether reason can verify Catholic teaching on this point. Is it possible that sexual relations that are not characterized by a one-flesh union across differences, and lacking procreation out of love, might also meet the creator's intentions for human love? The material discussed below suggests that the answer is no.

Allow me first, however, to suggest here that this discussion could benefit from more and better material than we presently have in order to achieve a full picture of the lives of men and women engaged in same-sex relations. We need a robust, highly intelligent, and honest dialogue, free of the intense pressures of the secular powers that be—and even of sometimes toxic intra-Church politics—that will grapple with *all* of the elements of the *reality* of same-sex attraction and behavior. Prominent Catholic voices who often write and speak elliptically in favor of same-sex relations would be performing a tremendous service—to the Church, to same-sex-attracted individuals, and to the common good—if they would agree to participate and encourage other fair-minded people to join such an extended, 360-degree conversation.

---

91 Kyle Harper, *From Shame to Sin: The Christian Transformation of Sexual Morality in Late Antiquity* (Cambridge, Mass.: Harvard University Press, 2013), 95, 99.

92 Joseph Cardinal Ratzinger, "The Church's Teaching Authority—Faith—Morals," in Heinz Schürmann, Joseph Cardinal Ratzinger, and Hans Urs von Balthasar, *Principles of Christian Morality*, trans. Graham Harrison (San Francisco: Ignatius Press, 1986), 45–73, 72.

On the basis of the material we presently have, however, I believe it makes sense to echo the conclusion reached by Richard Hays that it is doubtful at best that the current state of same-sex relations could meet Christian standards for adult romantic love. Hays arrives at this conclusion after reflecting upon his conversations with a close friend who succumbed to AIDS after being involved in same-sex relationships for twenty years. Hays characterizes his friend's experiences as sobering. Together they grappled with the fact that although some same-sex- attracted persons report that they find their relationships positive and loving, Hays's friend found same-sex attraction "complex" and often "tragic," involving sensations of "compulsion" and "affliction." His friend related that he found it a "hindrance to living [a life] committed to the service of God,"[93] and expressed anger at the LGBTQ community's push to "shift the ground of their identity subtly and idolatrously away from God."[94] Cameli would call this a substitution of the sexual for the spiritual—a setting aside of our true identity in God in favor of a limited, human-fashioned identity comprised primarily of our sexual interests.

Current qualitative and quantitative data tends to affirm Catholic theological insights, although one should be very careful not to cherry-pick studies or to make unnuanced statements. As noted above, a great deal more honest research and dialogue about same-sex attraction is warranted. Still, it is possible to say that the experience of same-sex relations is often associated with difficulties and dangers that undercut and destabilize the union between the partners and the well-being of any children involved. Here we must remind ourselves that opposite-sex relations regularly fall short of God's hopes for human love. Yet, their very structure better enables the partners to not only understand God's intentions for human life, but also to cultivate the love, dignity, happiness, freedom, and security that both the adults and children need.

We begin with some aspects of same-sex relations that point away from the presence of true union. Reliable data indicates that compared to opposite-sex couples, same-sex couples are disproportionately

93 Hays, *The Moral Vision of the New Testament*, 379, 399.
94 Hays, 379.

more likely to cohabit and less likely to marry.[95] They are also far more likely to engage in infidelity (and thus dramatically more likely to transmit sexual infections),[96] and far more likely to suffer violence within the partnership.[97] Same-sex marriages also dissolve at far higher rates than opposite-sex marriages, particularly among female pairs.[98] One study showed that same-sex couples (cohabiting and married combined) experienced a 3.1 times higher dissolution rate than opposite-sex cohabiting couples, and an 11.5 times higher chance of dissolution as compared to opposite-sex married couples.[99] The higher dissolution rate among females is very consequential for children given that married female households are dramatically more likely than male households to contain children (27 percent as compared to 9 percent).[100] One 2019 study in the US showed that 62 percent of young adults living in economically privileged lesbian households had experienced the dissolution of their parents' relationship; in the case of opposite-sex marriages, such couples are the least likely to dissolve.[101] In a 2020 study of 1.2 million children in

95 David Masci, Anna Brown, and Jocelyn Kiley, "5 Facts about Same-Sex Marriage," *Pew Research Center Fact-Tank*, June 24, 2019, https://www.pewresearch.org/fact-tank/2019/06/24/same-sex-marriage/.

96 See, e.g., Michael Shernoff, "Negotiated Nonmonogamy and Male Couples," *Family Process* 45, no. 4 (2006): 407–18, https://doi.org/10.1111/j.1545-5300.2006.00179.x. See also The Centers for Disease Control, "Sexually Transmitted Disease Surveillance, 2019," https://www.cdc.gov/std/statistics/2019/overview.htm (indicating that, in the case of some diseases, rates of transmission of sexually transmitted infections among men who have sex with men are up to forty-two times higher than the rates of infection among men who have sex with women).

97 Shanna N. Felix et al., "Lesbian, Gay and Bisexual Victims' Reporting Behaviors to Informal and Formal Sources," *Sexuality Research and Social Policy* 18, no. 2 (2021): 281–89; CDC National Center for Injury Prevention and Control, Division of Violence Prevention, "An Overview of 2010 Findings on Victimization by Sexual Orientation" (2010), https://www.cdc.gov/violenceprevention/pdf/cdc_nisvs_victimization_final-a.pdf.

98 Joseph Rauch, "The Mental Health Issues Lesbian Women Cope With," *Talkspace*, June 24, 2016, https://www.talkspace.com/blog/mental-health-issues-lesbian-women-cope/; "Why Lesbian Couples are More Likely to Divorce than Gay Ones," *Economist*, January 11, 2020.

99 Matthijs Kalmijn, Anneke Loeve, and Dorien Manting, "Income Dynamics in Couples and the Dissolution of Marriage and Cohabitation," *Demography* 44, no. 1 (2007): 159–79, 170.

100 Brian Glassman, US Census Bureau website, "Same-Sex Married Couples Have Higher Income than Opposite-Sex Married Couples," September 17, 2020, https://www.census.gov/library/stories/2020/09/same-sex-married-couples-have-higher-income-than-opposite-sex-married-couples.html.

101 Audrey S. Koh et al., "Predictors of Mental Health in Emerging Adult Offspring of Lesbian-Parent Families," *Journal of Lesbian Studies* 23, no. 2 (2019): 257–78, 257–58.

the Netherlands, 55 percent of children living with same-sex parents (mostly female couples) had experienced their parents' separation, as compared to 19 percent of children in opposite-sex households.[102]

Taken together—although more information would help to complete the picture—the above data point to same-sex-attracted persons having, on average, more difficulty in forming and sustaining relationships. Qualitative accounts illustrate this further. In a lengthy 2006 account of his attempt to construct a healthy, committed gay relationship, Catholic writer Ronald Lee painted a vivid picture of an environment that depersonalized and objectified men, and featured a great deal of obsession, addiction, substance abuse, loneliness, and depression. He referred to it as a "laissez faire free sexual market of the most Darwinian sort." Lee condemned whitewashed pictures of the lifestyle of gay men as having "almost nothing in it about the real lives of real homosexuals."[103]

A 2017 account in the intensely pro–LGBTQ rights *Huffington Post* paints a nearly identical picture of a Darwinian marketplace. Entitled "The Epidemic of Gay Loneliness,"[104] it portrays male homosexual milieux as prone to substance abuse, loneliness, depression, suicide, and suicidal ideation. Sex without intimacy seems more accessible than good friendships and social support: "You go from your mom's house to a gay club where a lot of people are on drugs and it's like, this is my community? It's like the f*king jungle." "I felt like a piece of meat."

While the author theorizes that promiscuity, drug abuse, and depression are a function of the stress of belonging to a minority or of gay men reenacting the bullying they once experienced, he also attributes these to excessive masculinity within the relationship: "Gay men are sh*ty to each other because, basically, we're men." "The challenges of masculinity get magnified in a community of men" because "masculinity is precarious. It has to be constantly enacted or defended or collected."

---

102 Deni Mazrekaj, Kristof De Witte, and Sofie Cabus, "School Outcomes of Children Raised by Same-Sex Parents: Evidence from Administrative Panel Data," *American Sociological Review* 85, no. 5 (2020): 830–56, 839.

103 Ronald G. Lee, "The Truth about the Homosexual Rights Movement: The Books Were a Front for the Porn," *New Oxford Review* 73, no. 2 (February 2006), https://www.newoxfordreview.org/documents/the-truth-about-the-homosexual-rights-movement-2/.

104 Michael Hobbes, "The Epidemic of Gay Loneliness," *Huffington Post*, March 2, 2017, https://highline.huffingtonpost.com/articles/en/gay-loneliness/.

A widely cited study claiming to support the theory that the dispro-portionate rates of illness and death that LGBTQ individuals expe-rience are largely a function of social biases was recently retracted because its key finding was found to be the result of a coding error. In reality, social stigma did not contribute to mortality in sexual minori-ties among the cohort studied.[105]

In sum, based upon the available information, it appears that same-sex unions suffer a deficit of the characteristics of permanent, faithful union for which God designed His daughters and sons. The gap between the creator's intentions and the human experience of love in connection with same-sex relations is also evident when the matter of children's well-being is brought into the frame, as it must be. The creation and education of children is an inseparable part of God's intention for adult romantic love. But the most credibly conducted research concludes that children in same-sex households experience problematic outcomes. Below, I consider how this unfolds.

First, although Christianity puts the creation, nurture, and well-be-ing of children at the heart of adult romantic love, alongside the couple's union, same-sex marriage proponents achieved state-rec-ognized marriage precisely by arguing that children are *extraneous* to adult romantic relations—that is, that there is nothing special about procreative couples that could possibly lead a state to take a special interest in the duration and stability of opposite-sex unions as compared to nonprocreative, same-sex unions. Rather, they argued, marriage is 100 percent about adults' civil-rights interests in gain-ing public approval of their unions as homosexual persons and their interests in the private satisfactions and state subsidies that accom-pany marital commitment. The Supreme Court agreed. Proponents thus engineered the Supreme Court's essentially anti-child holding in *Obergefell* that *no* state is allowed to value procreation more than its impossibility, and *no* state may value maintaining children's relations with the adults who procreated them more than it values severing children's relations with one or both natural parents in households headed by adults of the same sex.

---

105 See Mark L. Hatzenbuehler et al., "RETRACTED: Structural Stigma and All-Cause Mortality in Sexual Minority Populations," *Social Science & Medicine* 103 (February 2014): 33–41, 33 (stating that the "authors discovered an error in the study which, once corrected, rendered the association between structural stigma and mortality risk no longer statistically significant in the sample of 914 sexual minorities").

Second, physically severing children from their parents appears to harm children in the long run. The Christian pattern of adult romantic love takes strength and affirmation from nature's physically uniting the parents in the child's genetic makeup and from the parents' natural inclinations to care for their offspring. It also harmonizes with evidence that parents provide different gifts to children.[106] Same-sex parenting not only lacks these features, but suffers additional intrinsic disadvantages. Same-sex households with children regularly contain children born of a heterosexual relationship previously conducted by one of the adults; thus, the children are separated from a natural parent and living in a different family configuration. Some children in same-sex households were conceived with new reproductive technologies. These involved gamete donations or purchases and sometimes surrogate mothers. All are fraught with the potential for strife between the adults involved, and, in the case of surrogacy, with possible physical and psychological harm to surrogates.[107] Every child in a same-sex household is removed from one or both natural parents and from opposite-sex parenting that would otherwise teach him or her to "recognise the value and the beauty of the differences between the two sexes, along with their equal dignity, and their reciprocity at a biological, functional, psychological and social level."[108]

The difficulties such children experience should not surprise observers, according to sociologist Mark Regnerus. Prior to the same-sex marriage movement, it was well accepted that children benefit from ongoing relations with their biological parents because of their genetic connection to both parents and because of the sexually complementary parenting available to them. Children suffer, relatively speaking, when these advantages are lost. The benefits from ongoing relations with biological parents are measured especially by comparison with children's outcomes in step and adoptive households.[109] This is because household instability is a well-documented

---

106 See, e.g., Catherine Pakaluk and Joseph Price, "Are Mothers and Fathers Interchangeable Caregivers?" *Marriage & Family Review* 56, no. 8 (2020): 784–793.

107 Jennifer Lahl, "Babies for Sale," *First Things*, May 22, 2020, https://www.firstthings.com/web-exclusives/2020/05/babies-for-sale.

108 Congregation for Catholic Education, "*Male and Female He Created Them*," 38.

109 Mark Regnerus, "Understanding How the Social Scientific Study of Same-Sex Parenting Works," *Roczniki Nauk Społecznych*, Poland (English title: *Annals of Social Science*) 48, no. 3 (2020): 43–60, 46, https://doi.org/10.18290/rns20483-3. Of course, this is not

and crucial pathway by which children come to experience different levels of well-being.

But same-sex households are more unstable than opposite-sex households, as described above. A 2020 study looking at nationally representative datasets for the US and Canada even suggested that having children tends to *de*-stabilize same-sex but *stabilize* opposite-sex couples. Dissolution rates for same-sex couples were far higher (by a factor of two to five times) when they had children, and were five times the rate of opposite-sex couples with children.[110]

Thus, it should be expected that the loss of biological connections and sexual differentiation will matter in same-sex households. The evidence suggests that it does. The work of Regnerus and others shows that children reared in same-sex households suffer emotional and other difficulties at higher rates than children reared by their married, biological parents.[111]

How then are there so many studies claiming "no differences" between children reared in same-sex and opposite-sex households? Regnerus summarizes the answer: the "alleged scientific consensus is the result of early and methodologically-limited evaluations that formed a politically expedient narrative."[112] Translating this, the first point to be made is that supporters of same-sex unions use a technique that "factors out" or "controls for" a crucial vehicle by which same-sex households create problems for children—their greater instability. In this way the data is easily manipulated to reach the conclusion that children in same-sex households fare no differently than children in opposite-sex households.

Second, as chronicled by Regnerus, advocates of same-sex unions regularly rely on other faulty research techniques to reach the

---

in the least intended to disparage caring for children who need parents by means of adoption; rather, it criticizes laws *intending to create* households where any children present will always be separated from one or both natural parents.

110 Douglas Allen and Joseph Price, "Stability Rates of Same-Sex Couples: With and Without Children," *Marriage & Family Review* 56, no. 1 (2020): 51–71, 60–62.

111 Mark Regnerus, "How Different Are the Adult Children of Parents Who Have Same-Sex Relationships? Findings from the New Family Structures Study," *Social Science Research* 41, no. 4 (2012): 752–70; Corinne Reczek et al., "Family Structure and Child Health: Does the Sex Composition of Parents Matter?," *Demography* 53, no. 5 (2016): 1605–30.

112 Regnerus, "Understanding How the Social Scientific Study of Same-Sex Parenting Works," 47.

conclusion that children living in same-sex households have identical or even better outcomes than children reared with their biological parents. They use small and unrepresentative or nonrandom samples, permit self-selection of willing participants who have a prior awareness of a study's goal, or use parents' subjective reports rather than objective facts gathered about children. All of these undermine the validity of these studies' conclusions.[113]

This brief review of the currently available data on same-sex households indicates that the absence of the Christian pattern of love—involving union across differences leading to procreation—matters. It matters both for the adults involved and for their children's experience of freedom, dignity, and happiness.

In conclusion, when expressing their refusal to cooperate with same-sex behaviors, including same-sex marriage, Catholic institutions might communicate: *No one should be surprised that a Christian teaching about human love defers to the word of God, accepts His created design, and is demanding. All Christian teachings about love share these traits. Regarding same-sex relations, Catholics adhere to the pattern of adult romantic love that the creator designed for human beings, which involves two sexes with differences meant to create the conditions for a communion of persons who make a sincere gift of self that is procreative, and whose union and fidelity is meant to express the radical love of Christ on the cross. On its face, this pattern is uniquely capable of reminding us that we are limited as human beings and made for going out of ourselves, across differences, in relationships involving the giving and receiving of different gifts. From these relationships new life emerges and children find homes that best respond to their vulnerabilities and protect their futures. This pattern is made by God and therefore somewhat mysterious to us, but is not ours to overthrow no matter how much the Church will suffer for standing by it. This pattern has been supported and taught by the Church for two millennia. Currently available scientific and experiential data support its wisdom. They indicate that the absence of complementary union and procreation in same-sex relations cause suffering both for the adults and the children involved. But the Church is always and sincerely ready to welcome and accompany all persons and would welcome a complete and honest discussion with persons experiencing same-sex attraction.*

113 Regnerus, 48–56.

Transgender Drugs and Surgeries

THE CURRENT SITUATION

The notion that a person should be free to self-define a sexual identity, regardless of the person's actual sex, and has the right to pursue body modification—using drugs or surgeries—in order to align body and identity, is sweeping the nation. This observation is not the least bit histrionic.

The two root beliefs underlying this phenomenon are the claim that human beings must possess the autonomy to reject even their given, biological reality as male or female in favor of a self-defined sexual identity *and* that they have the correlative right to obtain "affirming" medical and surgical interventions on demand. Sometimes these beliefs follow an experience that the current medical establishment labels "gender dysphoria," defined by the American Psychiatric Association as the distress caused by a mismatch between a person's self-perceived identity ("gender identity") and his or her sexed body.[114] But sometimes they do not—autonomy with respect to sexual identity is the underlying demand.

About one million persons or 0.003 of the US population today identify themselves as trans, gender-diverse, or gender nonconforming.[115] This figure has climbed steadily since at least 2007, with cases skyrocketing among adolescents and young adults. In 2017, the Centers for Disease Control reported that nearly 2 percent of teens identified as transgender.[116] A more recent study in one urban school district (Pittsburgh) found that 10 percent of high schoolers identified as trans or gender-diverse.[117]

---

114 American Psychiatric Association website, "Help with Gender Dysphoria," November 2020, https://www.psychiatry.org/patients-families/gender-dysphoria.

115 Esther L. Meerwijk and Jae M. Sevelius, "Transgender Population Size in the United States: A Meta-Regression of Population-Based Probability Samples," *American Journal of Public Health* 107, no. 2 (2017): e1–e8, e1.

116 Michelle M. Johns et al., "Transgender Identity and Experiences of Violence Victimization, Substance Use, Suicide Risk, and Sexual Risk Behaviors Among High School Students—19 States and Large Urban School Districts, 2017," *Morbidity and Mortality Weekly Report* 68, no. 3 (January 25, 2019), 67–71, https://www.cdc.gov/mmwr/volumes/68/wr/mm6803a3.htm.

117 Kacie M. Kidd et al., "Prevalence of Gender-Diverse Youth in an Urban School District," *Pediatrics* 147, no. 6 (June 2021), https://doi.org/10.1542/peds.2020-049823.

Many who identify as transgender will seek medical intervention, including puberty blockers, cross-sex hormones for children as young as thirteen or fourteen, surgery to remove male- or female-associated body parts, and a lifetime of hormone treatments to maintain changes in sexual appearance.

The rise in cases of transgender identification and the demand for drugs and surgeries to affirm the patient's desired identity legally impact Catholic institutions in ways that are similar but not identical to same-sex marriage because both involve conduct that clashes with Catholic norms. Increasingly, state and federal laws and rules are interpreting or amending existing laws to forbid adverse decisions on the basis of a person's gender identity with respect to employment, public accommodations, housing, and education. Such laws may cover educational facilities, including housing, bathrooms, and dressing rooms. Insurance laws might require coverage of, and health care providers might be required to provide, gender-affirming drugs and surgeries.

THE RAP AGAINST THE CHURCH
AND SUGGESTED RESPONSES

Critics of the Church have generally acceded to the idea that a person's sexual identity is determined by his or her subjective belief, and not by his or her actual sex. Critics also seem to believe that a loving response to a person's subjective belief requires cooperation with it. They certainly don't see any harm in such cooperation. Thus, when Catholic institutions refuse to affirm a transgender identity, they are mostly lambasted as "cruel," and only occasionally as "unscientific."

The Catholic response is a mix of scripture in very close dialogue with reason. Its most complete presentation appears in a 2019 document issued by Pope Francis's Congregation for Catholic Education,[118] although it is also treated in *Amoris Laetitia* and *Laudato Si'*.[119] Like all Catholic engagement with the subject, it begins with the demand that persons suffering gender dysphoria be treated without any unjust discrimination and with tremendous compassion given how complex

---

118 Congregation for Catholic Education, *"Male and Female He Created Them."*

119 Francis, Post-Synodal Apostolic Exhortation *Amoris Laetitia* (March 19, 2016), 56; Francis, Encyclical Letter *Laudato Si'* (May 24, 2015), 155.

and painful their situation often is.[120] Here it should be mentioned again that not all persons adopting trans identities would claim to have experienced gender dysphoria; rather, many are simply asserting a right to determine their sexual identity free of any relationship to their biological sex.

Catholic institutions need to be prepared for the reality that the punishments meted out to persons disagreeing with the new orthodoxy respecting transgender identity are nothing short of brutal. But reason has not entirely fled the scene. There continues to exist a critical mass of voices who are both respectful of persons claiming a transgender identity but also unwilling to accept the general notion that sexual identity can be subjectively determined; they are thus skeptical about or opposed to medical interventions intended to change a person's secondary sex characteristics. These voices need encouragement.

The Church's response is in three major parts, which again reflects its reliance on both faith and reason. The first emphasizes the sovereignty of God and His decision to create two sexes. The second stresses the link between one's sex and one's sense of dignity, self-understanding, and personal development. And the third concerns the relationship between accepting one's sex and achieving the relationships for which human beings are created. In light of these teachings, it is logical to conclude that cooperating in the denial of a person's sex harms the person in each of these aspects: in their relationship to God, in their individual identity, and in their capacity for intimacy.

Documents of the universal Church on this subject are theologically and philosophically complex. I will do my best to articulate their wisdom using words that Catholic institutions might communicate easily to courts of law and to the court of public opinion.

The first point is rather straightforward. Each human being is made by God and not self-made. Thus, each person should respect what God has made and not "manipulate" human nature "at will."[121] Genesis reminds us that God's design for the two sexes is "good" (Gn 1:21). In the garden, human beings were in complete harmony with their bodies—"naked yet they felt no shame" (Gn 2:25). God has not

---

120 Congregation for Catholic Education, *"Male and Female He Created Them,"* 15, 16.
121 Benedict XVI, "Address of His Holiness Benedict XVI to the Bundestag," September 22, 2011.

fashioned persons with the "wrong" bodies. In the New Testament, Jesus recalls the Genesis account of a two-sexed creation made for a one-flesh union.

The second point is closely related to the first. The sex God gives each person is vital for each person's understanding of herself and her own dignity. It is vital for personal development along the vocational path that God provides. People grow and develop—at the biological, physiological, emotional, and mental levels—in relation to their sex, which conditions to some extent their thoughts, hopes, reflections, memories, relationships, capacities, and interests, among other things.[122] One's sex is also related to spiritual development, given that each person is a unity of body and soul. Human bodies and souls are meant for one another; thus, sex applies to the unified subject.[123] A person's vocation (i.e., God's call and her response), way of life, way of communicating with others, and way of feeling, expressing, and living human love are all inseparable from her sex. It conditions a person's "progress towards maturity and insertion into society."[124]

Testimony from women who felt completely "other" among men even after extended cross-sex treatments testify to the wisdom of these observations. A young woman who reversed her "transition," which she pursued in the belief that it would cure her familial and psychological problems, stated:

> But the further my transition went, the more I realized that I wasn't a man, and never would be. We are told these days that when someone presents with gender dysphoria, this reflects a person's "real" or "true" self, that the desire to change genders is set. But this was not the case for me. As I matured, I recognized that gender dysphoria was a symptom of my overall misery, not its cause.[125]

---

122 Paul C. Vitz, "Men and Women: Their Differences and Their Complementarity; Evidence from Psychology and Neuroscience," in *The Complementarity of Women and Men: Philosophy, Theology, Psychology & Art*, ed. Paul C. Vitz (Washington, D.C.: The Catholic University of America Press, 2021), 182–216.

123 Deborah Savage, "Woman and Man: Identity, Genius, and Mission," in Vitz, *The Complementarity of Women and Men*, 89–131, 105.

124 Congregation for the Doctrine of the Faith, *Persona Humana: Declaration on Certain Questions Concerning Sexual Ethics*, December 29, 1975, I.

125 Keira Bell, "My Story," *Persuasion*, April 7, 2020, https://www.persuasion. community/p/keira-bell-my-story.

This same woman was also quoted in a 2020 court opinion from the UK:

> I started to have my first serious doubts about transition. These doubts were brought on by for the first time really noticing how physically different I am to men as a biological female, despite having testosterone running through my body. There were also a lot of experiences I could not relate to when having conversations with men due to being biologically female and socialised in society as a girl. There was an unspoken "code" a lot of the time that I felt I was missing. . . .
>
> I started to realise that the vision I had as a teenager of becoming male was strictly a fantasy and that it was not possible. My biological make-up was still female and it showed, no matter how much testosterone was in my system or how much I would go to the gym. I was being perceived as a man by society, but it was not enough. I started to just see a woman with a beard, which is what I was. I felt like a fraud and I began to feel more lost, isolated and confused than I did when I was pre-transition.[126]

Medical science confirms that a person's sex is determined from conception and is genetically present in every cell of the person's body.[127] It is also manifested in the person's endocrinology, anatomy, and neurology.[128] Differences between the sexes are thus also manifested in the brain and even in the ways that diseases affect the person.[129] The tiny number of persons born intersex does not falsify

---

126 Bell v. Tavistock and Portman NHS Found. Trust, [2020] EWHC (Admin) 3274 [80–81] (High Court of Justice, Queen's Bench Division).

127 Theresa M. Wizemenn and Mary Lou Pardue, eds., *Exploring the Biological Contributions to Human Health: Does Sex Matter?* (Washington, D.C.: The National Academies Press, 2001), 28, 50, https://pubmed.ncbi.nlm.nih.gov/25057540/. See also, Kalpit Shah, Charles E. McCormick, and Neil E. Bradbury, "Do You Know the Sex of Your Cells?" *American Journal of Physiology: Cell Physiology* 306, no. 1 (2014): C3–C18. https://doi.org/10.1152/ajpcell.00281.2013.

128 See also Larry Cahill, "Why Sex Matters for Neuroscience," *Nature Reviews: Neuroscience* 7, no. 6 (2006): 477–84; Larry Cahill, "His Brain, Her Brain," *Scientific American* 292, no. 5 (2005): 40–47; Doreen Kimura, "Sex Differences in the Brain," *Scientific American* 267, no. 3 (1992): 118–25; Vitz, "Men and Women: Their Differences and Their Complementarity."

129 See J. Budziszewski, "The Meaning of Sexual Differences," in Vitz, *The Complementarity of Women and Men*, 9–34.

this data; and even the typical statements of intersex persons ("I am both or neither sex") and of persons claiming a transgender identity ("I am the other sex") reinforce the reality of sexual differences.[130] One's individual identity is also tied to sex because individuals cannot come to understand who and what they are without the existence of an "other." Psychology robustly confirms this. In the words of the Congregation for Catholic Education: "It is precisely the direct encounter between another 'you' *who is not me* that enables me to recognise the essence of the 'I' who is me. Difference, in fact, is a condition of *all cognition*, including cognition of one's identity."[131]

This applies in particular to the development of children, particularly their need for both a mother and a father to construct their identity. Again, in the words of the Congregation for Catholic Education, "Psychoanalytic theory demonstrates the *tri-polar value* of child-parent relationships, showing that sexual identity can only fully emerge in the light of the synergetic comparison that sexual differentiation creates."[132]

The third crucial function of sexual identity is relationship formation. Catholic teaching speaks about this a great deal. Our sex shapes our relations with all others. It enables the realization of the reciprocity and complementarity between the sexes—not only that which can make new life—but that which can enrich the world at large. It is differences that create the possibility for giving gifts.[133]

Denying sexual differences would preclude marriage and the one-flesh union.[134] It would obscure humans' understanding of God's love for us and ours for him, presented in the Bible as a bride-bridegroom relationship. It may even upend the entire "architecture of the faith," which depends on the existence of both male and female and their interaction.[135] And that depends on understanding sex, marriage, and parenting relationships as pointing beyond themselves to reveal

---

130 Congregation for Catholic Education, *"Male and Female He Created Them,"* 24–25.
131 Congregation for Catholic Education, 26–27 (emphasis in the original).
132 Congregation for Catholic Education, 27.
133 Savage, "Woman and Man: Identity, Genius and Mission," 110.
134 Congregation for Catholic Education, *"Male and Female He Created Them,"* 2, 21, 28, 34.
135 Gerard V. Bradley, "Catholic Schools and Transgender Students," *Public Discourse*, February 9, 2021, https://www.thepublicdiscourse.com/2021/02/73853/.

the identity of God, and of human persons as *imago Dei*—as persons designed for connection across differences, close union, gift-giving, and the generation of new life.

As with same-sex relations, while more scientific research would be extremely helpful, what we know so far harmonizes with what is portended by the theology and reason related to sexual identity; to wit, that the acceptance of the transgender project does not represent love of neighbor, but rather impairs the dignity, health, freedom, and happiness of human persons. It appears, in fact, that the willingness to affirm transgender identity is the result of political and cultural pressure, not the application of sound medical reasoning or well-informed care for the suffering person.

Scientists do not even know what causes gender dysphoria,[136] let alone how to treat it in a way that more likely than not helps a patient. The American Psychiatric Association has acknowledged that there are no highly reliable studies demonstrating the efficacy of transgender "medicine."[137] An important 2020 British case (later, sadly, overturned on appeal) denying the possibility that minors can give informed consent for transgender medical "treatments," observed that "the evidence base for this treatment is as yet highly uncertain."[138] In fact, the evidence suggests that rates of suicide for those who do and those who do not undergo transgender surgeries are roughly the same. A 2011 long-term Swedish study, despite finding *early* improvement in mental health and suicidality among "transitioners," found long-term that their suicide risk was nineteen times higher than the

---

136 Paul W. Hruz, "Deficiencies in Scientific Evidence for Medical Management of Gender Dysphoria," *Linacre Quarterly* 87, no. 1 (2020): 34–42, https://doi.org/10.1177/0024363919873762.

137 The APA Task Force wrote that the "randomized double blind control trial is the study design that affords the highest quality evidence regarding the comparative efficacy of various treatment modalities; however, no such trials have been conducted to address any aspect of the treatment of GID [gender identity disorder]." In spite of the "lack of evidence of the highest quality relevant to the treatment of GID," the APA proceeded to recommend changes based on "clinical consensus" and weak "available evidence." William Byne et al., "Report of the American Psychiatric Association Task Force on Treatment of Gender Identity Disorder," *Archives of Sexual Behavior* 41, no. 4 (2012): 759–96, 764–67, https://doi.org/10.1007/s10508-012-9975-x.

138 *Tavistock and Portman NHS Found. Trust*, 138. This case was overturned on appeal at Bell v. Tavistock and Portman NHS Found. Trust, [2021] EWCA (Civ) 1363, Appeal No. C1/2020/2142 (September 17, 2021).

general population.[139] A 2020 long-term study from the Netherlands found that the number of suicide deaths among those undergoing transgender surgery was higher than in the general population, with the average time to suicide being just over six years *after* the transition began.[140] In August 2020, the *American Journal of Psychiatry* issued a rare "correction" to a previously published study that had claimed gender-affirming surgeries resulted in less utilization of mental health services in the long-term. In fact, a reanalysis of the data "demonstrated *no* advantage of surgery in relation to subsequent mood or anxiety disorder-related health care visits or prescriptions or hospitalizations following suicide attempts."[141]

According to one particularly thorough review of existing literature, some of the limitations of this literature regarding treatments for gender dysphoria include a lack of randomized prospective trial design, very small sample sizes, recruitment bias, short study duration, high subject dropout rates, and reliance on questionable "expert" opinion.[142] There is also lack of long-term follow-up of patients who have undergone transgender treatments. Britain's National Health Service recently changed its guidelines to reflect a more cautious approach in the face of whistleblower complaints and a high-profile lawsuit alleging that the gender clinic of the National Health Service pushed adolescents toward transition with minimal mental health screening or treatment. As part of the lead lawsuit against this clinic, it was revealed, for example, that children were allowed to undergo transitioning medicine after just a few hours of consultation with doctors. It was also revealed that doctors were relying on adolescents' assertions that they really didn't mind if the treatment meant that they would never be able to have children or a normal sex life. A UK High Court concluded: "Children of this age cannot understand the

---

139 Cecelia Dhejne et al., "Long-Term Follow-Up of Transsexual Persons Undergoing Sex Reassignment Surgery: Cohort Study in Sweden," *PLOS One* 6, no. 2 (February 22, 2011), https://doi.org/10.1371/journal.pone.0016885.

140 C.M. Wiepjes et al., "Trends in Suicide Death Risk in Transgender People: Results from the Amsterdam Cohort of Gender Dysphoria Study (1972–2017)," *Acta Psychiatrica Scandinavica*, 141, no. 6 (2020): 486–91, https://doi.org/10.1111/acps.13164.

141 "Correction to Bränström and Pachankis," *The American Journal of Psychiatry* 177, no. 8 (August 1, 2020), 734 (emphasis added), https://ajp.psychiatryonline.org/doi/10.1176/appi.ajp.2020.1778correction.

142 Hruz, "Deficiencies in Scientific Evidence for Medical Management of Gender Dysphoria," 34.

implications of matters such as the loss of the ability to orgasm, the potential need to construct a neo-vagina, or the loss of fertility," and, "There is no age-appropriate way to explain to many of these children what losing their fertility or full sexual function may mean to them in later years."[143] Finally, the court noted the high percentage of cases in which gender discordance resolves itself without treatment, citing an expert who wrote: "In children who express gender discordance, the majority will experience reintegration of gender identity with biological sex by the time of puberty in the absence of directed medical or societal intervention. . . . The most recent studies report desistance rates near 85 percent."[144]

Another sign that transgender affirmation does not enact love of neighbor is the unwillingness to explore its galloping increase among young women and autistic youth. Adolescent girls who are socially isolated have preexisting mental health issues or who are on the autism spectrum are particularly vulnerable to transgender social contagion. They self-diagnose "being transgender" as the source of their psychological or social difficulties and become convinced that transition will relieve their distress and solve their problems.[145] Researcher Lisa Littman first described this phenomena, dubbed "rapid-onset gender dysphoria" (ROGD), in a 2018 study.[146] Parents reported a common fact pattern in adolescent girls who succumbed: isolation, excessive time online, "trans" or "non-binary" peers, preexisting mental health issues, exposure to the "trans" narrative followed quickly by "coming out," and demanding that parents "affirm" the new identity. The upsurge in ROGD tends to occur mostly in girls at around the age of fourteen, which is an age that has been identified by developmental psychologists to be particularly susceptible to peer influence.[147] Similar phenomenon have been observed in a number of countries.

143 *Tavistock and Portman NHS Found. Trust*, [2020] 93, 144.

144 *Tavistock and Portman, NHS Found. Trust*, [2020] 49, 75, 76. See also Hruz, "Deficiencies in Scientific Evidence for Medical Management of Gender Dysphoria," 36.

145 See generally Abigail Shrier, *Irreversible Damage: How the Transgender Craze is Seducing Our Daughters* (Washington, D.C.: Regnery, 2020).

146 Lisa Littman, "Correction: Parent Reports of Adolescents and Young Adults Perceived to Show Signs of a Rapid Onset of Gender Dysphoria," *PLoS ONE* 14, no. 3 (March 19, 2019), https://doi.org/10.1371/journal.pone.0214157.

147 Laurence Steinberg and Kathryn C. Monahan, "Age Differences in Resistance to Peer Influence," *Developmental Psychology* 43, no. 6 (2007): 1531–43, 1531–32, https://doi.org/10.1037/0012-1649.43.6.1531.

People on the autism spectrum are also three to six times more likely to identify as transgender or non-binary. This is true internationally, ranging from a low of 9.4 percent of transgender referrals in the Netherlands to 26 percent in Finland. In addition, three in four transgender-identifying teens have co-occurring mental illnesses.[148]

In conclusion, when declining to affirm a transgender identity, Catholic institutions might communicate: *No one should be surprised that a Christian teaching about human beings accepts God's created design and demonstrates special solicitude for vulnerable people. God does not mistakenly put a human being in the wrong body, even though people suffering identity distress come to believe that this is so. Faith and reason are harmonious here. It is empirically evident that vulnerable people are susceptible to the echo chamber that today supports transgender drugs and surgeries. At the same time, no evidence shows that transgender-identifying individuals are generally helped by treatments altering their sexual appearance; on the contrary, a great deal of evidence indicates that many of these treatments cause serious, lifelong physical and emotional harm in violation of basic bioethical principles. "Trans-affirming" drugs and surgeries alter a vulnerable person's understanding of his or her relationship with God and harm individual development and personal relationships. A more effective love of those suffering identity distress or who otherwise believe that sex is subjectively determined would reject interventions directly harming them and providing no demonstrated advantage. It would also take the time to address the full range of their struggles.*

Conclusion

As Catholics, it appears that we are being asked to reprise the role we played at the beginnings of Christianity: that of an unmistakably countercultural force revealing the nature of human love in the arena of sexual expression as God designed it, in the face of seemingly

---

148 Riittakerttu Kaltiala-Heino et al., "Two Years of Gender Identity Service for Minors: Overrepresentation of Natal Girls with Severe Problems in Adolescent Development," *Child and Adolescent Psychiatry and Mental Health* 9, no. 1 (2015), 1–9, https://doi.org/10.1186/s13034-015-0042-y.

insurmountable odds.[149] The Church is quite familiar with this pattern, even as it will always remain somewhat mysterious to its members. In some sense it is not difficult to penetrate how a two-sexed humanity made for procreative, faithful, and permanent union suggests and advances so many of the traits of human love that promote happiness in marriage and in all human relations: recognizing one's limitedness, bridging the divide from "the other," learning to give as well as receive, understanding equality alongside diversity, achieving synergies through union, creativity, and steadfastness, and so on.

But it is also difficult to understand why God set up the universe in this precise way. Why is marriage so central? Why is sex simultaneously pleasurable, ripe for exploitation, and consequential for both the couple and the continued existence of human society itself? And why do so many, many people—single and married, same- or opposite-sex attracted, with or without gender dysphoria—struggle with God's design, even as we acknowledge that all are impacted by original sin?

There is little doubt today that God's design for sex, marriage, and parenting requires additional reflection and better communication. Opinion in the US is shifting against it. Our best hope is to articulate our conclusions about sexual responsibility in ways that demonstrate their source in the imperatives to love God and one another. This no silver bullet—obviously not in the current environment! But it is better than what we have been doing. It also happens to be true. It respects and is worthy of both our tradition and our audience. It enjoys scientific support. It really fosters happiness and a sense of dignity and freedom. And perhaps it will advance the cause of knowledge and holiness at a time in human and salvation history in which these are the questions that are shaking the world and in which the answers are apparently linked and important to understanding God's love for us and ours for Him and one another.

At the same time, our speaking about this design will almost certainly cause offense, even when we express ourselves with the utmost delicacy, positivity, and respect for every person involved. And make no mistake about it, we will have to pay for taking up this

---

149 Carl R. Trueman reaches a similar conclusion in his book, *The Rise and Triumph of the Modern Self: Cultural Amnesia, Expressive Individualism, and the Road to Sexual Revolution* (Wheaton, Ill.: Crossway, 2020), 405–7.

particular cross, whether we achieve or fail to achieve the religious freedom protections that current law is willing to provide us. The next chapter both sums up the case for taking up our cross anyway, and doing so in a way that takes advantage of the opportunities offered us in typical contests pitting religious freedom against a certain understanding of sexual expression.

- 8 -

FINAL
THOUGHTS

THERE IS NO PATH TO THE OTHER SIDE OF THE CURRENT STORM over the Catholic Church's teachings on sexual responsibility except "through." No matter how tired we are of the world's obsession and our need to respond. No matter that sexual responsibility is not the Church's preoccupation. No matter that the cost to us could be significant.

"Through" requires at least clear, positive, and sufficiently thorough explanations of these teachings; in particular, how they are part of a total way of life that responds to God's extraordinary love for us and to His invitation to love Him and our neighbors. These explanations cannot be addressed only to same-sex-attracted persons, women, and those with gender dysphoria, but to absolutely everyone.

Catholics have no idea what lies on the other side of the storm—whether greater acceptance of our ideas or even more vehement rejection followed by legal and reputational punishment. That is not in our control. We can only control our response to the challenge.

It is more than tempting to mouth agreement with the current sexual orthodoxy and let the storm pass. It is also tempting to stay silent about the heart of things and instead complain that Catholic "rules," or the bureaucracy, or the bishop, demands this or that response to a law requiring cooperation with this orthodoxy. We might even win at law with such a limited position. And of course, some Catholics believe that the teachings are wrong in the first place and will say so. But these responses will leave people to suffer—especially already-wounded and vulnerable people—and cause the disappearance of one of the last voices that can explain their suffering and point to a better way. These responses can also advertise a Catholic institution's fear and/or its lack of commitment to its own supposed beliefs. Today, even if a religious institution aims only at living its beliefs as a community, and even if its only goal is to serve those in need, a government might attempt to impose its sexual orthodoxy upon it anyway. Well-funded interest groups, reporters and pundits, famous academics, and globally powerful corporations will be all over every channel of prestige media to loudly support this demand. There is no hiding.

As suggested throughout this book, a positive response that communicates the Church's teaching and keeps in mind all of the persons involved—especially vulnerable persons—should incorporate several elements. No individual element is complex, but each is important. It would be very helpful if institutional representatives thoroughly understood and *meant* each of them.

The first part of the response reminds listeners what the institution *is*. It is not merely an organized effort to provide education or health care or social services. It is, rather, a community of people who are responding to Christ's call to love Him and one another by doing as He did: healing the sick, serving the poor, and spreading the Good News to the ends of the earth. Its employees, services, and operations endeavor to manifest Christ, and to generate a communal life that provides a glimpse of the inbreaking of the Kingdom of God. The institution will fall short along the way, and will have to ask forgiveness and try again.

A second part of the response addresses the particular problem at hand. If it involves an employee, first assure the listener that the institution is not in the business of surveilling employees or judging souls. But in order to be a community that is responsive and obedient to Christ and witnesses to Him in the world, it must separate from employees who insist that the institution, not the employee, must change. If the problem involves an unacceptable mandate affecting operations or services, assert confidently that it contradicts the institution's mission to love God and one another in the provision of health care or social services or education. But don't stop there.

Third—and here is where both bravery and prophecy come in—articulate *how* the sexual responsibility norm at issue serves love of

God and neighbor, as described in chapters 6 and 7. The institutional leader might wish to prepare the listener for what's coming by stating that Christian love is demanding: whether inside or outside of the family sphere, it asks for great sacrifice, puts God first, holds the body to be sacred, and respects God's sovereign will for creation. Thus the leader will need to "turn the other cheek," "love the enemy," pick up the stranger strewn in her path and pay for his care, and for good measure lay her life down for her friends. Why wouldn't love in the family sphere be equally demanding? After all, our romantic partners and our family members are the people we are *most* likely to deeply and indelibly affect for good or for ill over the course of our and their entire lives.

Finally, regarding the precise sexual norm at issue, state the positive standard established by God and the obvious necessity—as with any good thing—to preserve the good by rejecting what harms it. The positive standard involves two sexes with differences requiring them to move beyond their individual limitations to offer a sincere, permanent, and faithful gift of self and to form a communion that is open to new life. This faithful union is a template for all human love and provides a privileged glimpse of the radical love of Christ on the cross.

I think it would be wise to add, humbly and truthfully, that not even at this moment in history does the Church fully understand why God fashioned love in this way. It is mysterious and often difficult to achieve. We fall short. But this design is not ours to contradict, disdain, or ignore. It is the creator's divine plan.

It is no surprise that the creator's divine plan can be incredibly beautiful and life-giving. It provides care for the vulnerable, as well as authentic experiences of freedom, belonging, dignity, respect, and happiness. People receive the radical, permanent, faithful, sacrificial love they crave. The weak evade exploitation. A vast trove of human experience and empirical data points to all of this. Reserving sexual intercourse for marriage can allow a person to experience the permanence and fidelity of true love and its link to caring for vulnerable new life. Avoiding contraception can preserve the horizon of "tomorrow" that is intrinsic to sex, and help to avoid using and objectifying another person. Choosing life instead of abortion can promote respect for the sacredness of every single life on earth, especially the weakest. It can transform an individual into a parent who understands life as loving service. Abstaining from same-sex relations can deepen one's relationship with the God of creation, and increase the person's understanding of every person's essential poverty and interdependence. It can heighten appreciation of the good of communion across differences and the creative power of love. Finally, grappling with gender dysphoria while avoiding transgender drugs and surgeries can deepen one's acceptance of God's creative authority and His vocational call, as well as human beings' utter dependence upon Him. In today's environment, each of these realizations and choices is more than a small miracle. Increasingly, each appears to require a form of heroism. Each manifests the meaning and the power of love as God intended it.

If Catholic institutional leaders believe what the Church teaches, they can play a role in ameliorating the suffering caused by contemporary sexual orthodoxy. Today, the opportunities to do this will all too often arise in the context of contests over sexual expression laws. These contests will persist even while the Church's own sexual abuse crisis and cover-up is still unfolding, even while the powers that be continue to brook no dissent, and even while Catholics are increasingly inclined to doubt whether Catholic "wisdom" on sexual expression matters can really be true.

There are a number of opportunities for Catholic institutions to speak in the course of typical contests pitting religious freedom against sexual expression laws. First, religious freedom lawsuits involving a services or operations mandate begin with the complainant's assertion that its free exercise is "burdened" by the law at issue. Here, Catholic institutions will want to avoid thin and defensive statements that "the bishop made me do it," or "we have a rule we can't break." Instead, they should explain the religious nature of the institution and how the law will damage or even destroy its mission, its identity, and its religiously determined communal life. The law would force the community to disobey Christ and to witness against Him; it would also destroy the community's ability to display the interpersonal relationships of love, sacrifice, and service obtaining in the reign of God. The law would do this by commanding the institution to violate Christ's Great Commandment to love God and neighbor by way of providing mandated services or operations that do the opposite.

In short, the institution is arguing that the law transgresses the "church autonomy" doctrine as it is described in the *Our Lady of Guadalupe* case. The institution's very life, its internal operations and its faith and doctrine, are usurped in favor of the state's sexual orthodoxy, which maintains its own beliefs about the content of love, dignity, freedom, and health. But it is never enough for a Catholic organization to plead "church autonomy" without additional discussion of its Christian roots and mission, nor without communicating how the sexual expression issue at hand is linked to these, as described especially in chapters 6 and 7.

Second, some religious freedom suits involve an institution's claim that religion is a "bona fide occupational qualification" for a particular position. Here again, the institution needs to go further than the claim that the employee is a "minister." It should describe in full the role he or she plays in responding to Christ's invitation to serve others, witnessing Christ to others, and helping to shape a community whose interactions show forth the reign of God. This material should also include the empirical conclusions from chapter 4 that evidence the importance of even a single employee to the maintenance and transmission of the religious identity of an institution.

Assuming that a court has accepted a religious institution's claim about the burden the law would impose, the state still can enforce the law if it can show a compelling state interest exercised by means that are least restrictive of religion. Although in some cases—as in First Amendment suits involving neutral and generally applicable laws—the state is currently required to show only that it is pursuing a legitimate state interest by rational means, the Catholic institution has another opportunity to teach at this juncture. Surprise! It will require a fair amount of courage.

This "opportunity" involves the Church claiming that *its* sexual responsibility norms *better* achieve the goals that the state claims that its laws pursue. Remember, in cases involving sexual expression laws, the state ordinarily claims that it is vindicating citizens' dignity, equality, freedom, and health. But also remember that the Church holds that *its* norms vindicate the same things in a more effective way, and it also has the empirical data to support this position. The Church holds that the state's separation of sex, marriage, and children, its promotion of abortion and contraception, and its support for same-sex relations and transgender drugs and surgeries, do not have a good empirical track record. The nation is experiencing more abortion, more sexually transmitted diseases, more divorce, more nonmarital parenting, the separation of children from their parents, and a great deal of associated physical and mental distress. Further-more, the dearth of marriage and marital parenting among the poor is significantly responsible for growing and hardening gaps between socioeconomic and racial groups in the US.[1]

Let me analogize the task and the opportunity confronting Catho-lic institutions to those that applied to the religious complainants in two famous cases decided by US courts. In the first, *Wisconsin v. Yoder*, the state of Wisconsin tried to show that it had compelling reasons for burdening the religious beliefs of Amish parents about their chil-dren's secondary school education in order to advance the formation of self-sufficient adults and contributing citizens. But the US Supreme Court held that the Amish scheme—which involved training children in productive work beginning in their teens in order to support their later self-sufficiency—actually realized the state's goals as well as or better than mandatory additional education.[2]

In a second case, *Rader v. Johnston*, about a public college that required freshmen to live in an on-campus dorm—and forbade them from living in a Christian Student Fellowship house across the street—the college claimed a compelling interest in fostering pluralistic inter-action and mutual interpersonal acceptance. However, in an opinion upholding the students' right to live in a Christian dorm, the court stated, among other things, that the Christian housing actually *better* accomplished the state's interests. It fostered unity among a more diverse array of students than did the university's own dorms, includ-ing among international students and students of color.[3]

Catholic institutions should take a page from the holdings in these cases. They should argue that the state cannot show a compelling interest achieved by means that are least restrictive of religion by imposing its rules upon the institution. Rather, the institution should

1 W. Bradford Wilcox and Anna Sutherland, "Less Marriage, More Inequality," Insti-tute for Family Studies website (blog), April 14, 2016, https://ifstudies.org/blog/less-marriage-more-inequality/.

2 Wisconsin v. Yoder, 406 U.S. 205 (1972).

3 Rader v. Johnston, 924 F. Supp. 1540 (D. Neb. 1996).

be left free to observe its norms because *these* can empirically claim to better promote equality, dignity, freedom, and health. This is a bold move, but worth a try. If it succeeds, Catholic institutions would be permitted to remain a light for the community. At worst, the states' claims will have been undermined to some degree.

Finally, there are those cases discussed in chapters 1 and 7 in which the state attempts to charge a Catholic institution with discrimination based upon an employee's "status"—as same-sex-attracted, or as single, or as transgender-identifying. But in all such cases, the institution is basing its personnel decision on the person's conduct and not their status. As already discussed, some courts recognize this distinction and others conflate the two, even though it makes no sense. No matter what happens, it is important for Catholic institutions to at least educate courts and the public about the fact that they do not discriminate based upon a person's sexual inclinations, desires, or beliefs. Instead, when an employee's *behavior* contradicting Catholic norms becomes public, the institution chooses to act in response to that behavior, not his or her status. The institution should make this crystal clear more than a few times even if the court involved will ultimately refuse to make the distinction.

Each of the above moves in a religious freedom lawsuit requires a fair amount of bravery today. At some level, this should strike the thoughtful Catholic as surprising. Only recently, Catholics and the powers that be were on the same page about which sexual and familial behaviors promoted human well-being.

Perhaps, though, it is this very recent unanimity that has left some Catholic institutions somewhat flat-footed in today's storms. They were not previously forced to articulate the goods of an opposite-sex, procreative union, to the degree necessary today. Discrete elements of this formula were denied bit by bit, but then . . . suddenly . . . *entirely*, and with a vehemence suggesting that the former consensus never existed, and that its continued adherents are stark raving mad, and cruel to boot! Even sincerely observant Catholics are sometimes surprised that the Church continues to teach its Catholic sexual responsibility norms in the face of such widespread disregard.

The task before the Church is therefore clear. It seems increasingly undeniable that Christianity is being asked to step up at this time in history to preserve individual and community well-being in the realms of sex, marriage, and parenting. This work can also promote insights into the various human and divine truths that romantic and familial relations are designed to illuminate. Even small Catholic institutions can't duck and run. They are potentially one of the few lights to their communities on these matters. They maintain the personal relationships within which hard conversations can be had in fellowship and love. They are an essential part of the larger, necessary movement in the Church to engage in sophisticated, ongoing inquiry and dialogue about Christian marital norms—a movement involving the contributions of theologians, philosophers, scientists, and others. It is a movement that invites honest and thorough dialogue with dissenters and that can ultimately illuminate the human and divine truths that these personal relationships point to.

I hope this book has provided not only some of the substance, but equally importantly, some of the inspiration necessary for such a movement. Even as I was writing it, I was often overwhelmed by the radically demanding nature of Christian love. But I also grew in appreciation for the wisdom and kindness of the Christian norms. To borrow (yet another) thought from Father Luigi Giussani, I came to see these norms as part of God's loving "pity" for human beings after the Fall. This is the spirit in which the Church can move forward, even as there is apparently no avoiding the offense that some will take from its faithfulness to its teachings. Just the opposite is intended.

ACKNOWLEDGMENTS

A BOOK THAT CROSSES THIS MANY DISCIPLINES and features so many footnotes could not have been written without the help of many people. First and foremost, I thank my husband and children for their patience with me as I filled our kitchen table and our small study with stacks of books and articles, and devoted hundreds of hours to writing.

Thanks to my top-flight research assistant Sarah Christensen and my amazing reference librarian Peter Vay, both at the Antonin Scalia Law School. I peppered both with relentless requests and neither ever complained. Not even once. I also thank the Antonin Scalia Law School for a series of summer research grants that enabled me to spend several years of summers writing this book.

I owe a great debt to fellow scholars and friends for sharpening my thinking and writing at conferences and during one-on-one exchanges, and for providing me more than a few expert sources: Gregory Black, Gerard Bradley, Archbishop Charles Chaput, Catherine Duggan, Maureen Ferguson, Mary Hasson, John Martino, Theresa Notare, Martin Nussbaum, Mark Regnerus, David M. Smolin, Ian Speir, and W. Bradford Wilcox.

Faculty and students at various presentations of some of the material in this book offered helpful comments and suggestions. I am grateful to them and to their organizers. Thanks therefore to James R. Stoner, Jr. at the Eric Voegelin Institute and to the other organizers of the Constitution Day address at Louisiana State University. Thanks also to organizers of the religious freedom colloquy sponsored by the

Pontifical John Paul II Institute for Studies on Marriage and Family at The Catholic University of America and the Alliance Defending Freedom.

My gratitude to the *Connecticut Public Interest Law Journal* and the *Texas Review of Law and Politics* for their permissions to use in this book material previously published in their journals.

I also want to thank the amazing scholars whose works I drew upon so heavily. I thank God for your intellects! These include especially Pope Benedict XVI, Dorothy M. Brown, Louis J. Cameli, Pope Francis, Luigi Giussani, Kyle Harper, Richard B. Hays, Barbara Mann Wall, Elizabeth McKeown, Pope St. John Paul II, Sarah Ruden, Heinz Schürmann, Rodney Stark, Carl R. Trueman, Hans Urs von Balthasar, and many others whose works pepper my footnotes and text.

And finally, I thank the staff at The Catholic University of America Press for so expertly handling the publication of this book.

INDEX

FAITH AND REASON FOR EVERYONE

FROM THE CATHOLIC UNIVERSITY OF AMERICA PRESS
https://www.cuapress.org/faith-and-reason-for-everyone/

Jared Staudt, *Renewing Catholic Schools*
(Catholic Education Press)

"This book should be in the hands of every Catholic educator in America. It explains why renewal in our schools' Catholic identity and mission is necessary and offers many practical suggestions on how to bring about this conversion."

—Archbishop J. Michael Miller, CSB

Sarah Bartel and John Grabowski,
A Catechism for Family Life

"I can testify that this book contains the questions Catholics are asking here and now about sex, marriage, and family life, and sourced answers they can trust."

—Helen M. Alvaré, George Mason University

Don J. Briel, Kenneth E. Goodpaster, and Michael J. Naughton,
What We Hold in Trust: Rediscovering the Purpose of Catholic Higher Education

"I applaud the work of these three authors for addressing the threat of secularization of Catholic institutions. Although primarily focused on Catholic higher education, their insights and offerings are applicable to all Catholic ministries."

—Sr. Mary Haddad, CEO & President,
Catholic Health Association of the United States

Bishop Robert Barron,
Renewing Our Hope:
Essays for the New Evangelization

"Bishop Barron's special genius, vivid throughout these marvelous essays, is his gift of making the 'new evangelization' more than just pious words, but the seeds of a new and fulfilling life in Jesus Christ."

—+Archbishop Charles J. Chaput, OFM, Cap.

Thomas Joseph White, OP,
The Light of Christ: An Introduction to Catholicism

"White is one of the brightest and most articulate theologians writing today. This book is an intelligent and spiritually alert introduction to the principal themes of Catholic theology. Both beginners and serious academics will find much to savor in its pages."

—Bishop Robert Barron

Msgr. Martin Schlag,
Handbook of Catholic Social Teaching

"In this exceptional volume, Monsignor Martin Schlag provides a one-stop-shopping overview, and it deserves to be widely read, studied, pondered, prayed over, and, perhaps most importantly, acted upon."

—John L. Allen Jr., Editor, *Crux*

Andrew V. Abela and Joseph E. Capizzi,
A Catechism for Business, 3rd edition

"A welcome compendium of magisterial teaching on topics relevant to business managers and leaders . . *A Catechism for Business* is a reference book that every Catholic would benefit from, whether or not they work in business."

—*The Catholic Social Science Review*

Edward Condon, *Death, Judgment, Heaven, and Hell: Sayings of the Fathers of the Church*

"Edward Condon has provided a most sure and efficacious tool in restoring and keeping a right view of things by collecting the sayings of the Fathers of the Church, those most authoritative interpreters of the Word of God, regarding the last things. I commend most highly his work, even as I am most grateful to him for it."

—Raymond Leo Cardinal Burke

Edward Hadas, *Counsels of Imperfection: Thinking through Catholic Social Teaching*

"This is certainly the best survey of Catholic Social Teaching I have ever encountered."

—Stephen Bullivant, Director of the Benedict XVI Centre for Religion and Society, Saint Mary's University, London

Anthony Lo Bello, *The Origins of Catholic Words*

"It is unlike any dictionary you have ever read, or any encyclopedia you are ever likely to read. Fun, feisty, and cuttingly edgy, it is nothing less than the words made fresh."

—Joseph Pearce

Heidi Giebel, *Ethical Excellence: How to Achieve It*

"A wise, charming, practical, and entertaining account of what moral excellence is and how we all can move toward it. This book offers not only clarity of understanding but more fulfilled lives and deeper happiness—for ourselves and for our children, students, and fellow citizens."

—Anne Colby, author of *The Power of Ideals*

John Gavin, SJ, *Mysteries of the Lord's Prayer.*
Foreword by George Weigel.

Pope Benedict XVI, *Called to Holiness*

Pope Benedict XVI, *A Reason Open to God*

Mike Aquilina,
The Holy Mass: Sayings of the Fathers of the Church

Adrian Reimers, *Hell and the Mercy of God*

Reinhard Hütter,
John Henry Newman on Truth and Its Counterfeits

Ryan N.S. Topping,
*Renewing the Mind: A Reader
in the Philosophy of Catholic Education*

Cardinal Angelo Scola,
Betting on Freedom: My Life in the Church

Fr. Daniel Cardó, SCV, *The Art of Preaching*

Fr. Thomas Weinandy, OFM Cap.,
Jesus Becoming Jesus (3 volumes)

More at https://www.cuapress.org/faith-and-reason-for-everyone/.